Contents

Acknowledgements

Early versions of some of these chapters were given as papers at the Newcastle-upon-Tyne meeting of the British Shakespeare Association. For that opportunity, we would like to thank the organisers and, in particular, Kate Chedgzoy. We are also grateful to Stephen Buhler, Stephen Cavanagh, Tobias Döring, Ewan Fernie, Douglas Lanier, Kenneth Rothwell and Adrian Streete for relevant and productive conversations. At Edinburgh University Press, Jackie Jones has not only been a supportive and facilitative editor: she has also played an importantly creative role. Final thanks are due to the Publications Fund at Queen's University, Belfast, which contributed towards cover costs, and to our stalwart band of contributors with whom it has been a pleasure to work.

Introduction

Mark Thornton Burnett and Ramona Wray

Shakespeare's Happy Endings, a spoof documentary produced as part of
the BBC's 2005 'Shakespea(Re)-Told' season, concludes with a scene
outside Holy Trinity Church, Stratford-upon-Avon.[1] Here, the erstwhile
presenter, Professor Simon Starkman (Patrick Barlow), greets William
Shakespeare (Kevin Eldon), welcoming him as the 'man of the millennium' and announcing a surprise celebration in honour of the famous
guest. Unfortunately, the church is closed: the vicar has forgotten about
the party, no one has bothered to turn up and, in a sublime rendition of
bardic demythologising, Shakespeare is reduced to kicking at the doors
and battering at a window in an attempt to gain entrance. The drama-
tist's inability to make a connection with his renowned place of nativity
is part of a comic collision between what Shakespeare has come to signify
(the commodified rhetoric of the industry) and the 'reality' of an early
modern writer revealed as an embarrassing and confused unsophisticate.
Certainly, many at the turn of the twentieth century would lend their
voices to this debunking assessment. Writing in 1999, Gary Taylor
contended that 'Shakespeare's reputation . . . has passed its peak of
expansion, and begun to decline', resulting in a diminution of the Bard's
'cultural authority'.[2] Richard Burt, surveying the field in 2000, goes one
step further, arguing for 'the end of the Shakespearean' or what he terms
'the Shakespeare apocalypse'.[3]

Lending some support to these views is the smaller number of major
Shakespeare films produced in the immediate post-2000 period. If the
1990s represented the heyday of the Bard's screen revival, the 'noughties'
have thus far been marked by a less voluminous, or at least less obvious,
corpus of screen 'Shakespeares'. Yet, as *Shakespeare's Happy Endings* also
attests, the Bard's name is still one to conjure with; his works continue to
reverberate; and the plays persist as repositories of lore and tradition even
as they are reworked as salient signifiers of meaning and knowledge.

A brief look at the International Movie Data Base confirms this, with some seventy-six 'Shakespearean' titles being listed between 2000 and 2005 as either in production or having already been released.[4] Some of these retain the familiar contours of the multiplex-oriented, star-encrusted feature; others take the form of the so-called 'spin-off' or appropriation, and it is in part towards an appraisal of such varieties and versions of Shakespeare that the current collection is directed. Shakespeare, in the post-2000 period, moves among and between a range of screen incarnations, which encompass adaptations, documentaries, cinema advertisements, post-colonial reinventions and mass media citations, and which test the boundaries of conventional idioms and mediums.

Typical of that twenty-first-century realisation of a screen Shakespeare is an advertising campaign launched by the H&M fashion empire in late 2005. *'Romeo and Juliet' by David Lachapelle*, a six-minute film, constitutes a loose rehearsal of Shakespeare's play and is aired both in cinemas and as a playable clip on the H&M website.[5] Unfolding in an urban, US environment, the film privileges the fetching attire and appearance of the two leads, Juliet (Tamyra Gray) and Romeo (Gus Carr), mediating its vision of a millennial romance via encrypted reference to a Shakespearean textual authority. Crucial here are the glimpse of the graffiti-sprayed name of 'Paris', which indexes the 'original', the image of Juliet on a fire-escape substituting for the balcony, and the reflection in a window of a billboard announcing a film entitled *The Lady Doth Protest*.[6] These invocations of a not simply circumscribed 'Shakespearean' represent the authenticating rationale for the film, the culture of conjuration and pastiche within which *'Romeo and Juliet' by David Lachapelle* affirms its particular logic. And, as the urban environment reveals itself as New York, a further summoning of the Shakespearean comes into view, with *West Side Story* (dir. Robert Wise and Jerome Robbins, 1961), itself a revisiting of *Romeo and Juliet*, being instanced as another inner-city parable that takes the play into modernity. This *Romeo and Juliet* is acutely responsive to, and self-conscious about, the 'sources' of its own existence and the histories of revision that intercede in, and give shape to, its imaginative possibility. Both the ghostly background of *West Side Story* and the titular presence of the fictional Shakespeare film *The Lady Doth Protest* suggest that in *'Romeo and Juliet' by David Lachapelle* the screen pasts of Shakespeare are a function of his current comprehensibility; that is, the ways in which the Bard has been packaged and transmuted through film are the precondition for the work's accessibility and applications, however displaced they might be from their early modern contexts and associations. What transpires in the wake of the authorial, material Shakespeare becomes the conceptual template whereby the play is made familiar.

Hence, it is peculiarly apposite that the film should make a point of consistently invoking other Shakespeare and Shakespeare-related screen outings. The emphasis on fashion – in this case, jeans – is of a piece with the film's reminder of the lineage of Shakespeare's popular culture visibility. The opening menu, for instance, discovers Romeo and Juliet standing against a graffiti-sprayed image of a flaming rose: at once, the composition harks back to the panoply of interrelated flaming hearts and logos deployed in Baz Luhrmann's *William Shakespeare's 'Romeo + Juliet'* (1996), thereby elaborating a context in which it is the icon rather than the word that is prioritised. The Luhrmann film is instanced again in the sequence showing the heroine as a descending angel (an allusion to the appearance of Claire Danes as a Botticelli-inspired angel during the party-masque), while Michael Almereyda's *Hamlet* (2000) lurks behind the fleeting capture of a photo montage adorning the walls of Juliet's bedroom. Films already inscribed with the market stamp of youth culture and urban angst lend their reputations to Lachapelle's advertising utterance, pointing up a modality of articulation and reception in which Shakespeare is 'hip' and in which an affiliation with the Bard is as cool and current as the acquisition of the latest designer label.

Interestingly, where *West Side Story* and *William Shakespeare's 'Romeo + Juliet'* privilege urban life as an ethnic war zone involving, respectively, Puerto Rican and Polish American youth, and Anglo and Latino rival groupings, *'Romeo and Juliet' by David Lachapelle* subscribes to a vaguely and ambiguously racialised constituency that belies any straightforward identification. Described on the H&M website as a 'true icon' who 'appeals to a wide range of ages and ethnicities', Gus Carr (Romeo) might be characterised as Asian or Latino or a combination of the two; similarly, although black, Tamyra Gray (Juliet) inhabits the aesthetically whitened extreme of the Afro-American experience. Ethnic specificity is not the point; instead, it is the notion of a free-floating and cross-cultural ethnicity defined by transatlantic parameters that *'Romeo and Juliet' by David Lachapelle* asks its audience to countenance. In this connection, the film brings to mind what Mary C. Beltrán has described as the 'new Hollywood racelessness': in action movies such as *Romeo Must Die* (dir. Andrzej Bartkowiak, 2000) and *The Fast and the Furious* (dir. Rob Cohen, 2001), she argues, 'mixed-race individuals' who nevertheless subscribe to a 'white ethos' embrace 'identities that are achieved through the . . . sharing of music, fashion and cultural forms . . . rather than by [an acceptance of] former ethnic . . . allegiances and in-group prejudices'.[7] Such a vision of 'cultural *métissage*', to adopt a formulation of Ronald Niezen, is, as Beltrán goes on to suggest, a reflection of 'contemporary shifts in US demographics' as well as 'concerns regarding . . . the nation's burgeoning . . . creolization'.[8] *'Romeo and Juliet' by David Lachapelle* models itself along the lines of these 'raceless' narratives: devotion to a product, if only briefly, is seen to be preferable to absorption in a community, and expectations about conflict are resolved in the spectacle of an ethnically diluted, and accessory-driven, homogeneity.

On the one hand, a 'raceless' *Romeo and Juliet* would seem to lend credence to notions about Shakespearean universality as it is mediated through the mechanisms and accompaniments that characterise film in its post-millennial manifestations. Thus, the Lachapelle film features a soundtrack of two songs, one of which, 'When I First Saw You', is performed by Mary J. Blige. This 'confessional singer', the website informs us, is possessed of 'an inner strength' and 'raw honesty [that are] used to tackle . . . personal pain, [so that her] uncompromising recordings reveal the universality of [her] heartaches and demonstrate the healing power of music'. Arresting here is the implied juxtaposition of the singer and the heroine, to the extent that this *Romeo and Juliet* becomes, in some senses, Juliet's story or, at least, her attempt at the articulation of suffering and psychological reparation. But more striking is the idea that the confessional form, because it rests upon a Shakespearean 'original', is listened to over and above the confines of the film's New York locations. Emerging from the construction of a narrative free of clearly demarcated ethnic markings is the representation of a personal journey that achieves a transcendently communicative efficacity. The song relies for its presumed effect upon Shakespeare, and Shakespeare is the guarantor of its 'soulful' appeal.

On the other hand, to argue for a 'universal' *Romeo and Juliet* is to ignore the details of any film's political and ideological underpinnings. *'Romeo and Juliet' by David Lachapelle* is no exception to this rule for, as much as the film gestures towards a whitened value system that traverses the restrictions of place and history, so does it betray both the structures of thought that lend its conceptions shape and the larger contemporary contexts that inform its mindset. Originally a clothing outlet founded in Stockholm in 1947, H&M has subsequently grown into a worldwide consortium, with stores in over twenty countries across the US, Canada and Europe. New York's flagship H&M store opened in 2005 with a timeliness that, given the Lachapelle film, cannot have been unintended. For all of its Swedish antecedents, then, H&M is a fashion empire distinguished by a global frame of reference and, as we will see, by particularly American representational methods and interpretive tendencies. For example, Tamyra Gray, who both plays Juliet and performs the other song on the soundtrack, 'And I Am Telling You I'm Not Going', is a former near-miss winner of *American Idol*, the syndicated pop contestant show that has recently entered its fifth season on the Fox television channel. Part of a global export network, *American Idol* testifies to the competitive cult of manufactured celebrity that characterises the US in the twenty-first century even as it expresses an illusion of traditions of meritocracy that contributed to the nation's ideological complexion.

Perhaps the most revealing moment of 'And I Am Telling You I'm Not Going' comes when, in a seemingly innocuous diegetic detail, the song lyrics interact with the filmic image. Previously, Romeo's killer is identified as a gunman who, from a passing car, unaccountably aims a fatal shot at the hapless lover. Because the killer is hooded, and the audience is granted only a brief glimpse of his eyes, a parallel is afforded with the infamous Carl Juste photograph 'Mask' (1994), which shows an anonymous hooded Haitian migrant detained at the US military base at Guantánamo Bay, Cuba.[9] The reminder of 'Mask' encourages further identifications, not least with constructions of Muslim and/or Islamic extremists: the stereotype of the lone, crazed assassin has in the US, in particular, acquired a fearful currency. The point is that this does not connote the ethnic gang disputes of the ghetto or, indeed, of previous film versions of *Romeo and Juliet*; rather, the hero's death is symptomatic of the attitudes informing American foreign policy, and participates in what Ken Booth and Tim Dunne have termed elsewhere 'a global war against terrorism'.[10] Crucially, the gunman appears as a black 'other': his is the film's most conventionally ethnicised appearance. Yet, towards the end, another view of the – now police-escorted – killer is granted. The hood is pulled back and the countenance is repentant as the lines from the Tamyra Gray song sound: 'We're part of the same place, / We're part of the same time, / We will share the same love, / We both share the same mind'. Ostensibly, the 'we' are the star-crossed lovers themselves; however, judged alongside such fundamentalist rhetoric of identicalness, 'we' simultaneously signals the born-again spirit of US patriotism. The moral conversion of Romeo's murderer makes sense inside this framework, the assumption being that the American people, regardless of ethnic affiliation, share a common goal and must band together against the outsider. At a deeper remove, the assassin's repentance, and the suggestion that he has already been punished, justifies the aggressive military tactics of the Bush administration. In the post 9/11 moment, there can be no differences, only unity: racial alterity is absorbed or incorporated, and 'racelessness' comes to serve a politically expedient purpose. The quotation from *The Merchant of Venice* – 'I will buy with you, sell with you, talk with you' – that adorns a shop awning is in keeping with this orientation, suggesting, as it does, fraternisation rather than rejection, intercourse rather than ostracisation.[11] But, in a rare instance of ironic counterpoint, the Shylock citation also works against itself, alluding to earlier US relations with Iraq, a history of trade in armaments, and a complicity in the engendering and perpetuation of authoritarian regimes. *'Romeo and Juliet' by David Lachapelle* styles itself to rehearse the concerns of a world in which US attitudes and actions are often dominant, at the same time as it dispassionately withdraws from the informing determinants that are among the conditions of its own production.

Ultimately, of course, both the evident presence of Shakespeare, and the more muted reminder of US foreign policy, must give way in the film to its primary directive, which is to sell the product. Here, Shakespeare comes into his post-millennial own, being mortgaged to, and deployed in promoting, the narrative's commercial requirements. *The Merchant of Venice* quotation is a subliminal part of this imperative: so, too, is the shop awning reference to *The Two Gentlemen of Verona* – 'Win her with gifts' – and the general equation of romance, youth and the designer lifestyle.[12] Contrary to the hood, which obscures the identity of the gunman, the jeans worn by Romeo and Juliet have an individuating effect. That, at least, is the claim of the film's website, which states: 'Each &denim pair are different . . . created . . . for the fashion of today and the one we will honour tomorrow'. As this parodic recasting of the language of the marriage service suggests, the '&denim' range of jeans is conceived of internally rather than externally, as the carrier of a sublime virtue rather than the demonstration of a must-have materiality. Jeans with the H&M label, therefore, are 'true . . . companions in long and honest relationships': they are purveyors not so much of momentary needs as timeless realities. There is a purposeful blurring here with one cultural construction of Shakespeare: like the Bard, whose works live on in the popular imaginary, '&denim' jeans will survive vicissitude. Or, to put it another way, the wearer/consumer enjoys a personal and permanent connection with his/her clothes, filling out the vacant space preceding the '&' and responding affirmatively to the invitation to buy the item and complete the romantic circuit.[13] Canonically entrenched ideas about the ageless applications of Shakespeare recur in the part of the menu devoted to the jeans themselves. Different styles are represented, variously, as 'loyal', 'classic' and 'original': the descriptors deployed suggest that, by acquiring a particular garment, the consumer partakes of, and comes to inhabit, precisely that Shakespearean attribute. To enjoy '&denim', it is implied, is to become acculturated, to claim a past that has a present purchase and an assured future. Inside this semiotic structure, all is geared towards facilitating the interested party and bolstering an impression of his/her buying power. Such a process is hinted at in the on-screen message at the close, 'With Love From H&M', which equates the experience of watching the film with the receipt of a gift. Yet, within this economy, to be so honoured is simultaneously to enter a system of debt and exchange whereby the primary act of giving must be responded to and repaid. *'Romeo and Juliet' by David Lachapelle* endows consumers with 'values' that span more than one cultural category, that privilege and implicate in the interests of broadcasting the '& denim' range's multivalent irresistibility.

Given the interplay between recollection and fantasy that makes up *'Romeo and Juliet' by David Lachapelle*, it is unclear which of the film's endings is granted priority. The penultimate sequence discovers Juliet seizing Romeo's mobile phone in order to shoot his assassin, yet the final composition displays the lovers reclining on a bed, barely moving as they gaze at each other adoringly. Vengeance is entertained, but so, too, are ideas about resurrection, survival, a shared approach to death and the embrace of an alternative reality. The confusion is, in fact, integral to the broader workings of the film: via the selection of jeans the consumer is encouraged to make particular narrative choices. Viewers are placed in the position of mixing and matching various readings of Shakespeare's play as part of the process whereby the desirability of the product is reified. Thus, it is not so much the case that, as the website informs us, 'the importance of fashion yields to the forces of true love'; rather, the ending(s) of the film reveal how a conservative construction of Shakespearean 'love' is the instrument through which 'fashion' is affirmed: the consumer is empowered at the level of narrative in order to be targeted in the extra-filmic economy. Because of these narrative layerings, *'Romeo and Juliet' by David Lachapelle* emerges as no straightforward filmic statement. It represents a collocation of texts to be decoded as much as it appears as a cross-media tie-in for the latest initiative of the global garment industry. A work in which Shakespeare is himself a brand or an implied icon, this *Romeo and Juliet* is part homage, part imitation, part trailer, part promotion, part PC experience. As such, Lachapelle's 'film' illustrates in abundance the signature features of Shakespearean filmmaking in the new millennium.

The essays assembled in the present volume confirm that Shakespeare is a magnet for negotiations about style, value and cultural identity. At the same time, the reverberations set up by his name facilitate screen reflections upon the operations of history and the nature of representation – the legacies of the past as they play themselves out in present circumstances. Shakespeare, the chapters argue, is frequently made understandable via an intertextual apparatus; that is, an always-already mediatised Bard is put into the service of discussions about, variously, place, locale and class in a range of contexts. The lineages through which Shakespeare is constituted in the post-millennial moment facilitate explorations into race, ethnicity and multiculturalism, across nations and formats, even as they shore up the romantic charge of his works' deployments. Indeed, it is precisely because of Shakespeare's prior and continuing absorption in popular culture that, in filmic guise, his plays are enabled to broach a spectrum of local and global twenty-first-century concerns, from the dangers of terrorism to the workings of a 'McDonaldised' world. And, as Shakespeare's association with authority and authenticity are the cues for film production, so, too, is his cultural leverage reinforced by his being marketed as a mystery that is still to be deciphered, despite the knowable qualities that his plays appear to epitomise.

As *Shakespeare's Happy Endings* suggests, culture after the millennium is still drawn to, if not haunted by, popular constructions promising to illuminate Shakespeare as author. Richard Dutton's provocative opening essay in this collection addresses *In Search of Shakespeare*, arguing that the persistent privileging of the presenter, Michael Wood, is key to the 2003 series' initiative – to 'discover' the Bard through subjecting him to a rigorous 'searching' process. Moving nimbly between scholarly accretions and media interpretations, Dutton analyses the ways in which Shakespeare's life is transformed into a 'whodunit' through the documentary's zealous use of unscripted conversation, insets of performance and stylised images. The result, it is argued, is the production of 'a Shakespeare for the twenty-first century', one who was always 'unseen', self-effacing and purposefully elusive both in his writing and in his material relations with authority. The thesis that this is a politicised Shakespeare, whose need for dark secrecy captures the mood of the present moment, chimes unerringly with Mark Thornton Burnett's contention that Shakespeare and surveillance are familiar post-millennial bedfellows. For him, Shakespeare on screen is penetrated by the broader strategies and methods that define and control the subject in modernity; hence, in post-2000 film versions of *Hamlet*, Burnett argues, surveillance is everywhere apparent as a practice that bespeaks cinema's sensitivity to the relations between incarcerating visual regimes and a terror-haunted world. Concentrating on three very differently produced *Hamlet*s which, nevertheless, share surprisingly similar thematic connections, Burnett shows how new modes of seeing are integral to the endeavour to establish both forms of political understanding and possibilities for social and cultural emancipation. In this way, through representation of the organisational bases of surveillance, these *Hamlet* films draw a heightened attention to the ways in which Shakespeare and optical systems of power form part of a symbiotic and mutually reinforcing dialectic.

Just as Burnett detects a marked change of emphasis in post-2000 versions of *Hamlet*, so does Richard Burt find *Stage Beauty* (dir. Richard Eyre, 2004) to be a twenty-first-century transfiguration of its twentieth-century precursor, *Shakespeare in Love* (dir. John Madden, 1998). He suggests that the film's interest in the fortunes of *Othello* in an imaginary Restoration theatre argues both for a break in an earlier filmic tradition interested in stagings of Shakespeare and for a 'post-post-colonial Shakespeare', a Bard enmeshed in a still unfolding trajectory of racial impersonation and parody. Consistently, racial marking has a subversive edge, avers Burt, who positions the film's challenge to prevailing cinematic codes governing race as part of a responsiveness to a newly transnational Shakespeare. Close analysis of 'fakery' and performance aesthetics inside a global film industry allows Burt to claim convincingly and controversially that *Stage Beauty*'s final effect is unwittingly to point up the inherent provinciality of the forms through which a raced Shakespeare might adequately be transmitted. Courtney Lehmann's understanding of provinciality occupies a contrasting register, moving as it does from the workings of race to a grammar of place. Her contribution, alive to the interplay between time and history that identifies the post-millennial Shakespeare, argues that, in *My Kingdom* (dir. Don Boyd, 2001), a 'post-nostalgic' yearning for a Liverpool that was is held in ideological equipoise with the shaping realities of late capitalism and post-9/11 paranoia. The city, Lehmann suggests, is a place poised at a crossroads made up of regret for an earlier glory, and aspiration for rehabilitation and improvement. It is such a doubled perspective that permits the film to read *King Lear* according to a twenty-first-century paradigm that involves fascinating reflections upon the formation of global polity and anticipations of a reinvigorated species of postmodernity.

In their chapter, Susanne Greenhalgh and Robert Shaughnessy address intersections between the local and the global, the urban and the rural, and the 'native' and the 'migrant' in order to pinpoint the multicultural status of the contemporary Shakespeare. Focusing on British television's evolving prioritisation of ethnicity and multiculturalism as essential modalities for Shakespearean interpretation and dissemination, their discussion ranges impressively across documentaries, dramas, adaptations, educational programmes and musical scores. In a Britain where colour-blind casting and the multicultural performance of Shakespeare have become increasingly normative, Greenhalgh and Shaughnessy make a case for the operation of a genuinely new dynamic of cultural 'fusion' in a growing body of post-2000 Asian work. Small-scale productions of Shakespeare, such as *Twelfth Night* (dir. Tim Supple, 2003) and *Indian Dream* (dir. Roger Goldby, 2003), give way in the next chapter to globally marketed and multiplex-targeted screen realisations. The subject of Samuel Crowl's chapter is *The Merchant of Venice* (dir. Michael Radford, 2004), a film which secured international distribution via MGM and Sony Classics and which, it is suggested, displays in its ideological orientation an intriguing essentialist alliance with some recent literary criticism, including Stephen Greenblatt's best-selling *Will in the World*. Crowl posits the importance of a relation that both demonstrates the symbiotic relationship enjoyed by film and literary analysis and marks a significant turning-point in attitudes towards, and constructions of, Shakespeare's play. The twenty-first-century *The Merchant of Venice*, the essay concludes, is striking for playing up the perils of a global system in which religious revivals, and sectarian intolerances, are everywhere apparent. Complementing and complicating the perspective of Radford's film is the first full-length Shakespeare film to be made in New Zealand and the first full-length Māori Shakespeare film. Catherine Silverstone's discussion of *The Maori Merchant of Venice* (dir. Don Selwyn, 2001) demonstrates some of the tensions that inhere in 'intercultural' performances of Shakespeare, where Shakespeare's texts are produced in the context of local knowledges and traditions. While *The Maori Merchant of Venice* takes pains to showcase Māori language (*te reo*) and heritage, it does so unevenly and uncertainly: traumas of past tensions and inequities are conjured in the effort to bypass memory and imagine a better, 'intercultural' future. Indeed, it is as an articulation of the 'future-past' that the film functions most cogently, with histories of land dispossession and violence being revived in the same moment as a post-millennial impulse towards mutually satisfactory integrationist policies is formulated.

An essay that deals with the legacies of colonisation is followed by one devoted to exploring a filmic reworking of what has come to be regarded as a salient colonial statement – Shakespeare's *Henry V*. Almost twenty years ago, Kenneth Branagh's *Henry V* (1989) kicked off the Shakespeare film boom of the 1990s, but, as Sarah Hatchuel writes in her contribution, Peter Babakitis' *Henry V* (2004), in conception, method and execution, is intriguingly nuanced by comparison. Available only inside the conference and convention circuit, the film draws upon the popular genre of docu-drama and mobilises pre-existing media representations of the invasion of Iraq in order to promote a sense of historical realism. At the same time, Hatchuel argues, the use of digital stylisation in the realisation of Henry counters moves towards verisimilitude and creates a distancing effect: the two forms co-exist in a tense rapport that underscores an ultimately mythologised reading of the protagonist at the new millennium. If Babakitis is one of the many directors defining himself in complex opposition to the Shakespeare films of the 1980s and 1990s, then this is a procedure also common to the numerous 'spin-off' Shakespeare films that have proliferated since 2000. As Carolyn Jess-Cooke argues in her chapter, screen 'Shakespeares' after the millennium, despite internal differences and international market distribution, are marked by a curious homogeneity and indebtedness in the extent to which they cannibalise, sequelise and entertain a 'repetition compulsion'. This, following recent developments in cultural theory, Jess-Cooke labels 'McDonaldisation', which she defines as a commercialising rehash of the work of a Hollywood film industry marked by a general poverty of imaginative energy. Yet her essay argues against a summary dismissal of the films discussed in that they make available routes though cultural diversity, throw light on the imperial legacies of the present era, draw a necessary attention to the politics of reterritorialisation, and establish discursive fields within which Shakespeare might be newly negotiated. In this way, Jess-Cooke's argument imaginatively appreciates the significance of 'spin-offs' for an understanding of what Shakespeare 'means' in, and to, popular culture in the twenty-first century.

It is precisely such an absorption in popular culture that Ramona Wray elaborates in her discussion of the 2005 'Shakespeare (Re)-Told' season. Addressing the latest Shakespearean incarnations, Wray argues for a contemporary purchase on Shakespearean comedy, one capable of accommodating the genre's characteristic intransigence in exciting and original ways. Jointly foregrounding identical popular television genres, character types and contemporary media debate, *Much Ado About Nothing* and *The Taming of the Shrew*, Wray argues, demonstrate an assured sense of modern equivalents for Shakespearean comedy and a considered awareness of the ways in which post-feminist understandings operate. Particularly distinctive, in a transformed sexual economy, are the means whereby modern-language adaptation is capable of pushing into productive proximity early modern constructions of gender and twenty-first-century reflections upon life-work balance and male-female relations. Both adaptations suggest the ongoing vibrancy of the Shakespearean word, the utility of his applications and the complexion of his current manifestations. They point, too, to constructions of Shakespeare that are more thematically demanding, and less ironically strident, than the conclusion to *Shakespeare's Happy Endings* would appear to offer. Despite views to the contrary, Shakespeare has been drained neither of 're-telling' potential nor of the energy of his imprimatur. His 'endings' are not so much the stuff of millennial unhappiness as they are the material for an unfolding series of interrogations and interpretations, a sequence of screen Shakespeares that promises a new chapter, another beginning.

Notes

1. The 'mockumentary' was first broadcast on BBC4 on 29 November 2005.
2. Gary Taylor, 'Afterword: The incredible shrinking Bard', in Christy Desmet and Robert Sawyer (eds) (1999), *Shakespeare and Appropriation*, London and New York: Routledge, pp. 198–9.
3. Richard Burt, '*Shakespeare in Love* and the End of the Shakespearean: Academic and Mass Culture Constructions of Literary Authorship', in Mark Thornton Burnett and Ramona Wray (eds) (2000), *Shakespeare, Film, Fin de Siècle*, Basingstoke: Macmillan, pp. 226, 227.
4. http://www.imdb.com/name/nm0000636.
5. http://www.hm.com/uk (the film is available under the '&denim' menu option). All further references are taken from this website and appear in the text.
6. The title, of course, is adapted from Gertrude's response to the players in *Hamlet*, in *The Norton Shakespeare*, Stephen Greenblatt, Walter Cohen, Jean E. Howard and Katharine Eisaman Maus (eds) (1997), New York: W. W. Norton, III.ii.210.
7. Mary C. Beltrán (2005), 'The New Hollywood Racelessness: Only the Fast, Furious (and Multiracial) will Survive', *Cinema Journal*, 44.2, pp. 56, 57, 59.
8. Ronald Niezen (2004), *A World Beyond Difference: Cultural Identity in the Age of Globalization*, Oxford: Blackwell, p. 40; Beltrán, 'New Hollywood Racelessness', p. 50.
9. Edwidge Danticat (2005), 'Inspiration: Pictures with Meaning', *The Guardian Weekend*, 5 November, p. 122.
10. Ken Booth and Tim Dunne (2002), 'Worlds in Collision', in Ken Booth and Tim Dunne (eds), *Worlds in Collision: Terror and the Future of the Global Order*, Basingstoke: Palgrave, p. 20.
11. *The Merchant of Venice*, in *The Norton Shakespeare*, I.iii.29–30.
12. *The Two Gentlemen of Verona*, in *The Norton Shakespeare*, III.i.89.
13. Here, again, '*Romeo and Juliet*' by David Lachapelle recalls Baz Luhrmann's *William Shakespeare's 'Romeo + Juliet'*, with the '&' of the design label self-consciously echoing the '+' of the earlier filmic title.

Chapter 1

'If I'm right': Michael Wood's *In Search of Shakespeare*

Richard Dutton

Two Woods

There are two Michael Woods. One, we infer from the book that accompanies the TV series *In Search of Shakespeare* spends many hours in libraries and consulting leading scholars.[1] Although his book is not disfigured with conventional academic annotation (it is aimed at a middlebrow, not a highbrow readership), it records its extensive debts to scholarship and to solitary reflection. And it is scholarship that is commendably up to the minute. If there is nothing strictly new here, there are many details – for example, John Shakespeare's prosecution for illegal wool-dealing, the latest twists in his possible association with Hoghton Tower in Lancashire, the possible association of *Cymbeline* with the investiture of Prince Henry as Prince of Wales – that are not yet established in conventional biographies. And the whole emphasis on the first Elizabethan age less as a world of letters celebrating its Virgin Queen than as a religious police state, riddled with spying and insecurity, is very much in tune with the politicised literary studies of recent decades. This is the Michael Wood with two Oxford degrees, one a research degree in Anglo-Saxon history: a learned, bookish man, accustomed to the solitude of writing – so, in that respect, not all that unlike his subject here. William Shakespeare must have spent a high proportion of his life writing, poring over his Ovid, his Holinshed, his Plutarch, then writing again. It is a challenge to any biographer to instill drama and excitement into the life of – of all things – a writer. Yet this Wood – let us call him the scholar Wood – does so admirably in his book.

But the challenge is all the greater when the biographer is working in the medium of film, where the target audience is much larger than that envisaged by the book. This audience will probably be characterised as predominantly lower-middlebrow, worldwide (at least, throughout the

English-speaking world, and especially North America), with a short attention-span, and needing to be fed visuals as much as words – though happily it can be distracted for quite long periods with vistas of 'Olde England'. It is in the context of the film series (and previous series he has made) that we find the *other* Michael Wood, an extrovert presenter Mr Hyde to the desk-bound scholar Dr Jekyll. Like most scholars, the first Wood is largely absent from the pages of his book, even as he quietly imposes his personality upon them. But the presenter Wood is omnipresent, both verbally and visually. The formula 'In Search of . . .' is not merely a metaphor. On screen, this really is the tale of a physical search – for documents, for places, for associations – and this Wood is with us every step of the way: earnest, enthusiastic, photogenic. It is not that he avoids libraries and archives – these, after all, are where the key documents live. But where scholar Wood must read, absorb, ruminate, presenter Wood promptly talks us (and their curators) through their significance, a source of instant illumination. He invokes academics and other experts continually in the course of his search, but their expertise is never allowed seriously to disrupt what is essentially *his* narrative flow (even when it sometimes masquerades as dialogue). There is still, to be sure, something of the scholar in the presenter Wood: this is a man who can decipher Elizabethan secretary hand at sight and offer impromptu translations of Latin. But it is never a scholarship that is worn heavily or allowed to seem hard work, nor to offer much in the way of doubt or debate – distractions anathema to the gods of popular film.

So, although the book and the TV series were clearly written and devised by one and the same man – they cover much (not all) of the same material, with similar emphases – they are actually very different beasts. The scholarly underpinnings of the series, which are rarely allowed to register there, are clearly visible in the book, which also has the space to allow more material than can go on air, despite the very generous four hours allowed – an epic in TV documentary terms. This is, as I shall discuss, partly the result of the decision to include in the series elements for which there could be no print equivalent – notably snippets of performance and passages of conversation – which absorbed time entertainingly but perhaps not all that instructively. What follows is largely an account of the TV series and presenter Wood. If I am sometimes less than reverent about his screen mannerisms, please do not misinterpret this as disrespect for the project as a whole, which at its heart offers us a serious and considered Shakespeare for the beginning of the twenty-first century.

Style

The series defines itself, both thematically and stylistically, in the sequences immediately before and after the opening credits of Episode One. The former gives us skyscapes of modern London at night and then of the starkly lit, reconstructed Globe on the Bankside, before which Wood (handsomely sinister in a black leather bomber-jacket) announces that: 'This is a historical detective story, an Elizabethan whodunit', promising us an investigation into the life of Shakespeare 'set against the turbulent times in which he lived'. The credits roll. We are in sunny deciduous woodland, on an unmetalled road, where Wood (now wearing a more casual light-brown jacket and knapsack, which will figure repeatedly hereafter) has an apparently unscripted encounter with a young boy:

BOY: Where are you going?
WOOD: We're walking up the ancient road. It's one of the old roads of
        England.
BOY: Are you walking all the way there?
WOOD: Yes.

These sequences set the filmic parameters of what follows. We are always unmistakably in the here-and-now, at the beginning of the twenty-first century. We are on a historical quest, but it is one that will be conducted in the present, often with the aid of material artefacts – notably documents and buildings – which may derive from the past but which clearly have an identity in contemporary culture. The woody lane may evoke 'Merrie England' or the Forest of Arden but it does not pretend to be, or even to represent, them: a caravan from which the boy has evidently emerged holds us in the present, as does the earnestly enthusiastic figure of Wood himself, a historian far too hip to be mistaken for a figure from the past towards which he walks. The series will end with Shakespeare being described as 'a man whose works are a bridge between the world we have lost and the world we have become', a formulation that neatly encapsulates the series' own handling of history as a process of finding bridging moments between past and present – a formula made for the medium of TV, where it is possible to talk about the past and simultaneously look at the present. We see a fair amount of Wood walking as if in Tudor England, but we also often see him taking the train or the Underground (less often in a car) in our second Elizabethan age. When we hear the story of Marlowe (described at one point as 'gay, hip, iconoclastic') being arrested in Flushing, the pictures dwell on an anonymous figure on a Harley Davidson. When we hear of James VI & I setting off south to claim the throne of England, the pictures we see are of a train, on a bridge on the East Coast line.

This is a stylisation that has little place for historical reconstruction or pastiche. There are no actors here pretending to be Shakespeare, or mouthing words ascribed to him: we are denied an actorly presence, such as that of Joseph Fiennes in *Shakespeare in Love* (2000) or of Tim Curry in the John Mortimer-scripted *Life of Shakespeare* (1978).[2] Anything in that mode would inevitably announce itself as fiction, with a freight of its own, at odds with the Wood search. By the same token, we have become accustomed in recent years to a form of TV history in which action is provided by grainy or soft-focus footage of costumed actors, perhaps riding or fighting (but not speaking from a prohibitively time-consuming and expensive script). There is *almost* none of that here, though there is an intriguing exception when we hear of Edmund Campion and his fellow Jesuits being smuggled into England in 1580 and see an appropriate ship at sea with huddled figures in the dead of night. (We immediately cut back to a much more typical Wood in a car at the floodlit port of Dover.) Similarly, TV history commonly resorts these days to computer simulations as a cheap substitute for grandeur or action. Again, these are largely conspicuous by their absence here. There is a small exception in the final episode where, to evoke James I's 1604 ceremonial entry into London, we see computer graphics of the triumphal arches under which he rode, and superimposed on them indistinct footage of a twentieth-century coronation. But again, these are exceptions that prove the rule.

No, this is not history by fictional or technological reconstruction. Nor does it have any truck with postmodern musings about the medium and the message, or the complicities of representation. It stands by the idea of actuality, of empirically knowable truth. Or, to put it another way, it stands by Michael Wood. As I have suggested, Wood is on-screen for a large part of the time, and is the focus of attention throughout. Even when, for example, actors appear to perform sequences from plays, we see cut-away shots of the audiences' response – and Wood is invariably in the audience. This is no surprise to anyone familiar with Wood's earlier work, much of which follows a similar formula: *In Search of the Dark Ages, In Search of England, In the Footsteps of Alexander the Great* – the common denominator is always Wood himself, comfortably at home with the camera, articulate, casually, but probably expensively, dressed. Like Knowledge in the morality play of *Everyman*, he willingly undertakes to act as the common man's guide through a difficult world: 'Everyman, I will go with thee and be thy guide, / In thy most need to go by thy side'.[3] He never trails his qualifications, but he exudes authority and conviction. He *knows* how to read evidence.

This is a particularly daring tactic to adopt in respect of Shakespeare, so much of whose life remains inscrutable, unknowable and overladen with myth. Wood knows as much, and occasionally admits it. But his characteristic reaction is to make light of it. So, for example, when faced with the actuality of the entry in the Bishop of Worcester's Register (27 November 1582) of the grant of a marriage licence to William Shakespeare and Anne Whateley (not Hathaway), he does not – like Anthony Burgess in his *Shakespeare* (1970) – leap to the conclusion that Anne Whateley was Shakespeare's true love, whom he was only prevented from marrying by friends of the pregnant Anne Hathaway's family (who then made sure he did the honourable thing). Rather, he suggests an overworked and confused clerk, who had been dealing with Whateleys in another connection and here made a simple mistake. It is a common-sense solution, frequently followed by other biographers. But when a similar matter-of-factness is applied to other matters – sometimes without even revealing that a judgement of this sort has been made – the effect can be more worrying. So in the first episode, about Shakespeare's early years, Wood is pictured in the King Edward VI School at Stratford, saying: 'William was taught in *this* school-room'. This is very likely, but it is more than we actually know. As an alderman of the town, and sometime bailiff (Wood says 'mayor', a more familiar term though not strictly accurate), John Shakespeare was entitled to have his sons educated free in the town's grammar school. But the records of the school for the period are missing, so we have no concrete proof. Again, that Shakespeare attended that school is common-sense likelihood, but there is room here for 'probably'. The issue becomes more critical slightly later when (after tracing the likely source of John Shakespeare's notable early wealth and standing as 'a brogger – an illegal wool-dealer') Wood links the end of that illicit trading with the end of William's education: 'his father took him out of school early. At the age of fourteen he found himself cut off from the chance of higher education and the chances of going to university'. This is in fact considerably more than we know or might guess. Yes, John Shakespeare fell on hard times, and William certainly did not go to university. But to state categorically that he did not complete the humanist curriculum of a grammar school is to make a serious claim for which there is no evidence. Baconians, Marlovians and Oxfordians have traded on the supposed implausibility of Shakespeare becoming the writer he did without a university education: to have him leaving school this early is to play into their hands.

To be fair, such lapses are rare.[4] But another instance gives more indication of how potentially misleading such apparent certainties can be. In the third episode, we are told that 'only days after *The Dream* was played before the Queen, Southwell was hanged, drawn and quartered at Tyburn'.[5] This claim is made in order to accentuate the distance between Shakespeare as a writer of popular and courtly theatre and the Jesuit Robert Southwell, author of religious poetry: it also tacitly draws a picture of Queen Elizabeth as a pleasure-loving monarch, at a time when many people were being put viciously to death in her name. But we have no evidence that *A Midsummer Night's Dream* was ever played before her: that it *may* have been is tied in with extensive suppositions (which Wood does not pursue) about it having been written for some aristocratic wedding which Elizabeth might have attended. But this itself is contentious, and besides we have no absolute certainty that the play was written before 1598. Wood, in fact, has been economical with the truth because it conveniently underscores what we may describe as the principal thesis underlying the series. He may want to give the impression that he is walking up 'the ancient road' to encounter what he finds in the historical record with an open mind, in a spirit of impartial factuality: he sees the document, and it reveals its truth to/through him. But it is not, and cannot be, as simple as that. The historical record (as Shakespeare's own history plays demonstrate only too well) can be – quite legitimately – read many ways. In this instance, as in many others, Wood is predisposed to read the record firstly and most insistently in the light of the religious conflicts of the early modern era (the driving force behind 'the turbulent times in which he lived'), and to search for Shakespeare within these.

Substance

This is all rather more elegantly outlined in the book, which opens with a prologue in which John Shakespeare, as bailiff of Stratford, is called upon to obliterate the medieval (and so Catholic-tainted) wall paintings in the town's Guild Chapel. The work is done but only amounts to a thin whitewashing, which might conceivably have been reversed had English history performed yet another religious U-turn in the tortuous sequence that ran from Henry VIII through Edward VI and Mary to Elizabeth. (On screen, Wood knowingly sums up the Tudors as 'a dysfunctional family if there ever was one' – and, unlike many earlier historians, he does not exclude Elizabeth from that judgement; in the book she is characterised as 'brilliant, vulnerable, psychologically damaged' (p. 69).) This is posited as a central metaphor: William Shakespeare born into a deeply

Roman Catholic world, the world of English myth and memory to which his mother's Arden family was certainly attached and to which John Shakespeare also (apparently) subscribed in setting his hand to a Jesuit-borne Spiritual Testament. This world was constantly in friction with Elizabeth's police state of a Protestant regime, though the intensity might vary depending on circumstances. But it proved to be fighting a lost cause, so that (whatever William's personal convictions) the whitewash had effectively triumphed by the end of his life, a bridge had been irrevocably crossed and there could be no going back. All of this is certainly in the TV series, but it is not established with quite the same polish or centrality in the first episode, doubtless because in televisual mode other themes and issues were vying for early positioning. I mentioned earlier the actors: they have to be introduced. Also, in a work trailed as a 'whodunit', it is important to come quickly to the plot, to the evidence which will be encountered and how it will be investigated. So we move quickly to the record of William Shakespeare's baptism, which of course gives us dates, places and persons – the building blocks of the plot. Significantly, in line with the stylisation I described earlier, we do not see a re-enactment of the events behind that register entry. Instead, we see shots of a modern baptism (one of the first 'bridging moments') intercut with woodcuts of Elizabethan ones. This is a world we have lost; but it is also where our own world begins.

In the TV series, therefore, religion at first seems only one of a number of preoccupations, but it quickly becomes apparent how central it is in the amount of air-time it consumes. 'Elizabeth's England must have been a schizophrenic place, the old religion still in so many hearts, and the new secular age waiting to be born. And young Will right at the heart of it'. This is very much in tune with Shakespeare studies in the wake of New Historicism and Cultural Materialism: we are less inclined to idealise, more to see in the great plays and poems violence, power struggles, tensions. This emphasis is, for example, largely responsible for the fact that fully half of the series (the first two episodes) are devoted to Shakespeare *before* he emerges in the written records as a playwright – that is, before he is identified as a member of the Lord Chamberlain's Men.[6] So, in the account of Shakespeare's family, significant emphasis is placed on the will of mother Mary's father, Robert Arden ('This is it, the document itself', Wood enthuses, holding the parchment like a holy relic). The point is that the will is unmistakably couched in the language of the Old Faith, a marker of how closely it can be tied to Shakespeare's immediate family on his mother's side. Similarly, the business of the entry of the wedding licence quickly passes over the Whateley/Hathaway confusion to focus on the fact that the bride is associated there, not with Stratford, but with Temple Grafton. Wood quickly identifies a reason (*the* reason?) for this: whereas the Stratford parson in 1583 was Puritan-leaning, John Frith in Temple Grafton was a hold-over from Queen Mary's reign, inclining to the Old Faith even if he maintained a façade of Anglican orthodoxy. He collected simples and medicinal herbs, like Friar Lawrence in *Romeo and Juliet*. Here was a priest who might conduct a marriage more in tune with the old ways.

The brief (and stylistically anomalous) reconstructed scene of the Jesuits at sea is, in this connection, obviously meant to mark a dramatic development: 'The time for compromise was over'. Catholics like the Shakespeares increasingly had to commit themselves to one camp or the other. This ushers in the tale of John Shakespeare's Spiritual Testament, discovered by workmen in the eighteenth century, transcribed by Edmund Malone, but then lost – and only verified when other versions of such documents came to light in the twentieth century. Wood is thus deprived of the truly talismanic bridging document – material evidence in the present of a significance in the past – but makes do with showing us a place (*the* place?) in the thatched rafters of the Shakespeare house in Henley Street where it might have been found. The narrative here is building to William's leaving home, at some point in the 1580s. The most popular anecdote about his doing so supposes that he left because he was caught poaching deer in the Charlcotte deer-park of the Warwickshire magnate, Sir Thomas Lucy. Pedantic history objects that Lucy had no deer-park at Charlcotte in Shakespeare's time, only an enclosure for rabbits. But more important for Wood is the fact that Lucy was one of the most important Protestant enforcers in Warwickshire, unswervingly loyal to Elizabeth's favourite, the Earl of Leicester, and to the Protestant ascendancy. Is it possible, Wood asks, that the deer-poaching legend remembers some friction between Shakespeare and the man who represented everything that threatened his family's culture? Episode One ends with an account of the arrest and barbarous execution of Edward Arden, the head of the old Warwickshire Ardens (an important relative, if not a close one, of Shakespeare's mother). He was done to judicial death by the Protestant authorities on no real grounds other than the fact of his faith. Of the effect of that execution, Wood claims special insight: 'As we shall see, Shakespeare never forgot'.

Episode Two opens 100 miles north of Stratford, at Hoghton Tower near Preston in Lancashire. Wood is in pursuit of the theory that Shakespeare may have been the William Shakeshafte mentioned, in connection with household theatricals, in the 1581 will of Alexander

Hoghton. This was first floated in the 1930s, relaunched with compelling new evidence by Ernst Honigmann in 1987, and has since been vigorously championed by Richard Wilson.[7] In a quintessential bridging moment, Wood greets the current family owner of Hoghton Tower, Sir Bernard de Hoghton (and cannot resist reminding him that he first visited 'in pursuit of Shakespeare' twenty years earlier – that is, before the current vogue for the theory): together they peruse the will.[8] We have been told that several of Shakespeare's presumed Stratford schoolmasters were Lancastrian Catholics (Lancashire being an even stauncher hotbed of Catholicism than Warwickshire); now we learn that 'William's Stratford teacher was a Hoghton man'. The beauty of the Hoghton theory is that it ties together so many features of the Shakespeare story: it fits one of the best attested of the early anecdotes, about him being 'a schoolmaster in the country' (which derives from William Beeston, son of the fellow actor, Christopher); it introduces him to key figures – not only the Hoghtons, but the Heskeths (Thomas Savage who helped finance the Globe was married to a Hesketh); and it provides him with an entrée to the world of theatre, firstly in noble households, but potentially also encountering professional troupes patronised by the great magnates of the north-west, the Stanley Earls of Derby. These key figures were all (and this is the glue that holds this all together) crypto-Catholics – as we may suppose the poet to be. Shakespeare certainly wrote for the players of the heir to the title, Ferdinando, Lord Strange, in the early 1590s, and many of these were later to join with him in the Lord Chamberlain's Men. As a theory, it has most things going for it – except proof.[9] Wood is surely right, however, in pointing out that it demonstrates how patronage networks worked at the time, especially in the Catholic underground, and how professional playing was still closely linked with entertainments in great households. 'So whether William was Shakeshafte or not, Lancashire is an important part of the story.'

Episode Two moves into the question of how Shakespeare became fully involved in the professional theatre, opting for the much favoured current theory that he might have joined the Queen's Men when they visited Stratford (to which he must have returned for his marriage and the begetting of his children) in 1587, having lost one of their principal players in a duel. His entry into London theatre is thus set against the backdrop of the defeat of the Spanish Armada, the military highpoint of the Elizabethan regime, which must have been an ambivalent moment for many Catholics. The propaganda war surrounding this is knowingly evoked with clips from *Fire Over England* (1937), a pro-rearmament vehicle in its day which now just looks naively patriotic. The 'imaginal'

Shakespeare at the heart of this dangerous world is characterised as 'funny, streetwise, sexy', but his Catholic upbringing is still not an exhausted topic.[10] Episode Three opens at Baddesley Clinton near Stratford, home of the Ferrars family, and relates the tale of pursuivant searches for Robert Southwell: Wood himself characteristically descends into the sewers where the Jesuit and his fellows (for the time being) escaped detection. This focus on Southwell is a telling mark of Wood's predisposition. Southwell is not even mentioned in Samuel Schoenbaum's *William Shakespeare: A Compact Documentary Life* (1977), which for an earlier generation was the most robust and reliable biography of Shakespeare. Wood, however, attaches a good deal of significance to a preface that Southwell wrote around 1592 and circulated in manuscript with his poems; it is addressed 'To My Worthy Good Cosen, Maister W. S.', whom Wood takes (he is not original in this, though the theory has not recently been fashionable) to be Shakespeare, who was indeed a very distant relative. The preface praises W. S. as a superior poet, but condemns him for 'playing with pagan toys' – that is, writing secular verse rather than spiritual poetry like his own. As Wood puts it, he 'took him to task on the role of the poet'. If Shakespeare really was W. S., Southwell's subsequent barbarous execution by hanging, drawing and quartering cannot but have challenged the very basis of the lifestyle he had chosen in writing for the stage and for money.

In 1593, however, that career choice was challenged in other ways. Severe plague closed the theatres and eventually led to the break-up of many of the established acting companies. Wood follows most authorities in assuming that Shakespeare's turn to writing narrative verse, in *Venus and Adonis*, was prompted by these circumstances. His choice of the third Earl of Southampton as dedicatee was, however, apparently dictated by a familiar agenda: 'the Southamptons leaned to the Old Faith', and there is discussion of the earl's mother harbouring Catholic priests at their various houses. This takes us to the fate of Southwell and, against footage of Beefeaters and the Tower of London, Wood observes: 'Easy to forget, isn't it, the dark side of Shakespeare's world? Southwell was one of 36,000 people who died on the scaffold or in prison in Elizabeth's reign, among them members of Shakespeare's own family'. It is here, however, that the strain of Wood's attempt to tell the full tale of Shakespeare, while giving the religious theme such prominence, really begins to tell, since his interest in Southampton quickly wanes – so quickly in fact that there is no mention of the *Rape of Lucrece*, the dedication of which most scholars agree is more warmly personal than that of *Venus and Adonis*.

This must be because another agenda now intervenes, all but derailing the religious one. The Stratford burial register in 1596 records the death of Shakespeare's son, Hamnet. This must, of course, have been a terrible blow: the death of his only son and male heir, all but mocking the family's efforts to establish its gentry, which came to fruition shortly afterwards with the grant of a coat of arms. (More primary documents are in the College of Heralds, a 'bridging' institution if ever there was one: in the book, Wood speaks of it having 'more than a faint whiff of Hogwarts, Griffender and Ravenclaw' (p. 167).)[11] But Wood sees in Hamnet's death one of the mainsprings behind the writing of the sonnets. This flows against the modern tide, which has increasingly seen Southampton c. 1593/4 as the likeliest of the sonnets' primary subjects. Jonathan Bate even invokes Occam's razor to stress, with italic emphasis, the strength of the case for Southampton: '*All candidatures for the fair youth with the exception of Southampton's depend on things not known to exist; it is not necessary to postulate any of these things as existing, since the origin of the sonnets can be explained with things we do know to exist.*'[12] Wood, however, eagerly follows the contra-flow created by Katherine Duncan-Jones in her Arden edition of the sonnets and biographical *Ungentle Shakespeare*, which resurrect the other principal candidate, William Herbert, from 1601 the third Earl of Pembroke.[13]

Wood marks his radicalism here with 'If I'm right' – a repeated formula of his, meaning 'there is an even bigger element of speculation about what follows than usual': 'the next spring Shakespeare got a commission from one of the great literary patrons, Lady Mary Herbert of Wilton. He was to write sonnets for the seventeenth birthday of one of her children'. The idea that Pembroke might have been the recipient of the sonnets (that is, Mr W. H., their 'only begetter', as the dedication perhaps has it) is hardly new. But Wood invokes it in a particular cause, which is not that of Duncan-Jones herself.[14] He does not exactly duck the issue that most of them were written to a man; indeed, he invokes the eminent Shakespearean, Stanley Wells, to delicately make the point that the Renaissance did not draw the same lines between hetero- and homosexual love that we do today. But Wood makes this secondary to the idea that Shakespeare was, in these poems, finding an outlet for bottled-up grief over his son: commissioned to write to urge young Herbert to marry and have children, he must have been reminded of the loss of his own male issue. And once he was over the rather mechanical commission which many identify in the first seventeen sonnets, his intense feelings for the 'fair youth' might well have been fuelled by complex feelings about the son who doubtless meant much to him, but whom (given his lifestyle, away from Stratford so much of the time) he had perhaps seen little of. Wood reads aptly and movingly from the sonnets in this vein as he wanders in the gorgeous, sun-drenched grounds of the Wilton estate. In fact, he is so dedicated to this thesis that he never specifically identifies William Herbert at all – only vaguely mentioning Mary Herbert's son; nor does he make the point, so often advanced by others who see Pembroke as the 'fair youth', that in 1623 Heminge and Condell were to dedicate the Shakespeare First Folio to him and his brother, claiming that they had 'prosecuted both [the plays], and their author living, with so much favour'.

This version of the passion behind the sonnets is the clearest – and most questionable – instance of Wood ('If I'm right') claiming to be able to read through the works themselves to the heart of the man. He carries this into the so-called 'dating sonnets', claiming 107 (with its 'The mortal moon hath her eclipse endured') as an unequivocal reflection on the death of Elizabeth, and claiming the disenchanted boast in 125 that 'I bore the canopy' as a reference to his role in the ceremonial entry of James I into London.[15] Both of these are perhaps more plausible if we accept Herbert as the 'fair youth', though such late dating would not square as well with the Southampton thesis, focused around 1593/4: the determination to read the sonnets in the wake of Hamnet's death thus has consequences within consequences. Plausible coherence diminishes even further when we consider Wood's candidate for the 'Dark Lady': Emilia Bassano/Lanier, first advanced with self-defeating arrogance by A. L. Rowse. Lanier is a fascinating candidate – apparently the former mistress of Shakespeare's theatrical patron, the first Lord Hunsdon, and a member of the Venetian Jewish Bassano family of musicians (and so plausibly both musical and dark-skinned, as the scenario of the sonnets seems to require). Wood also wants to make the point that Lanier is one of the earliest published women poets in England, whose *Salve Deus Rex Judaeorum* came out very shortly after Shakespeare's sonnets.[16] She is thus a particularly intriguing rival (alongside the *male* 'rival poet') in poetic matters as well as sexual ones. The real problem here is timing and circumstance: by 1597 the elder Hunsdon was dead, and there is nothing to associate Lanier with Pembroke or his circle. The 'Dark Lady's' belated narrative appearance in the sonnets would make much more sense, with Lanier in the role, around 1594, when Shakespeare retreated from Southampton and returned to the theatrical scene, for the first time associated with Hunsdon. Much of a Shakespeare biography is inevitably speculation, but it should be consistent speculation: you cannot simply pick and mix. In that sense, Wood's choices for the 'fair youth' and the

'Dark Lady' in the sonnets are not really compatible: each is plausible and intriguing in itself, but they do not add up. At the same time, the rather sketchy attention that Southampton and Pembroke actually receive here suggests the pressure Wood is now under to fit everything in.

We have not yet quite lost the religious theme, though it takes something of a back seat in the second half of Episode Three and much of Episode Four – until we reach the Gunpowder Plot, which is another major bridging moment. Most of the plotters are associated with Catholic Warwickshire and include men (like the leader, Robert Catesby) who came from families that Shakespeare must have known. To convey the import of the plot, we have pictures of a modern opening of Parliament and are told, in a particularly telling analogy, that it was 'nothing less than a Jacobean 9/11' (in intention: of course, it failed miserably). In another soundbite from contemporary affairs, Wood suggests that 'for Catholic England it was the end of history'. Yet for Wood's Shakespeare it hardly seems to have such resonance. He detects in the major tragedies a growing skepticism in matters of faith. In the book we read: 'By the time he wrote [*Hamlet*] around 1600, Shakespeare was . . . probably no longer a Catholic. But he never sounds like a Protestant' (p. 78). Although Wood acknowledges that some contemporaries (at least) felt that *King Lear* spoke to the cause of the Old Faith, he does not see in this Shakespeare's personal convictions. He makes the usual connections between *Macbeth* and the Gunpowder Plot, but more in the spirit of Shakespeare being playwright-in-residence for a King James obsessed with witchcraft and plots against his own life than in terms of making a personal statement. We do hear that his elder daughter, Susannah, was indicted for recusancy in the crackdown that followed the plot. But there is an odd sense that this theme, which has so dominated the series, has rather run into the sand.

This must in part be because Wood only argues for indirect connections between Shakespeare's writing and his Catholic upbringing, not for a sustained (albeit covert) commitment to its doctrines. He does make the point that many of his plays focus on an English history that was perforce a Catholic history, and that he often seems to evoke 'the holy women and good friars of Old England'. But he is not inclined to investigate closer connections: he tells us that John Speed in his *History of Great Britain* (1611) linked Shakespeare with the Jesuit propagandist Robert Persons in his depiction of Falstaff ('this papist and his poet'), but he does not want to pursue how such a claim might inform our reading of the character – who has been shown simply as a gloriously universal comic character. Wood justifies his emphasis on religious matters not because they open up a specific agenda in the writing, but because they offer a major insight into Shakespeare's psychology, or at least his psychic world. He is a notoriously anonymous and self-effacing author: we actually know a surprising amount about his business dealings, his London residences, his non-payment of taxes, but about the man and his personality we have little to go on beyond uncorroborated anecdotes, most recorded many years after his death.

These are mysteries we cannot unlock with an open-minded journey to the Public Record Office. The whole religious context, however, offers us the tantalising possibility of a way into the man's soul. If he was indeed brought up in a strongly committed Catholic household, he would have had to learn to keep his private convictions *intensely* private – like John Shakespeare's Spiritual Testament, secreted away in the rafters of the house. Wood comments on the preponderance of historical subjects in the plays: 'Writing critically about contemporary politics was impossible, so history was a way of articulating the pressure of the times'. That is, he characteristically expressed himself by indirections. At the same time, if he belonged to a Catholic circle that had to operate within the framework of a Protestant orthodoxy, he might have cultivated a particular sensitivity to the situation of strangers or outsiders: Wood focuses upon Jews and blacks, but the analysis might also stand, say, for bastards, or indeed for women who are not comfortable with the roles their culture imposed on them. More generally, such an upbringing might have inculcated a capacity for understanding more than one point of view at once, which is certainly a skill he brought to writing plays.

Distractions

These are interesting propositions, which deserve more attention than they actually receive here. This must in part be because they have to share screen time with other matters. It may be perverse to say so, of a series about the greatest playwright in the language, but the most distracting of these is the recurrent presence of actors. With no disrespect to the skills of those involved (mostly members of the Royal Shakespeare Company), their precise function in the wider narrative seems not to have been thought through. It is linked to Wood's determination to identify actual sites in which Shakespeare and his fellows acted. These include the location of James Burbage's original theatre in 'the wild and lawless suburbs of Shoreditch', tracked down (on camera: it is not in the book) behind what is now Crispins' veneer shop. There is, sadly, absolutely nothing theatrical now identifiable, but the actors are brought on to ooh and ah

about this sacred site. They have more to do in other sites. The most constructive instance is in the Guild Hall at Stratford, where they stand in for
the Queen's Men to offer us a flavour of the *Troublesome Raigne of King
John*, emphasising the patriotic Protestant message it contained, which
Shakespeare was to transmute when he later revisited the material. But in
other sites, such as the New Inn in Gloucester, the last surviving galleried
inn of the kind that Elizabethan actors regularly used, the modern actors
are really only there to give us snippets of Shakespeare's greatest hits – the
ass-turned Bottom, Falstaff and Hal in the Eastcheap tavern, Juliet
lamenting that Romeo was Romeo, and so on. The same is true at the
Globe – a simulation, of course, not the real thing – and in The Swan at
Stratford, which doubles for an indoor Blackfriars. Each of these sites
offers a bridging opportunity to investigate what it might have been like
playing in the round, or to use the kind of stage machinery we know to
have been available to the Elizabethans, or even to have customers sitting
on stage, as they did at the Blackfriars. But that was not the spirit of the
exercise: these are always modern actors, not theatrical archaeologists
making bridging leaps. In this respect, they serve a less focused purpose
than the historical documents with which they vie for prominence. The
clearest marker of this is that actresses play the female roles, as of course
they did not in Shakespeare's day. The business of boy actors and their
female impersonations is siphoned off into scenes of Stratford schoolboys
performing *Ralph Roister-Doister* in the old schoolroom above the Guild
Hall. This suggests how the Elizabethan humanist school curriculum
drew on drama, but in the context of demonstrating that performances
like this (cross-dressing and all) are still very much part of single-sex education in Britain – and so, implicitly, not all that remarkable. Apart from
one lingering shot of a lipsticked boy in a blonde wig, the series makes no
effort to plumb the depths of Elizabethan gender-construction or the
intense homosociality of its theatre.

So the actors are, in many ways, a distraction from the more serious
historical questions being asked by the series. There are further distractions in many of those whom Wood engages in conversation in the course
of his 'search'. Some of these are notable Shakespeareans and have (as in
the sequence with Stanley Wells and the sonnets) been drafted in to
offer – even if it is disguised as conversation – what is effectively a structured 'piece to camera', aptly summarising a key point. Some, like
Richard Wilson on matters at Hoghton and the property in the
Blackfriars gatehouse which Shakespeare acquired late in life, manage to
engineer their own pieces to camera out of not very helpful cues. Others
seem really rather wasted: Peter Blayney, for example, was apparently

brought over from Toronto to demonstrate his immense knowledge of the Elizabethan book trade by indicating a space outside St Paul's Cathedral where the stall of a bookseller who sold copies of *Henry IV* once stood. How much else finished up on the cutting-room floor? More generally, however, what we see is in the mode of Wood's encounter with the little boy at the very beginning of the series – apparently spontaneous and off the cuff, supplying atmosphere more than information. So we have former mayors of Stratford, engaged in conversation about John Shakespeare's activities in that role 400 years previously: if there was supposed to be a script here, they were not very good at sticking to it. Similarly, Lord Montagu of Beaulieu turns up as a descendant (or something) of Shakespeare's Southampton, to offer not very authoritative answers on such questions as whether the story that the Earl gave Shakespeare £1,000 might have been true. And various record keepers, from Stratford archives to the College of Heralds to the Public Record Office, are led in rather casual conversations that might, or might not, elucidate the documents in their keeping. There is a classic instance of this in the final episode where, in pursuit of the scarlet cloth issued for the entry of James I, Wood visits Ede and Ravenscroft, robe-makers to the Queen. He enters the shop, marvelling to camera that such places still exist, and asks an assistant – who almost certainly did not expect him, or his camera crew – where to find the man he had come to interview. That man doubtless knew in advance what was to happen, but there is little evidence of rehearsal: conversation circles amiably around red cloth, and makes its points in passing. It is as if the key issue is to keep the whole event spontaneous and unscripted. This is presumably meant to keep everything lively and informal, but it also has the effect of keeping authority quite firmly in Wood's hands: he is not about to allow hardened professionals to pontificate on their own terms, or even to suggest alternative lines of thought. They can help him on his way, but will not be allowed to upstage him.

This, then, is a Shakespeare for the twenty-first century. In 1978, John Mortimer produced a fictionalised TV Shakespeare who spoke to the era's hedonism and sexually liberated ways: the casting of Tim Curry, fresh from his triumph as the rampantly bisexual Frankenfurter in Richard O'Brien's *Rocky Horror Show*, was not accidental. Wood's unseen Shakespeare is the product of a religious Cold War which ended in a (failed) 9/11 explosion – a set of circumstances which made of him 'writer, actor, director . . . the artist-in-chief of the Elizabethan state. In the Elizabethan police state, theatre . . . had a thrilling and dangerous power'. He is unseen because ('If I'm right') he was as self-effacing in his writing as he was in dealing with authority, constantly shifting digs in London, or retreating to Stratford, as occasion demanded. Though we cannot actually see him, he is visible to us all (not just specialist scholars) through the good offices of Michael Wood, to the very end Knowledge to our Everyman, and the only knowledge we really need.

Notes

1. *In Search of Shakespeare* is the title both of the four-part TV series, presented by Michael Wood, produced by Maya Vision and first broadcast on BBC2 in 2003 (and issued on video by BBC Worldwide Ltd the same year: BBCV7485); and of the book to accompany the series, written by Michael Wood and published by BBC Worldwide Ltd in 2003. My comments relate to the video, except where I explicitly refer to the book.
2. Also circulated on video as *William Shakespeare, His Life and Times* (1978).
3. *Everyman*, in A. C. Cawley (ed.) (1956), *Everyman and Medieval Mystery Plays*, London: Dent, ll. 523–4.
4. Wood is normally quite factually scrupulous. The gaps in his knowledge tend to show most around theatrical history. For example, when in the final episode he discusses the acquisition of the Blackfriars theatre by the King's Men, he seems not to know that James Burbage had converted the playing space there as early as 1596, and that the Children of the Revels had been playing there since 1599/1600. He also gives the date of the burning of the first Globe as 1614 when it was actually 1613. The book is more secure on both these points, but becomes oddly confused whenever it deals with Ben Jonson. For example, it is under the impression that he was working exclusively for Shakespeare's company around 1599/1600 (p. 227), which is just not true; and it bizarrely suggests that he 'perhaps lampoons Lovewhit [sic] in *Volpone*' (p. 315). Lovewit actually appears in *The Alchemist*, and it is very doubtful that he lampoons anyone. In the book Wood is also confused (p. 266) about the distribution of roles in masques between courtiers (who were almost invariably non-speakers) and professional actors. Other notable slips include having Shakespeare 'influenced by the debate over "humours" in Burton's *Anatomy of Melancholy*' (p. 240), which was not published until 1621, and describing Samuel Harsnett – then a lowly chaplain to the Bishop of London, even if he did eventually become Archbishop of York – as 'a Privy Councillor' (p. 276). But these are rare blemishes amid much solid historical research.
5. Again, the book is more circumspect: 'in 1595 or 1596, *A Midsummer Night's Dream* was played, perhaps before the queen at court in Greenwich' (p. 161). He is apparently thinking about the wedding of William Stanley, sixth Earl of Derby, though there is nothing actually to associate Shakespeare with the Stanleys after the death of William's brother, Ferdinando, in 1594.
6. As I shall suggest later, this leads to a palpable imbalance of material, especially in Episode Three.
7. Most notably in his *Secret Shakespeare* (Manchester: Manchester University Press, 2004).
8. If it was the real document, it was presumably brought over from Preston Record Office for the occasion. But it looks so much more authentic in the Great Hall of Hoghton Tower. I should acknowledge that Richard Wilson and I were colleagues for many years at Lancaster University, and that I was one of those who organised a *Lancastrian Shakespeare* conference in 1999, partly held at Hoghton Tower.

9. The Hoghton theory receives far less prominence in the book than in the series, because of a recent article by Robert Bearman (' "Was William Shakespeare William Shakeshafte" Revisited', *Shakespeare Quarterly*, 53 (2002), pp. 83–94), which demonstrates the prevalence of Shakeshafte as a name in the Preston region. Citing this, Wood claims in his 'Further Reading' that 'the "Shakeshafte" theory has not survived closer scrutiny' (p. 346). Of course, that very prevalence might explain why Alexander Hoghton would think of Shakespeare as Shakeshafte – just as, in an instance Wood shows, the clerk of the Revels Accounts thought of him as 'Shaxberd' – and Bearman is by no means the last word that Wood takes him to be.

10. A word rather favoured in the book, but eschewed on screen.

11. In Episode Four, the response of writers to the accession of James I as a philosopher/poet prince, who had use for their services, is compared to 'Cool Britannia'. The shelf life of such comparisons is very short.

12. Jonathan Bate (1997), *The Genius of Shakespeare*, London: Picador, p. 47.

13. Katherine Duncan-Jones (ed.) (1997), *Shakespeare's Sonnets*, London: Arden Shakespeare; (2001) *Ungentle Shakespeare: Scenes from His Life*, London: Arden Shakespeare.

14. Pembroke was a man of Protestant, even Puritan, leanings, which of course does not help the Catholic case. But Wood obviously thinks that a secondary issue in this context.

15. The 'mortal moon' has been interpreted in many other ways, including as a reference to the formation of the Spanish Armada, Elizabeth's survival of the supposed Dr Lopez plot (1594) and her outliving of her 'climacteric' year (1596); and while we know that Shakespeare and his fellows were awarded scarlet cloth for James' entry, there is no concrete evidence that they took part in it.

16. In the book, Wood explicitly describes Lanier as 'the first woman in England to publish a volume of poetry' (p. 201). Scholarship now accords Isabella Whitney that honour.

Chapter 2

'I see my father' in 'my mind's eye': Surveillance and the Filmic *Hamlet*

Mark Thornton Burnett

A recent editorial in *The Guardian* claims that governments are building 'a global registration and surveillance infrastructure' in the 'US war on terror'. The aim, it is argued, is 'to monitor the movements and activities of entire populations' in what has been termed ' "an unprecedented project of social control" '.[1] In keeping with the associations of the term 'warning' that appears in the header, the report is concerned less with the details of the scheme than with the seeming threat that an increased deployment of surveillance poses to civil liberties. Such a viewpoint makes a logistical sense in the light of the proliferation of surveillance practices that characterises postmodernity. Generally understood as the process of 'watching over', surveillance is now routinely evident in almost all aspects of everyday life, making itself felt in the use of credit cards, mobile phones and the internet, in the activities of voting, shopping and working, and in the operations of a range of public and private institutions and organisations, to the extent that the Western world has been dubbed both a 'maximum security society' and a 'superpanopticon'.[2] It was not always thus. The late eighteenth-century panopticon, as conceived and designed by English reformist Jeremy Bentham, imagined surveillance embodying itself primarily and ideally in the prison, in which a central tower surrounded by a circular perimeter of cells ensured at all times the visibility of the observed and the invisibility of the observer. This hierarchical discipline, which was modelled on contemporary beliefs in divine omniscience, depended, as Michel Foucault writes, on equations between 'security and knowledge, individualization and totalization, [and] isolation and transparency', thereby facilitating the smooth running of an optics of power.[3] By contrast, particularly in the wake of 9/11, twenty-first-century forms of surveillance are at once more diffuse and less localised, centred, as they are, not so much upon a single institution as upon plural information flows, multiple social systems and transnational information networks. Computers and cameras, rather than specific carceral domains, constitute the new surveillance landscape.

In this chapter, I discuss three film versions of *Hamlet* – Campbell Scott and Eric Simonson's 2000 release, Michael Almereyda's cinematic undertaking of the same year, and Stephen Cavanagh's 2005 Derry Film Initiative screen reading of Shakespeare's play. First shown on the Odyssey cable channel, Scott and Simonson's *Hamlet* is a made-for-television production set in the late nineteenth century and inspired by the heritage industry; in contrast, Almereyda's work represents a millennial, modern New York scene and is defined by its appeal to the art-house market. The Derry Film Initiative is a grassroots, collaborative organisation directed towards the development of a film industry in the north-west of Ireland, and its *Hamlet* appears as a raw, visceral feature urgently attuned to, and making extensive use of, politicised, present-day Londonderry locations. Differences notwithstanding, these films come together in being absorbed by, and endeavouring to tease out the implications of, postmodern surveillance practices. The play's concern with spying cedes place to a filmic grammar of looking and looks, to a visual regime in which surveillance is everywhere apparent. Such a filmic translation is sufficiently flexible, moreover, to allow for cross-reference and reflection: each *Hamlet*, for instance, invokes the prison and gestures towards the trajectory that has shaped surveillance in its various historical incarnations. Traversing the institutional and technological means whereby surveillance is organised, the filmic *Hamlet*s of the twenty-first century are acutely self-conscious in contemplating how, where and with what ideological effects the gaze originates. In this sense, they begin the process of mediating the connections binding surveillance and cinema, and implicitly conclude by suggesting that, in a terror-haunted world, film itself might constitute an optical disciplinary mechanism.

I

Because Campbell Scott and Eric Simonson's *Hamlet* (2000) uses Hempstead House, a magisterial Long Island residence constructed in 1912 by the Gould family, for its exteriors and interiors, the film immediately presents itself as surveillantly preoccupied. Designed in the style of a Tudor manor house, the property is dominated by two towers, which, within and without, allow for a range of observational opportunity. Maximum advantage is taken of a series of linked central halls which give onto each other, of banisters that permit wide-angle glimpses of the main staircase, and of eyelets in the Gothic stonework of the reception rooms; as a result, occasions both public and private become subject to scrutiny, and points of view assume an inquisitorial, inquisitive uniformity. Interior panopticism is matched by exterior surveillance suggestions: throughout, the film privileges shots of gargoyles that adorn the house's façade. Samuel Crowl writes that this ornamental stonework 'suggests the pressure of the ancient past', yet alternative interpretations come into play if we note the ways in which particular gargoyles are punctuationally deployed.[4] Thus, the countenance of a grave knight acts as a prelude to the appearance of the ghost; the figure of a jester marks the transition to Polonius; and the form of a fanged demon announces Ophelia's descent into madness. The effect, bolstered in part by upward shots that prioritise downward-looking gargoyles, is to suggest that all of the players are moulded according to surveillance modes: figuratively, each cast member is possessed of a deity – or nemesis – who watches over individualised segments of the proceedings. These surveillant forces are equally connotative of eventual extinction and subsequent memorialisation; in their stony and eroded passivity, the gargoyles bring skulls to mind and thus serve as predictive observers of mortality, of an action that has been foreseen before it has taken place. Camera work functions finally to construct an illusion of the gargoyles ringing the house, and this is taken up in a more general enlistment of 360° pans, which, particularly in the opening scene, sweep around the guards, reinforcing an impression both of constriction and an encircling eye. To be looked at in Scott and Simonson's *Hamlet* is, it seems, synonymous with being incarcerated.

But surveillance is not identically applied; it is also gendered and hierarchised. A pronounced sense of a controlling, entrenched and authorised vision is embodied in Claudius' (Jamey Sheridan) line that Hamlet should remain in 'the cheer and comfort of our eye'; because the sentiment is preceded by a scene in which Polonius (Roscoe Lee Browne) inspects and then burns legal papers, the implication is that the King's public role depends upon private servants who function both as his eyes and executioners.[5] In this construction of Elsinore, then, although surveillance is a common denominator, carefully gradated levels of power define its ownership and extent. Crucially, Hamlet (Campbell Scott) himself is invariably excluded from surveillance's operations, as when he is filmed against portraits of his father, uncle and mother: he is discovered as metaphorically overseen by this trinity of the ruling elite, which suggests that, even at the level of inanimate representation, the protagonist is a target of enquiry. The symbolic import of the images is crystallised when Hamlet takes down from the wall the portrait of Claudius, only to find that he has accidentally pinioned himself beneath it: despite the comic hubris of the episode, vividly realised here is the notion that the prince is in thrall to, and dominated by, the King's gaze, and in such a way that he is rendered immobile. A parallel scene of the visual enforcement of inaction occurs when Polonius announces, 'Perpend, I have a daughter' (II.ii.105–6), and opens a door to reveal Ophelia (Lisa Gay Hamilton) standing in the neighbouring hall. The interpolated sequence discovers a silent Ophelia spectated upon by her father, Claudius and Gertrude (Blair Brown): she is depicted as aware of being looked at but unable to rebuff the examination, with her physical impassivity reinforcing a sense of her objectified utility. Indeed, in the spatial economy of the film, Hamlet and Ophelia are frequently dovetailed. Both are glimpsed looking through the latticed windows of their rooms as if yearning for something beyond their perimeters: the parallel montage is vital in constructing a kinship between the characters at the same time as it suggests the existence of a defended state composed of separate gaol-like units. The difference between Hamlet and Ophelia in Scott and Simonson's film, however, is that the latter remains within the purview of the court while the former attempts to break out. Incorporating a number of *Hamlet*'s visual motifs, including windows, the representation of the protagonist's 'To be or not to be' soliloquy is both thematically resonant and dramatically energetic. Unsuccessful in finding solace in the book he is reading, Hamlet smashes his spectacles on a table and proceeds to cut himself with a sliver of glass as he intones the famous words. At once the episode harks back to the second appearance of the Ghost and its bloody seizure of the sword from Hamlet's hands: the recapitulation of the image of a mutilated body emphasises a recurring bond between father and son that expresses itself in injured corporeal extremity. But, in the same moment, the scene of Hamlet's self-laceration signifies a paradoxical attempt to achieve clarity of insight by breaking the forms of visual technology. Physically, within the film's fiction, Hamlet will move beyond a political apparatus of seeing and illusions through suicide; symbolically, he will counter the practice of Claudius' regime by smashing its optical manifestations and instruments.

That Hamlet's 'To be or not to be' soliloquy leads to no obvious change in his circumstances is testimony to the inflexibility of the state's investment in surveillance. For, throughout the film, surveillance methods and measures are abundantly in evidence, as when the camera lingers over the magnifying glass displayed on Polonius' desk or when the cupboard that is deployed to eavesdrop upon Hamlet becomes the coffin in which the counsellor is temporarily 'stowed' (IV.ii.1). Even the Ghost (Byron Jennings) appears complicit, all too often entering the narrative accompanied by gusts and whispers that represent uncannily aural and acoustic surveillance signatures. In the light of the film's surveillant emphasis, and its intermittent reorganisation of the narrative structure, linguistic features that in the play are specific in their range of meaning take on an added depth of reference. The 'To be or not to be' soliloquy, for instance, is repositioned so that it comes before the ironic exchange between Hamlet and Polonius, with the effect that the protagonist's designation of the counsellor as 'honest' (II.ii.176) appears a barbed and accusatory charge. The suggestion, reinforced by the film's staging, is that Hamlet knowingly performs his reflections upon suicide for an unseen audience even as he is simultaneously engaged in addressing an interiorised agenda. 'Honest', in this context, is translatable as 'practising surveillance', the term illuminating not so much an (early modern) sense of sexual morality as a (postmodern) idea of visual machination and political intrigue.

'To speak to you like an honest man', Hamlet announces to Rosencrantz (Michael Imperioli) and Guildenstern (Marcus Giamatti) soon afterwards, 'I am most dreadfully attended' (I.ii.268–9). The recapitulation of the term at this point functions to consolidate the surveillant associations of an exchange in which Hamlet berates his 'good friends' (II.ii.240) for their part in a system that encloses in order to view and views in order to enclose. Hence, although Hamlet is represented throwing leaves out of an upper conservatory window, he is still, in his own words, in 'prison' (II.ii.241) and unable to leave his domestic 'confines' (II.ii.245). The point is underscored by the film's intercutting between Hamlet's reflections and Hempstead House's architectural interior features. As Hamlet pauses to extol the 'brave o'erhanging firmament' (II.ii.300), for instance, the camera pans to reveal a ceiling criss-crossed with Gothic tracery. This is less an open 'canopy' (II.ii.299) than the closed bars of Hamlet's gilded cage. Or, to put it another way, the pattern on the roof is the psychological analogue to Hamlet's condition, 'bounded in a nutshell' (II.ii.254). Yet the exchange with Rosencrantz and Guildenstern is simultaneously animated by the one moment in *Hamlet* when the protagonist attempts to turn the tables on his onlookers. A telescope is prominently displayed in the conservatory, a place that Hamlet retreats to as an observatory. Deploying the telescope to espy the players gives Hamlet, in the film's construction of his character, the idea of the play-within-the play: a technology of magnification provides the prompt for a performance of detection. Claudius' crime will be spied out via theatre, and, in Hamlet's idealised conception of drama's power, surveillance practices will be disastrously redirected.

As both play and film illustrate, however, *The Mousetrap* achieves only a limited success. Apart from his English sojourn, Hamlet remains – and particularly so in Scott and Simonson's reading of Shakespeare's play – an inmate who is rarely 'out in the air' (II.ii.206). Such, at least, is the impression afforded by the film's conclusion in which Hamlet is discovered as a solitary, encircled figure at the start of the duel in a visual composition that replicates the earlier physical situation of the guards and the Ghost. Indeed, the Ghost reappears in this climactic scene, reminding an audience that this patrolling spirit has been as much a practitioner of surveillance as its living counterparts. In part because the duel takes place in one of Hempstead House's central halls, many of the film's surveillance motifs come together here, including material properties such as the portraits and spy cupboards, and cinematic manoeuvres such as downward shots that privilege a hierarchical gaze. But that gaze belongs neither to Claudius nor to the survivors of his reign; rather, it is appropriated by Fortinbras (Sam Robards) whose point of view, in a continuous take, tracks the progress of Hamlet's dead form from the interior hall to the exterior gardens. The filmic operation signifies a narrative opening of the windows, the barriers that have ensured Hamlet's enclosure, and a breaking-down of boundaries and perimeters. Fortinbras is still represented as all-seeing and surveillant, but the 'sight' (V.ii.406) he authorises is one that moves easily between inside and outside, and that is not shaped by the stony faces of a bleakly predetermined historical destiny.

II

Fully inserted into the revolutions of postmodernity, Michael Almereyda's *Hamlet* (2000) pushes further a concern with observers and the observed, finding capital both in new technologies of representation and a filmic preoccupation with a world in thrall to visual introspection and examination. Covert glances and investigative stares are the norm, and even seemingly innocuous references to sight are compromised in the moment of their articulation. This is keenly exemplified in Gertrude's plea to Hamlet to 'let [his] eye look like a friend on Denmark': not only does Diane Venora, who plays the Queen, sport impenetrable sunglasses at this point, but her delivery of the line is accompanied by the action of winding down a blacked-out limousine window.[6] The request for a kindly transparency from one whose own gaze appears purposefully concealed sounds warning bells, suggesting that the film imagines vision as inhabiting a state of epistemological duplicity and uncertainty. Given these emphases, it seems entirely apposite that, during the 'closet scene', the prime question Hamlet (Ethan Hawke) directs at his mother is 'Have you eyes?'.[7] The arraignment ironically reprises the earlier mother-son encounter and, taking energy from the film's conception, draws a heightened attention to the need for clarification and illumination. In fact, what allows these – and other such lines – to reverberate is the context of surveillance within which they are placed, Hamlet reacting not so much to his mother's failure to see as to her willing, and subsequently unwitting, involvement in the technological spy-games of Claudius' (Kyle MacLachlan) brand of panoptical rule. If, according to Anthony Giddens, surveillance constitutes a historically particularised 'supervision of the activities of subject populations in the political sphere' which has its 'basis [in] administrative power', then Almereyda's *Hamlet* pursues the implications of this construction: the film elaborates surveillance as an administrative undertaking that has political import, and pursues connections between the late capitalist ethos and the control of the individual subject.[8] It is no accident, for example, that Rosencrantz (Steve Zahn) and Guildenstern (Dechen Thurman) are discovered as comically creeping up on an unaware Hamlet (he represents a surveilled, while they function as surveillers), or that the protagonist's playing of his 'vicious mole of nature' soliloquy should be captured on the CCTV system of the Elsinore Corporation. Both moments are gathered into, and overshadowed by, the opening shot of, in Barbara Hodgdon's words, 'Manhattan's canyon of skyscrapers at deep twilight': although the camera angle looks up, it is clear that the bank of faceless buildings looks down, the implication being that an anonymous institutional gaze is as omnipresent as it is invisible.[9]

Invariably in the film, acts of looking and recording, which are symptomatic of the information-gathering tendencies of surveillance, are elaborated as unwelcome and invasive. Typical is the way in which Hamlet shrinks from the *paparazzi* at the première in a scene that is returned to in the glimpse of a row of photographers at the duel: the glare of the camera outlaws claims to privacy and frames every social interaction as a public event. The film's prioritisation of the media reminds us that, in the early twenty-first century, surveillance all too often has a corporate face or, at least, to cite David Lyon, is deployed by large-scale 'companies' and 'organizations' aiming to 'influence [and] manage . . . certain persons or groups'.[10] Little wonder, then, that the logo of the Elsinore Corporation is both a camera shutter and a species of eye that snaps open and circles shut, freezing activity and collecting data in the interests of administration and categorisation. The spiral-like motion of the camera shutter, which is represented on two occasions, forms an alliance with related circular structures, from the hotel rooms the characters inhabit to the crescent-shaped galleries of the Guggenheim Museum, which, no less powerfully, are imaged as surveillance apparatuses. Christopher Dandeker writes that contemporary forms of surveillance are intimately dependent upon 'the physical design of the . . . built environment', and his statement accords with *Hamlet* in the extent to which the film depicts all of its spaces, both corporate and non-corporate, as available for inspection and centred upon the visibility of the occupant.[11] In fact, what *Hamlet* demonstrates is that the open, plate-glass interiors and exteriors that decorate the narrative are as much prisons as they are the architectural manifestations of a surveillance culture; as Samuel Crowl notes, commenting upon the film's 'description of the world', all of the major players are 'trapped in the prisonhouse of those enormous skyscrapers'.[12] The inescapable impression, in this version of Elsinore, is that the subject must fail to control his or her social existence, that the role of the individual is assessed as a function of the collective, and that release from the carceral gaol is prevented by the surveillant nodes of which it is constituted.

Arguably in reaction to the ways in which the operations of the eye are placed at the service of an inscrutable order, Hamlet and Ophelia (Julia Stiles) are discovered as taking up the accoutrements of contemporary visual technology as a means of demarcating personal domains. A shared predilection for, in Alessandro Abbate's words, 'objects of mechanical reproduction' means that the two are inevitably cast in an identical representational mould: thus, Ophelia takes a photograph of Laertes' leave-taking, while Hamlet films Claudius' inauguration.[13] The technological parallel signals, in fact, a deeper subjective affiliation, with Hamlet and Ophelia being tied at psychological as well as practical levels. Both have three bids at suicide, and, at the second attempt, Ophelia's diving into the swimming pool is explicitly linked with Hamlet's placing of a gun next to his head in the film's editing of events. But the insights that technology affords are not imagined in a wholly pejorative light. Particularly in the case of Hamlet's experiments as an 'indie'-style filmmaker, his rehearsals on his video diary of cultural fragments and traces of lived experience are granted an emancipatory and empowered significance. Crucially, the protagonist plays with film in an endeavour to pinpoint the 'mystery' (III.ii.357) of things, and it is here that the image of a stealth-bomber from the Bosnian crisis, which we see on Hamlet's monitor, underscores a key narrative point. Brief as it is, the suggestion of an engine of covert destruction, which is simultaneously an instrument of surveillance, brings to mind the movement of Claudius as he 'stole / With juice of cursed hebona in a vial, / And in the porches of [Old Hamlet's] ears did pour / The leprous distillment'.[14] Poison and vision, and stealth and death, join in an unsettling arrangement in the protagonist's laptop performance. An individually strategic use of technology, in short, is the means whereby Hamlet will root out the rotten core at the heart of Elsinore, the implication being that the portable PC serves the role of the postmodern 'prophetic soul' (I.v.41). Commenting on the particular inflections of Almereyda's *Hamlet*, Sarah Hatchuel writes that 'the eyes are poisoned by modern technologies', and it is against the backdrop of such a possibility that the protagonist's film-within-a film, which substitutes for the play-within-the play, has a critical effect.[15] Because Hamlet's version of *The Mousetrap* is a 'silent short', it operates essentially at a visual level, to the extent that its patchwork of stock footage, cartoons and movie clips comprises an assault on Claudius' optical faculties. The corporate camera of Elsinore is challenged by the amateur cinema of its prince, with the choice of the filmic medium functioning as an ironically apposite comment on some of the means whereby the powers of the state are perpetuated.

In addition to raiding popular culture for material for his public debut as a filmmaker, the private Hamlet screens clips from his own history in order, as Courtney Lehmann observes, 'to locate an image that will unify his internal and external reality'.[16] One such image discovers Old Hamlet (Sam Shepard) ice-skating and placing his hand over the camera lens, suggesting not only that the former CEO is more media-shy than his fraternal replacement but that Hamlet's will to know and revivify through film is ultimately inefficacious. In this sense, Hamlet's surveillance system falls singularly short of adequately situating his experience, and coheres with Kirstie Ball and Frank Webster's argument that 'the construction of files on persons does not mean that one "knows" them in any conventional sense'. 'Faced with an expansion of surveillance', they write, 'it is as well to remember' that we are not necessarily granted 'access to the inner workings of the mind . . . surveillance can . . . set the surveiller still further apart from the surveilled'.[17] This, at least, is the impression precipitated by sequences that appear to testify to the fact that the accumulation of representation can never bypass the loss of the originary object of desire. By the film's finale, however, an alternative perspective has been afforded, for, in death, Hamlet is discovered reviewing in a composite montage the chief events both of the film and his life. What is distinctive here is the seamless incorporation of the action the audience has 'watched' and the anterior 'past' *Hamlet* has invoked. Uniquely, multiple narrative elements are integrated, and in such a way as to generate a further film-within-a film, one that, significantly, unfolds in a continuous temporal sequence and not according to stop-and-start logistics. Incarcerating circularity has ceased, to be superseded by a representational method that is as much reflective of what has been as it is purposefully directed to futurity.

Earlier in the film, we were granted a glimpse of a photograph of a teenage Hamlet surrounded by clothes, the suggestion being that an impersonation of others or a penchant for dressing-up were favourite pursuits, yet here there is no ambiguation of identity, or continued donning of an 'antic disposition' (I.v.180), only the visual declaration of a definitive 'I'. The story that the protagonist is empowered to tell is also one that is framed by looks of mutual gazing between Hamlet and Ophelia, which implies reconciliation after death or at least some species of romantic affirmation. In short, Hamlet puts his 'sights' into a coherent order, seeing properly and communing successfully with his new-found sense of self. This, of course, is patently unlike the improper, surveillant seeing of Polonius (Bill Murray), who, at his death, is represented placing a hand over one eye in a composition that is identically replicated in a later shot of a cover picture of Fortinbras on *Wired* magazine. The grim joke is that in a culture in which the majority of the players are at some point or another wired – either Laertes (Liev Schreiber) via the electronic score counter at the duel, or Ophelia through the bugging mechanism, the 'wiretap' being one of the most eagerly deployed 'communicational measures' of contemporary surveillance systems – Hamlet, in expiration, is finally unwired, becoming the master of a 'natural' technology.[18] This is one of the first times in the film that we see him unharnessed, in Michael Anderegg's words, from 'the world of electronic reproduction' and free of his filmic devices.[19] It is a feeling, physical body with which an audience is left, not the artificial form that Hamlet was in danger of becoming. In this sense, the particularised protagonist of the end emerges as an altogether alternative creation to the haunted everyman of the film's poster, which, in a wry allusion to James Cameron's *The Terminator* (1984), displays skyscraper windows displacing, invading and inhabiting the Hamletian countenance. In the naturalised corporeal ontology that Hamlet eventually masters is suggested a rejection both of the multinational company's surveillance/control policies and the perils inherent in the cyborg machine.

III

Like Almereyda's film, Stephen Cavanagh's *Hamlet* (2005) is concerned with recollection and the pressures of the past on the present. But here the similarity ends, for, in this Londonderry-based production, the question of memory is deeply riven with disputes and irresolutions specific to a Northern Ireland context. One has only to instance the Saville Enquiry set up to ascertain what 'actually' happened on 'Bloody Sunday', 30 January 1972, when thirteen marchers were killed in Derry by the parachute Regiment, to appreciate that, in Ian McBride's words, 'there can be no sense of identity' in Ireland 'without remembering' and that 'the interpretation of the past has always been at the heart of national conflict'.[20] Cavanagh's *Hamlet* reveals its sensitivity to these and related issues by purposefully reworking the play's structure into a series of flashbacks and reminiscences. Thus, Horatio's (Anthony Doherty) account of the Ghost to Hamlet (Stephen Cavanagh) from I.ii is spliced in with the supernatural action as it unfolds (I.i), while Laertes' (Chris Simpson) agitations for revenge are juxtaposed with retrospective reflections upon his arrival. Such reorganisation is of a piece with a culture in which what is seen is crucial to what is recalled, to the extent that surveillance has become an important tool whereby history in Northern Ireland might be adequately accessed and assessed. This *Hamlet* makes a virtue of surveillance, in fact, with the existence of an observational system being implied, first, in the very design of the city: originally a seventeenth-century garrison town, Londonderry is organised around a central square from which radiate axial streets, the surrounding walls having a roughly diamond-like shape. It is an evocatively panoptical architectural concept. (An early modern map of the city's street plan is flashed on screen in the opening sequence in an eerie anticipation of the aerial surveillance shots, and police thermal image scans, of postmodernity.)[21] The distinction of Cavanagh's *Hamlet*, however, is that the walls, studded with bastions, watchtowers and gunloops, which historically enabled the gaze to be directed outwards (as in the famous siege of Derry in 1688–9) become, in this version of Shakespeare's play, a means to look inwards at the city's interstitial complexities. Indeed, so emphatic is the orientation that surveillance is reified into a principal narrative component: each character, it is suggested, periodically possesses the camera, and in such a way that techniques of observation appear a general condition. (The difficulty of disentangling live recording from video footage serves only to enhance the film's overall impact.) Who has the camera at any given point becomes the commander of the interpretive act and, by extension, of a mission of historical recovery. All is encapsulated in Horatio's opening speech which, wrenched from the play's conclusion, asks 'What is it you would see?' (V.ii.367).

What is seen in Cavanagh's *Hamlet*, then – or, rather, what is not seen – is of inestimable value, and perhaps nowhere more obviously than in the appearance, or non-appearance, of the Ghost. Because the Ghost (Tony Brown) only ever features as a foggy, wraith-like presence that, forever out of reach, is barely caught on camera, it appears even more 'questionable' (I.iv.43), with the excision of the spirit's speeches augmenting a sense of its unknowability. Crucially, the Ghost exists in and through the mechanism of film, and there is more than a pun intended in the coming of the 'apparition' (I.ii.211) and the operation of the apparatus that manages to register a version of its image. Yet existing, or not existing, in 'haunted media' complicates the Ghost still further, for, as Jacques Derrida remarks, using an appropriately cinematic metaphor, 'the spectre is also . . . what one imagines, what one thinks one sees and which one projects – on an imaginary screen where there is nothing to see'.[22] Hinted at here is the notion that the camera, and its creations, are never 'reliable' records, since all that is produced is a sense of the viewer or user's fantasy and wish-fulfilment. Interrogating the status of technologically mediated vision in this way and, by implication, surveillance, *Hamlet* works no less powerfully to query whose point of view is prioritised at any given time. During the opening sequence, for instance, as Horatio insists upon the primacy of the 'sensible and true avouch / Of mine eyes' (I.i.60–1), we are granted a glimpse a helicopter hovering overhead. Although Horatio's position is entertained, so, too, is the perspective of the British military, for chopper surveillance was, and is, one of the chief means through which army 'security' is maintained in 'troubled' Northern Irish locations. A species of 'eye of God' is set against the viewpoint of the 'man on the ground'; the two are placed in implicit conflict; neither is allowed wholly to dominate the filmic frame.

Further distinguishing Cavanagh's *Hamlet*, then, is the way in which surveillance is invariably politically freighted. Hence, when an audience is treated to shots of CCTV cameras and Derry's walls, which respectively suggest surveillance in postmodern and early modern manifestations, these represent far from ideologically blank images, since, in view of their context, they are, to adopt Slavoj Žižek, 'always-already symbolized' with local resonances.[23] Similarly, the deaths of Rosencrantz (Colin Stewart) and Guildenstern (Martin O'Brien), which are captured on CCTV, appear symptomatic of the tit-for-tat killings that characterise the turf warfare of the island. From political surveillance to culture politicised is a small step. Such is the reverberative quality of Londonderry that the very act of the city's representation is politically communicative. The line 'This bodes some strange eruption to our state' (I.i.72) is accompanied by a wide-angle shot of the city at night which features a conflagration in the distance. On the one hand, the composition suggests a relatively straight-forward and narrative-specific equation between the interruption of the Ghost and the subsequent destabilisation of the political situation. On the other hand, because the fires represented are almost certainly the bonfires that are lit in Londonderry on 18 December to commemorate the closing of the gates and the commencement of the siege (an effigy of Lieutenant-Colonel Robert Lundy, the unpopular governor, is burned on this date), the 'eruption' is hardly 'strange'; rather, as an annual event and a ritualistic replaying of the past, it is all too familiar.[24] The Ghost in the play may be occasional and particular but, in the Derry Film Initiative *Hamlet*, disruption 'to our state' is a constant. The Ghost's inseparability from local politics is granted its most strident articulation in the camera's frequent focusing upon an emblem of a skeleton, which is deployed to suggest both Old Hamlet and the protagonist's desire to see into the 'heart' (III.ii.357) or origin of his circumstances. Yet, because a skeleton also features as one of the devices on the coat of arms of Londonderry (the heraldic insignia are glimpsed on several occasions), additional themes, centred upon law, possession and succession, themselves Hamletian preoccupations, are allowed to circulate. Images are of particular importance when, in the wake of the Ghost's wordless (non)-appearance, the action lingers upon a poster emblazoned with the header 'Treason? Something is rotten in the state'. Under the image of Old Hamlet is the caption 'Murdered?'; under the image of Claudius is the caption 'Murderer?' This pithy visual substitution for the Ghost's revelation brings to mind the historical role of murals in Northern Ireland, which have been, and are still, devoted to and commemorate such political concerns as the hunger strikers, the routes taken by the parades, the disbanding of the RUC and the perceived double-dealing of Westminster. The Northern Irish mural makes visible and transparent what are sometimes thought to be matters of state security or secrecy; in the same way, the hidden crime of Old Hamlet's death is broadcast in the symbolic iconography of *Hamlet* in the form of a public smear campaign.

This is in sharp contrast to the more covert ways in which Claudius (James Lecky) is represented as attempting to consolidate power. Quickly, Rosencrantz and Guildenstern are established as Claudius' technological accomplices, and the fact that their scenes are filmed in an underground location, suggestive of a besieged mentality, serves only to reinforce a sense of an illegal operation and conspiratorial surveillance activity. In the meeting between Hamlet and his 'schoolfellows' (III.iv.204), Ness Woods in Londonderry are mobilised as an apposite natural equivalent to the protagonist's reflections upon 'this goodly frame the earth' (II.ii.298). However, because we do not see Hamlet in this exchange, only his point-of-view shots of Rosencrantz and Guildenstern, the effect is to establish the pair as the 'piece of work' that 'is a man' (II.ii.303), as 'friends' (II.ii.273) who are 'foul and pestilent' (II.ii.302) in their intrusiveness. Moreover, in that an audience is encouraged to concentrate on the scanning of Hamlet, it becomes apparent that Rosencrantz and Guildenstern's mission is to collect information about him: they therefore take on the contours of practitioners of 'dataveillance', which Wolfgang Ernst has defined as the 'reconnaissance' or tracking of 'data'.[25] Ironically, the invisibility of Hamlet makes urgent the need to place him in a visibility that will be the precondition for his classification. Nowhere is Hamlet more obviously the target of a classificatory imperative than in the representation of his being confined to 'Admissions Clinic A' of Derry's Altnagelvin Hospital. Here, the discovery of mental institutionalisation, or a state response to 'lunacy' (II.ii.49), is granted a familiar inflection by the simultaneous CCTV unfolding of Polonius' (Dominic Stewart) interrogation, which functions to cast him as a type of chief constable interviewing a political prisoner. The scene's setting reminds us that, historically, the panoptic principle was applied across a range of institutions, and not simply the prison; as Michel Foucault argues, 'doctors were . . . the first managers of collective space', adding, 'disciplinary partitioning . . . in the psychiatric asylum . . . [and] the hospital [allowed] . . . a constant surveillance to be exercised'.[26] The mad Ophelia (Simone Kirby), too, is confined to a hospital ward in a later sequence which bears comparison with the early image of her own interrogation by Polonius. Infantilised by her father, Ophelia is realised as the 'baby' (I.iii.105) with which she is associated (she is seen holding a doll), reinforcing the implication that her childlike status prevents her from being a camera-bearer. (There is an interrelationship in *Hamlet* between the scopic disempowerment of women and a larger refusal to allow them technology.) The use of CCTV in the interrogation of Ophelia, and the detail of Hamlet cradling a doll during his psychiatric sojourn, suggest that both she and he are meted out similar punishments and treatments at the hands of an abusive surveillant paternalism.

Quite how much resistance is allowed in *Hamlet*, then, is debatable. Yet there are moments of dissent, and alternatives proposed to the state-sanctioned investment in surveillance, as when, for instance, Claudius

retires to a toilet to confess, only to be filmed from above in the cubicle
by Hamlet: the protagonist's shot both replicates and parodies the
CCTV-like and hierarchical organisation of the King's visual policy. In
addition, given the particularly self-conscious point of view introduced
at this point, Claudius' 'shuffling' (III.iii.61) before God becomes a confession to a mechanical apparatus and thus a rehearsal of the ways in
which, in the surveillance-saturated world of postmodernity, according
to David Lyon, 'what once we might have revealed, consciously, about
ourselves to someone we trust – friend, doctor, priest, therapist – may
now be involuntarily disclosed by electronic means to organizations or
machines that we cannot know'.[27] Filming his own perspective, Hamlet
is frequently seen deploying a grainy black-and-white, which is in sharp
contrast to the colour-laden palette enlisted in the 'official' and com-
memorative moments of Claudius' sovereignty. This not only allies
Hamlet with a radical and revolutionary convention of filmmaking; it
also constructs him as embodying an economic alternative to Claudius'
brand of glossy and high-resolution representation. But the most obvious
strategy of resistance is arguably the use of Irish in the staging of the 'To
be or not to be' soliloquy, which, shot to the accompaniment of torch-
light wielded by Hamlet, functions at the narrative level to frustrate
Claudius' designs. As the director states, 'Hamlet has the idea that
Claudius is listening, and he doesn't want to be understood. He doesn't
want his intentions to be transparent from what he says'.[28] Because
Hamlet is figured in darkness here, and is seeking to direct a beam on
suspected eavesdropping, he inverts one of surveillance's key characteristics; as Kirstie Ball and Frank Webster state, 'surveillance . . . strive[s]
to illuminate the observed, to shine a light on subjects whom it would
make transparent'.[29] Inversion is clear in other ways, however, and not
least in Hamlet's linguistic challenge to the surveillance tactics of the
regime and compromising of its acoustic methods. Irish language is also
important as a social/communal, as well as individual, modality of resistance. The first exchange (I.ii.160–1) between Hamlet and Horatio, for
example, unfolds in Irish, the presence of the non-English tongue
working as a verbal equivalent of what Philip R. Reitlinger terms
'encryption' or 'the scrambling of information to prevent unauthorized
persons from reading it'. 'Encryption', according to Reitlinger, is
frequently deployed by 'hackers' wishing to bypass surveillance: it provides 'nearly perfect protection for the privacy of . . . communications'
and the 'confidentiality of data', and is invariably attractive to those
pursuing a route around 'law enforcement'.[30] Aiming at an aural
invisibility, and shifting linguistic gear in the interests of countering

surveillance, Hamlet and Horatio are discovered as conversing so as to confuse the law and speaking in order to become inscrutable.

What grants Hamlet's efforts at counter-surveillance a revealing local purchase is the divided social and political context within which they are situated. That is, *Hamlet* insistently reminds its audience of Protestant and Catholic constituencies and of the differences that have historically obtained between these religious and cultural polarities. 'The Heroes' Mound' in the cemetery of St Columb's Cathedral in Derry, for instance, which substitutes for Old Hamlet's sepulchre, is scored with Protestant associations, marking, as it does, the mass grave of around 5,000 people who lost their lives during the siege. It functions as a potent reminder of the fact that, in Ireland, as Joep Leersen states, 'monumental history . . . gravitates to the register of national triumphalism'.[31] Protestant meanings are no less powerfully attached to the coat of arms, which, in addition to its other connotations, is deployed to recall the loyalist majority that, until relatively recently, dominated the city's oligarchy. But *Hamlet*'s political Protestantism is also developed to encompass suggestions that Claudius' form of government entertains extreme sympathies: the King, Rosencrantz and Guildenstern are all shaven-headed, which implies an alliance with such loyalist leaders as Billy ('King Rat') Wright and Johnny ('Mad Dog') Adair, whose splinter groups have been linked to murder, terrorism and conspiracy. Against the mobilisation of Protestant signification must be posited *Hamlet*'s circulation of Catholic iconography. Typical is the way in which Ophelia is represented as being forced to read 'A Prayer Book of Catholic Devotions' during her staged conversation with Hamlet; illustrative, too, are the votive candles and crucifix next to her hospital bed. As for Hamlet, his immersion in the rituals of Catholicism is hinted at in the scene in which, in an appropriation of the sacraments, he pours whiskey from his own glass into that of Claudius, intoning, 'Father and mother is man and wife, man and wife is one flesh' (IV.iii.54–5). Contrary to how it might appear, none of this is simplifying; instead, the film's absorption in loyalist and republican symbols is symptomatic of the discovery of a protagonist who vacillates around historically adversarial positions, of a bifurcated type who, speaking two languages, is fractured inside the communicative registers of his world. Hamlet in *Hamlet* inhabits neither London nor Derry but somewhere as yet unidentified between the two. (Both 'Derry' and 'Londonderry' are used as referents in the city in the interests of answering to the needs of each community: the film is responsive to this practice and thanks 'The People of Derry Stroke Londonderry' in the closing credits.) The chaotic sense of self with which the protagonist is seen to wrestle is, in fact, suggestive of broader difficulties of identity and identification in Northern Ireland, to the extent that Hamlet and his 'encrypted discourse' take on some of the properties of the 'melancholic and the migrant' as described by Homi Bhabha: 'wandering peoples who will not be contained within the *Heim* of the national culture, and its unisonant discourse, but are themselves the marks of a shifting boundary that alienates the frontiers of the modern nation', the critic writes, 'by speaking the foreignness of language split the patriotic voice of unisonance'.[32] Culturally and linguistically, Hamlet is similarly disunited: even the Irish he speaks is accompanied by subtitles in English, which suggest that, in the moment of aspiring to difference, he is made the same, or, rather, that despite moves to escape, he does not avoid being colonised, overwritten, subordinated. Derry Stroke Londonderry, two entities in one, is/are the governing context for the protagonist's plurality and singularity.

A sense of the implications of the film's Protestant/Catholic dialectic is necessary in order to pinpoint the ways in which it endeavours to mediate Hamlet's dilemma. In a telling postscript which partly precedes the duel proper, Hamlet, who is shot against a photograph of his father, delivers the justification for murder speech (V.ii.63–70) not so much as a reflection upon dispatching the perpetrator of a crime as an admission to selling out to the system he has cast himself against: this is because the protagonist appears as both shaven-headed and dressed in combat fatigues. Evocatively suggested is less the embrace of an alternative identification than a co-opting into authorised styles and symbols. The composition implies that, in ultimately defining himself inside a schema of kin and dominant politics, Hamlet seeks to erase, or at least to attempt to repair, a split sense of self. Interestingly, what this amounts to is a succumbing to a mode of surveillance, and it is useful, in this connection, to recall that Michel Foucault's proposed English (noun) translation for the French (verb) *surveiller* was discipline: in being 'watched over' as a soldier Hamlet will be disciplined. Herbert Dreyfus and Paul Rabinow state that 'the first model of . . . control through surveillance, efficiency through the gaze, order through spatial structure, was the military camp. Here, total organization and observation were possible'.[33] The appearance of Hamlet at this point suggests such an observational practice, even as his bearing (he holds a gun and stands to attention) points up a further dimension of surveillance culture, one that Foucault encapsulates when he writes that the trained body of the soldier constitutes the 'docile body' the state can control, in part because natural 'gestures and movements' are manipulated to suit overarching 'temporal imperatives'.[34] In a post-première public discussion, Cavanagh noted that the postscript to *Hamlet* was intended to invoke Martin Scorsese's *Taxi Driver* (1976), the image of the 'Vet' and the idea that American soldiers who fought in Vietnam shaved their heads before battle in readiness for death. To enter combat is thus to agree to a private suicide pact.[35] Certainly, *Taxi Driver* seems a resonant cinematic parable with which to conjure, and not least in terms of its surveillant emphases. For, in a film that is itself concerned with processes of looking and looks, not only is Travis Bickle a 'confined' Hamletian figure who, as Lawrence S. Friedman observes, is 'as divided from society as he is divided within himself'; he is simultaneously, to cite Lesley Stern, an instance of 'regimented training' and 'the ritualistic modification of the "docile" body into a machine body'.[36] Hamlet's agitation to escape politics is thus compromised by its self-defeatism; whatever means he utilises to counter surveillance he eventually dismisses; and if the self is knitted, this is at the expense of reinscribing a discipline characterised by unwelcome and potentially destabilising connections and influences.

Yet this is not to suggest that *Hamlet* is necessarily politically despairing. If *Taxi Driver* deploys a 'sacrificial motif' in order to underline 'purgation though destruction' and 'redemption through self-destruction', then, so might one Irish construction of history be described as 'redemptive, concerned with the promissory words and deeds of martyrs'.[37] Particularly in republican circles, such a vision would have a familiar and still active currency. Moreover, if Hamlet at the close appears hopelessly isolated, he goes on to be rescued and memorially reinvigorated via, to adopt a formulation of Ian McBride, 'social networks of communication' that depend upon acts of 'confirmation' undertaken by 'members of the community'.[38] This is implied in the culminating insertion into the film of Horatio's act of narrative recuperation: as the director states, '[the film] is about Horatio's testimony and his attempt to exonerate Hamlet – to tell his story, which is Hamlet's dying request. Horatio goes back, edits . . . the footage, puts it together, introduces it [and] . . . concludes it'.[39] Perhaps the most obvious expression of the perspective is in the final shot, a dawn image of Maurice Harron's 1992 DOE-commissioned bronze sculpture of 'Hands across the Divide' or 'Reconciliation', which is located in Carlisle Square, Londonderry, and features two male figures with hands outstretched. The doves that, in the film, fly over the sculpture strike an affirmative note, as does Horatio's overlaid comment that 'the morn in russet mantle clad / Walks o'er the dew of yon high eastward hill' (I.i.171–2). At the level of *Hamlet*'s inner workings, Horatio's upbeat remark absorbs the protagonist's defeatism, while his elaboration of emotional time replaces the deceased prince's relation to a military timetable: this is a personal discipline, not a soldierly chronology. At the level of *Hamlet*'s material and political contexts, the glimpse of 'Hands across the Divide' is of a piece not only with a recent attention in Derry to cross-community organisations and cultural regeneration and collaboration, but also with the 'new remembering' that has emerged in the wake of the peace process: this, Edna Longley describes as a 'positive engagement with the European legacies that condition the Northern Irish conflict; [a] critique of the morbid cultures of commemoration that inhibit its resolution; [an] insistence on the humanity of each victim; [a] recognition that "healing" is difficult and demanding'.[40] Yet, as Jacques Derrida remarks, reconciliation is a notoriously intractable philosophical concept, since, as he states, 'forgiveness forgives only the unforgivable. One cannot, or should not, forgive; there is only forgiveness, if there is any, where there is the unforgivable . . . [F]orgiveness', he concludes, 'must announce itself as impossibility itself'.[41] If forgiveness is impossible, and it is impossible to forgive, then those deconstructive qualifications are held in play in *Hamlet*. The hands of 'Reconciliation', we recall, reach out to each other but fail to touch (conflict continues unresolved); moreover, immediately before the appearance of the image of the sculpture, the camera dwells momentarily on a bonfire on a hillside in a clear reminder both of the film's earlier montage and of a spirit of segregation that ignores contemporary political moves to community and consensus. Horatio aims at the declaration of a redemptive possibility, referring to a modern memorial to assist him in the project. Yet, as his story makes clear, conflict is resistant to the healing powers that representation aspires towards, while the 'truth' is always in danger of falling prey to, and being distorted by, the pasts that have preceded it.

IV

Adopting Hamlet's admission to Horatio, this essay has explored the ways in which postmodernity 'sees' the past and Shakespeare; in so doing, it has addressed questions relating to the vision of the 'mind', establishing varieties of 'screen', whether these manifest themselves as lenses, cameras or computer and television monitors, as key to a drive to recover memory and establish authenticity. Arguably it is because postmodernity is dominated by representations and simulacra, many of which are communicated through technology, that *Hamlet*, a play devoted to 'origins' and 'originals', has proved so accommodating to 'screen' treatment. A further term for screening is surveillance and, in this regard, the *Hamlet* films of the twenty-first century absorb themselves in modalities of 'watching over' as part of a self-conscious negotiation with the medium of cinema itself. Anne Friedberg writes that 'the panopticon model has served as a tempting originary root for the inventions that led to cinema': the 'film spectator', she adds, 'is a subject with a limited (and preordained) scope' in that his or her 'immobility' invariably functions in relation to a 'confined spatial matrix'.[42] One might not want to push this thesis as far as Thomas Y. Levin does when he writes that 'surveillance has become *the condition of [cinematic] narration itself*'; however, it is certainly the case that film in general, and *Hamlet* films in particular, by detailing the practices attendant upon the postmodern 'eye', aid a deeper comprehension of a disciplinary society and the disciplines against which human agency is defined and within which it operates.[43]

The practices that are interpreted in *Hamlet* films extend, as well, to changes and continuities in surveillance as it is refashioned in response to global events. Shakespeare's play, for instance, is a timely parable to conjure in the light of the 'Pentagon's Terrorism Information Awareness Project (TIA)' which, announced in 2002, was, according to Kirstie Ball and Frank Webster, 'driven by a conviction that . . . order will be assured if all is known'. 'If only everything can be observed', they write, 'then, goes the reasoning, everything may be controlled . . . if surveillance can be thorough enough, then disturbances, [including] . . . the break-up of families . . . can be anticipated and the appropriate action taken to remove . . . them'.[44] Both reflective of such measures, and unwittingly anticipating them, *Hamlet* in its filmic guises discovers the temptations of such a scopic fantasy and the inevitable accompanying dangers. Yet this is not to suggest that the screen *Hamlet* is a passive refractor; rather, all three of the films explored here are actively engaged in the making of what might be termed new ways of seeing. In simultaneously giving voice to and qualifying the powers of technology, and thus cinema and its associated disciplines, *Hamlet* films ultimately effect a move away from the camera; this might not amount to a radical aesthetic, but it does constitute an ideal that modes of representational flexibility exist outside surveillance. That is, the postmodern incarnation of *Hamlet* on screen acknowledges that there are 'truths' to be grasped beyond the mediated gaze, and that forms of subjectivity, which might be termed sublime, are accessible despite the dominance of the surveillant realm. In this sense, a filmic preoccupation with surveillance is ultimately liberating, with the activity of observing and being observed paradoxically facilitating fresh optical perspectives. To a 'new remembering', then, there might well be married a 'new seeing', an understanding that transcends terror and terrorism, and the possibility of an emancipation that eschews controlling borders in order to embrace better cultural horizons.[45]

Notes

1. Richard Norton Taylor (2005), 'Warning on spread of state surveillance', *The Guardian*, 21 April, p. 17.
2. David Lyon (1994), *The Electronic Eye: The Rise of Surveillance Society*, Oxford: Polity, pp. 4–5; Gary T. Marx (1988), *Undercover: Police Surveillance in America*, Berkeley: University of California Press, p. 219; Mark Poster (1990), *The Mode of Information*, Cambridge: Polity, p. 97.
3. Michel Foucault (1979), *Discipline and Punish: The Birth of the Prison*, trans. Alan Sheridan, Harmondsworth: Penguin, p. 249.
4. Samuel Crowl (2003), review of Campbell Scott and Eric Simonson (dirs), *Hamlet*, *Shakespeare Bulletin*, 21.4, pp. 57–8.
5. *Hamlet*, ed. Harold Jenkins (1987), London and New York: Methuen, I.ii.116. All further references appear in the text.
6. Michael Almereyda (2000), *William Shakespeare's 'Hamlet'*, London: Faber, p. 14.
7. Almereyda, *'Hamlet'*, p. 81.
8. Anthony Giddens (1990), *The Consequences of Modernity*, Oxford: Polity, p. 58.
9. Barbara Hodgdon (2003), 'Re-Incarnations', in Pascale Aebischer, Edward J. Esche and Nigel Wheale (eds), *Remaking Shakespeare: Performance Across Media, Genres, and Cultures*, Basingstoke: Palgrave, p. 200.
10. David Lyon (2003), *Surveillance after September 11*, Oxford: Polity, p. 5.
11. Christopher Dandeker (1990), *Surveillance, Power and Modernity: Bureaucracy and Discipline from 1700 to the Present Day*, Oxford: Polity, p. 37.
12. Samuel Crowl (2003), *Shakespeare at the Cineplex: The Kenneth Branagh Era*, Athens: Ohio University Press, p. 190.
13. Alessandro Abbate (2004), ' "To Be or Inter-Be": Almereyda's end-of-millennium *Hamlet*', *Literature/Film Quarterly*, 32.2, p. 84.
14. Almereyda, *'Hamlet'*, p. 31; William Bogard (1996), *The Simulation of Surveillance: Hypercontrol in Telematic Societies*, Cambridge: Cambridge University Press, pp. 90–1.
15. Sarah Hatchuel (2004), *Shakespeare, from Stage to Screen*, Cambridge: Cambridge University Press, p. 30.
16. Courtney Lehmann (2002), *Shakespeare Remains: Theatre to Film, Early Modern to Postmodern*, Ithaca and London: Cornell University Press, p. 97.
17. Kirstie Ball and Frank Webster (2003), 'The Intensification of Surveillance', in Kirstie Ball and Frank Webster (eds), *The Intensification of Surveillance: Crime, Terrorism and Warfare in the Information Age*, London: Pluto, pp. 13–14.
18. Lyon, *Surveillance after September 11*, p. 68.
19. Michael Anderegg (2004), *Cinematic Shakespeare*, Lanham: Rowman and Littlefield, p. 179.
20. Ian McBride (2001), 'Introduction', in Ian McBride (ed.), *History and Memory in Modern Ireland*, Cambridge: Cambridge University Press, pp. 1–2.
21. This, at least, was part of a montage belonging to the film at its première showing at the Shakespeare Association of America meeting in Bermuda (19 March 2005). In subsequent showings (at the Derry Nerve Centre on 29 May 2005 and at the British Shakespeare Association Conference, Newcastle-upon-Tyne, on 1 September 2005), the sequence was removed.

22. Jeffrey Sconce (2000), *Haunted Media: Electronic Presence from Telegraphy to Television*, Durham and London: Duke University Press, p. 4; Jacques Derrida (1994), *Spectres of Marx: The State of the Debt, the Work of Mourning, and the New International*, trans. Peggy Kamuf, New York and London: Routledge, p. 100.

23. Slavoj Žižek (1999), *The Žižek Reader*, ed. Elizabeth Wright and Edmond Wright, Oxford: Blackwell, p. 73.

24. In a personal communication (31 May 2005), the director writes that the shot was in fact taken 'on the Catholic holy day known as the Feast of the Assumption [15 August], when bonfires are lit in Catholic areas, supposedly to celebrate the assumption of the Virgin Mary . . . in my view, the real intention of the fires is as a form of "answer back" to the tradition of [Protestant] bonfires'.

25. Wolfgang Ernst (2002), 'Beyond the Rhetoric of Panopticism', in Thomas Y. Levin, Ursula Frohne and Peter Weibel (eds), *CTRL [SPACE]: Rhetorics of Surveillance from Bentham to Big Brother*, Cambridge, MA: MIT Press, p. 463.

26. Michel Foucault (1980), *Power/Knowledge: Selected Interviews and Other Writings, 1972–1977*, ed. Colin Gordon, Brighton: Harvester, p. 151; Foucault, *Discipline*, p. 199.

27. Lyon, *Electronic Eye*, p. 19.

28. Interview between Stephen Cavanagh and the author, 4 April 2003.

29. Ball and Webster, 'Intensification of Surveillance', p. 13.

30. Philip R. Reitlinger (2000), 'Encryption, Anonymity and Markets', in Douglas Thomas and Brian D. Loader (eds), *Cybercrime: Law Enforcement, Security and Surveillance in the Information Age*, London and New York: Routledge, pp. 132, 135.

31. Joep Leersen (2001), 'Monuments and Trauma', in McBride (ed.), *History and Memory*, p. 208.

32. Homi Bhabha (1990), 'DissemiNation', in Homi Bhabha (ed.), *Nation and Narration*, London and New York: Routledge, p. 315.

33. Herbert Dreyfus and Paul Rabinow (1992), *Michel Foucault: Beyond Structuralism and Hermeneutics*, Hemel Hempstead: Harvester Wheatsheaf, pp. 156–7.

34. Foucault, *Discipline*, pp. 138, 151.

35. See note 21.

36. Lawrence S. Friedman (1999), *The Cinema of Martin Scorsese*, Oxford: Roundhouse, pp. 66, 81; Lesley Stern (1995), *The Scorsese Connection*, London: BFI, p. 53.

37. Friedman, *Scorsese*, p. 63; McBride, 'Introduction', p. 27.

38. McBride, 'Introduction', p. 6.

39. Interview between Stephen Cavanagh and the author, 4 April 2003.

40. Edna Longley (2001), 'Northern Ireland: Commemoration, Elegy, Forgetting', in McBride (ed.), *History and Memory*, p. 253.

41. Jacques Derrida (2001), *On Cosmopolitanism and Forgiveness*, trans. Mark Dooley and Michael Hughes, London and New York: Routledge, p. 32.

42. Anne Friedberg (1993), *Window Shopping: Cinema and the Postmodern*, Berkeley: University of California Press, pp. 19–20.

43. Thomas Y. Levin (2002), 'Rhetorics of the Temporal Index', in Levin, Frohne and Weibel (eds), *CTRL [SPACE]*, p. 583.

44. Ball and Webster, 'Intensification of Surveillance', p. 4.

45. I would like to thank Stephen Cavanagh for extending many courtesies to me during the making of *Hamlet* and for facilitating the writing of this essay. I am equally grateful to Adrian Streete for numerous stimulating conversations about Shakespeare and film.

Chapter 3

Backstage Pass(ing): *Stage Beauty, Othello* and the Make-up of Race

Richard Burt

'Othello was not a role of which I would be able to rid myself when I took off the makeup'.[1]

Laurence Olivier

Hearts of Darkness

Adapted from a stage play by Jeffrey Hatcher, and following in the wake of related films, *Stage Beauty* (dir. Richard Eyre, 2004) is a direct reply to the box-office success and Oscar-winning film *Shakespeare in Love* (dir. John Madden, 1998).[2] A review stating that *Stage Beauty* is 'sexier than *Shakespeare in Love*' is on the *Stage Beauty* official film website homepage, and the opening blurb on the back of the US DVD edition of the film reads 'This year's *Shakespeare in Love*!' The generic, narrative and thematic parallels between *Stage Beauty* and *Shakespeare in Love* are notable. Both are romantic comedies, and both share interests in feminism, the first professional woman actress, gender-bending, theatre, law, royal patronage and commerce. Both films invest in a behind-the-scenes romance between the actors performing together as the leads in a Shakespeare play; show how an artificial acting style gives way to a greater realism; respectively reveal Shakespeare and Ned winning a share in the acting company; and conclude with a death scene. *Stage Beauty* and *Shakespeare in Love* share two of the same actors, Rupert Everett and Tom Wilkinson, and both films are the products of US and UK collaboration, with American screenwriters and American actors – particularly the female leads Gwyneth Paltrow and Claire Danes – speaking with *faux* English accents.[3]

Despite *Stage Beauty*'s obvious connections to *Shakespeare in Love*, the paratextual material for *Stage Beauty* marginalises its citations of Shakespeare and occludes a significant feature of *Othello* – namely, race.

The trailer for *Stage Beauty* shows several shots of the final *Othello* performance, but no lines from the play are cited nor is the play named, unlike *Romeo and Juliet* in the trailer for *Shakespeare in Love*.[4] The *Stage Beauty* official film website, DVD menu, posters and production stills all significantly play up whiteness. For example, Maria or Mrs Maria Hughes (Claire Danes), who, as Desdemona, wears a costume with a large white ruff around her neck, appears on the film poster, DVD cover and DVD menu, with the ruff and Dane's face digitally touched up to appear as a luminescent white. If *Othello* is so central to the film, why marginalise it? This question invites similar questions about the film itself: why does Ned Kynaston (Billy Crudup) make his stage comeback by playing a black man? Why doesn't *Stage Beauty* address the first black actor to perform Othello as it addresses the first woman to act on the stage? Or why not have Ned be the first actor to do Othello in white-face?[5] Why does *Stage Beauty* choose *Othello*, thereby requiring that the protagonist be performed in blackface, rather than another play, such as *Antony and Cleopatra* (which is mentioned by Ned before the final death-scene performance)?[6] The blackface *Othello* is especially remarkable given casting practices for the role of Othello on television and film since Jonathan Miller's BBC *Othello* (1981) in particular and, more broadly, in Shakespeare films since Kenneth Branagh's *Much Ado About Nothing* (1993).[7] Along similar lines, we could ask why, if *Othello* is so important, are there no actors of colour in the film? Are we to assume that Restoration England was all white?

In response to these questions, one might argue that *Stage Beauty*'s Othello in blackface performance, and its lack of interrogation of race, make it a perfect example of what Katherine Eggert has inventively termed 'post-postcolonial Shakespeare'.[8] Trevor Nunn's 1996 *Twelfth Night* and Kenneth Branagh's 2000 *Love's Labour's Lost* recycle and recolonise for export purposes a racially inflected and already parodic post-colonial Americanised Shakespeare involving the musical, itself heavily indebted to African-American dance and blackface minstrel shows, which often cited Shakespeare. Evidence for an account of the film along Eggert's lines might be adduced by a sequence in the final scene of *Stage Beauty* that violates the conventions of classic cinema and links Eyre's film to an earlier English *Othello* film/theatre hybrid indebted to American minstrelsy: shots showing Claire Danes' face smudged with Crudup's blackface recall a longheld shot of Laurence Olivier's make-up smudging Maggie Smith's face in the death scene of Stuart Burge's *Othello* (1965). By locating Shakespeare in the Restoration so as to present an Othello in blackface, Eyre is able to do more nakedly, so the argument might go, what Branagh was doing when casting Adrian Lester in his American musical film adaptation of *Love's Labour's Lost*.

Unlike Nunn's *Twelfth Night* and Branagh's *Love's Labour's Lost*, *Stage Beauty* does not attempt to export Shakespeare by recolonising post-colonial American Shakespeare; rather, the film offers, through its citation of Burge's *Othello*, a genealogy of the failure of this post-post-colonial strategy (neither *Twelfth Night* nor *Love's Labour's Lost* did well at the box office, and neither did *Stage Beauty*) and points up the limitations of commercially successful post-colonial, transnational Shakespeare cinema as exemplified by *Shakespeare in Love*, a Shakespeare that can be romanticised precisely because the Bard is already fixed, no longer open to adaptation (here *Stage Beauty* abandons historical accuracy altogether) even in the Restoration. Against Madden's rather cheerful account of Shakespeare's maturation from impotent hack into potent genius, Eyre places a degraded English Shakespeare, signified via the reduction of *Othello* to key passages, the deployment of a central and cinematically weak cross-cutting sequence, and the use of darkness (blackface and behind-the-scenes sh(ad)ows are associated with labour, commerce and prostitution) and whiteness (as evidenced in set design, lighting and cosmetics, which are linked to stardom and the after-lives of stars). And, whereas Shakespeare's development into Shakespeare is already fixed by the end of *Shakespeare in Love*'s opening credit sequence, when Shakespeare signs his name as we spell it, *Stage Beauty* shows that rehearsal rather than textual revision allows for continuous innovations – or what the film calls 'novelty' and 'surprise'. Putting into question what passes as Shakespeare in cinema, *Stage Beauty* darkens *Shakespeare in Love* to mark its status as damaged goods and progressively whitens Olivier's *Othello* to distance itself from that actor's engagement with American minstrelsy, which has been perceived as racist in the US, at least since the Burge film was first released.[9] As if tracing the manifold links between filth as slime and sex in *Othello*, Eyre's film connects dirt, scuffs, bootblack and horse manure to allegorise the film's artistic freedom from fidelity to present transnational, cinematic Shakespeare, adapted or cited, as a matter of sloppy seconds.

Shakespeare in Love, Actually

To understand the centrality of race to *Stage Beauty*, and the film's blind spot to it, we first need to locate Eyre's film in the broader context of two genres, the Shakespeare play-within-the-film genre, in which characters in a film rehearse or watch scenes from a play, and the UK/US transatlantic romantic comedy convention that uses English and American actors and often includes a Shakespeare citation or reference.[10] The commercial success of *Shakespeare in Love* was due in large measure to its seamless fusing of these two genres to appeal to a broad middlebrow audience that enjoys the mall film and the art film. In *Film/Genre*, Rick Altman points out that film genre is typically established in two ways: in the one case, the critic sees common features among various films, then names the genre (*film noir*, for example) and amasses a list of films that belong to the genre; in the other case, a producer sees common features in earlier, commercially successful films and decides to make a film just like the others.[11] While the British romantic comedy is often a commercially successful, big-budget, mall film with a relatively short history, many of the same stars (such as Hugh Grant, Julia Roberts, Colin Firth, Renée Zellweger and Emma Thompson) and a producer's genre, the Shakespeare play-within-the-film genre is an often less commercially successful, low-budget, art-house film with a much longer history, a wide range of national cinemas and a critic's or fan's genre.

Produced by Miramax's Harvey Weinstein, and cleverly written to allegorise a fit between a behind-the-scenes romance and acting on the stage, *Shakespeare in Love* might be said to have fused and hybridised the genres sketched above, thereby allowing *Stage Beauty* to be promoted, if not produced, as another *Shakespeare in Love*. What is at stake in *Stage Beauty*, however, is an engagement with a cheapening of the commodities being offered up for sale, namely, love and Shakespeare, in a transnational film market represented most clearly by *Shakespeare in Love* but by no means confined to it. The UK/US romantic comedies are almost invariably peopled exclusively by white actors, and often allegorise their own import and export with references to travel, action in both countries and/or scenes in airports, such as at the end of *Love Actually* (dir. Richard Curtis, 2003). The witty tagline of *The Wedding Date* (dir. Clare Kilner, 2005), a blundering remake of *Pretty Woman* (dir. Garry Marshall, 1990), even more clearly lets the catty cat out of the bag: 'this love doesn't come cheap' refers to the price the gigolo charges the heroine for services rendered and emphasises how his love for her is priceless. Hence, we may read the citations of Shakespeare in these knowingly cynical romantic comedies, with their improbably fulfilled fantasies of upwardly mobile working-class women characters, as cultural capital on the cheap, in the throwaway form either of iconic references, as when the prime minister of England (Hugh Grant) mentions Shakespeare in a ludicrous defence of Britain during a conference with a US president (Billy Bob Thornton) like George W. Bush, or of burlesques, as when a *Richard III* musical is discussed at the end of *The Tall Guy* (dir. Mel Smith, 1989).[12]

While parasitically piggybacking on these trends and on *Shakespeare in Love*, *Stage Beauty*, in my view, thematises a disenchantment with the present state of affairs ('only the audiences are new', Ned says of his performances, a line Maria later quotes back at him). That is, Eyre uses *Othello* as a way of registering the film's own fakeness, its attempt to pass itself off as a new *Shakespeare in Love*. *Othello*'s infidelity is a clue, in other words, to *Stage Beauty*'s infidelity. As a variation on the emergent romantic comedy meets Shakespeare play-within-the-film genre, *Stage Beauty* resists the pressure to make Shakespeare signify in a romantic manner, a pressure that might be said to have increased since the success of *Shakespeare in Love*. Such a process serves further to limit, fix, marginalise and even occlude Shakespeare as he is folded back into the cheaper and more formulaic producer's genre of the UK/US romantic comedy. Hedging its bets in a kind of secret sharing with novelty and surprise, *Stage Beauty* remakes *The Dresser* (dir. Peter Yates, 1983) as *The Undresser* in order to extend the astonishingly diverse range of ways of dramatising Shakespeare in previous Shakespeare play-within-the-film examples, a diversity which perhaps explains the genre's longstanding appeal to a spectrum of directors and screenwriters, especially of European art films. Part of the diversity has to do with how much Shakespeare is dramatised and how much significance the dramatisation carries. The Shakespeare scenes elaborated in the film genre have a markedly transnational status as well. Scenes are sometimes performed in modern costume, sometimes in period costume, and lines are delivered either in English or in foreign translations.

Stage Beauty belongs to a particularly diverse sub-genre of Shakespeare plays-within-the-film (or within a television episode) that is specifically devoted to performances of the death scene from *Othello*. The diversity of the sub-genre comes, however, at the price of its visibility, its not being recognisable before *Shakespeare in Love* to anyone but a small number of Shakespeare film critics.[13] The Shakespeare scenes are typically subordinate elements, often incidental and sometimes seemingly invisible, in films that form part of an easily recognised genre such as detective fiction, melodrama, romantic comedy and so on. Regarding *Stage Beauty* as a transvaluation of *Shakespeare in Love*'s generic hybridity allows us to understand what is cinematically innovative about it – the decision to have a white actor play Othello in blackface and the refusal to read the love between Ned and Maria as a version of the love between Othello and Desdemona. In placing so little dramatic weight on the meaning of *Othello* for our interpretation of the characters in the film, *Stage Beauty* notably reverses a tendency seen in earlier films about actors doing Shakespeare that involve transitions from theatre to film and that engage transnational flows of immigration and emigration seen not only in *Shakespeare in Love* but also in *Les Enfants du Paradis* (dir. Marcel Carné, 1942), *A Double Life* (dir. George Cukor, 1947), *Shakespeare Wallah* (dir. James Ivory, 1965), *The Playboys* (dir. Gillies MacKinnon, 1992) and *In Othello* (dir. Roysten Abel, 2003), among others.[14]

Unlike these films, *Stage Beauty* daringly uses blackface and highlights whiteness and whiteface to question widely shared, unexamined assumptions about the alternating visibility and invisibility of race in Shakespearean transnational cinema. Racial marking has a subversive edge in *Stage Beauty*, I will argue, precisely because it challenges prevailing cinematic codes governing race, which, while intended to be anti-racist, have rigidified into a cinematic orthodoxy and critical dogmatism. Unlike Kenneth Branagh's *Love's Labour's Lost*, the ITV/PBS *Othello* (dir. Geoffrey Sax, 2001) or Michael Radford's *The Merchant of Venice* (2004), which excises Portia's racist line about Morocco's 'complexion', *Stage Beauty*, even while marking itself as an English film, does not safely adhere to the conventions of race-blind casting in English Shakespeare cinema. Though paratextual materials such as the film website, DVD menu and DVD edition of the film specify the US distributor, Lion Gates Films, and show its logo, the film proper begins with a shot of an address plaque on a brick wall of a London street which specifies the production company as Qwerty Films and lists a fake address in Soho. By connecting a raced Shakespeare to an aesthetic of cinematic degradation and fraudulent Shakespeare, *Stage Beauty* helps us to see more clearly that our assumptions about the ways in which race is marked in Shakespeare-related cinema are limited to national models of US and UK cinema and are thus quite provincial.

White Lies Beneath

To understand why Ned's return to the stage requires that he act Othello in blackface, we might begin by examining how race is set up as relatively fixed in relation to gender. After a performance of *Othello*, Betterton (Tom Wilkinson) tells male fans outside the theatre looking for autographs that 'I played the Moor'. When they look uncertain, he adds, 'No, I'm not really black'. The joke suggests that race is fixed in a way that gender is not, especially since Betterton's exit follows Ned's with

Miss Frayne (Alice Eve) and Lady Meresvale (Fenella Woolgar) and continues as the tease scene in the coach – is Ned a man or not? Does he have a 'thingie' or not? As the actor playing Othello, Betterton, it would appear, does not have a 'thingie' that interests either women or men.

The narrative of the film follows through a logic already in place in the contrast between the fans' reception of the actors: the phallic white star versus the castrated black male.[15] Betterton's 'thingless' Othello is already a castrated figure without fans or groupies. The kick in the balls given Ned at the instigation of Sir Charles Sedley (Richard Griffiths) and the two ladies Ned mocked is cross-cut with the precise moment Charles II (Rupert Everett) reads aloud the law prohibiting men from playing women on the stage, and the sequence ends with a medium close-up of Ned's hand, gesturing as did his theatrical dying gesture, fading to black. At the aptly named Cockpit Tavern to which he descends thereafter, Ned performs a song about a man with 'no balls at all'; significantly, this Pepys (no)show is interrupted when Maria enters bearing aloft a sack with five pounds to pay Mistress Revels (Clare Higgins) to release him. Ned takes off his dark coat before performing Othello's last soliloquy, dressed in a white shirt, before Charles II and his courtiers and guests. And, even when appearing in blackface as Othello, Ned's successful return to the stage continues the earlier separation of acting and sex seen when he and Maria are in bed together. Ned's question to Maria in this scene, 'How do you die?', does not involve a Shakespearean pun on 'die', but it is a show-stopper.

Similarly, at the end of the film, we cannot be sure, as Ned and Maria clasp hands and continue again to move their arms theatrically, whether they will actually have sex or, if they do, what kind of sex – straight or gay – it will be. Fully capitalising on its R-rating, *Stage Beauty* never shows us Ned's penis in the coach or at the tavern. The film cuts away in the former case, while Maria's entrance stops it in the latter. Pornographic sex is acted out after the shows. When a lord was represented as having sex with Ned, he was seen to be enjoying sex, or a fantasy thereof, with Shakespeare's characters. But Ned learns of this only after he has been rejected because he no longer plays Shakespearean roles. In the earlier rehearsal of the death scene after the episode involving the coach and the ladies, Maria pauses as Ned goes to kiss her, saying, 'She doesn't kiss him'. The pause has less to do with Desdemona than Maria's curiosity about whether Miss Frayne and Lady Meresvale feel Ned's 'cock'.

Ned's metaphorical castration is registered as well in theatrical terms. Charles II interrupts Ned and Maria's death scene to exclaim 'brava', and audience members follow suit, some adding, 'Mrs Hughes'. The narrative point – that the focus is now on her stage triumph rather than his – is reinforced cinematically. In a shot that precedes his beating, Ned's success as Desdemona was earlier registered by his being at the centre of the stage, flanked by Othello and Emilia on either side. By contrast, Maria is the subject of four medium close-ups, appearing alone in the frame; in addition, in three shots with Ned, she stands in the foreground, in very shallow focus, to Ned's right.[16] Ned is literally displaced.

Yet *Stage Beauty* does not oppose a fixed racial identity to malleable and ambiguous gender and sexual performances. Ned's 'castration' as a male star in blackface involves fakery and art, a reverse (and clearly a failed passing) of white as black. *Stage Beauty* does not contrast more or less convincing masquerades (none of the Othellos could pass as black) but more or less artistic masquerades. Blackness and whiteness take a variety of cosmetic forms in the film. The three men playing Othello all wear different make-up and costumes, as if the film were dramatising the history of the debate over the colour of Othello's skin – black or tawny – and the history of stage Othellos who chose one or the other skin colour.[17] Betterton wears partial blackface on his upper cheeks, nose and forehead, a beard and a red turban; the actor in Cockerell's tavern wears a darker, full-face blackface, no beard and a green turban; Ned wears a much lighter, two-toned blackface (tawny and black), does not wear a beard and sports a white turban. Blackness is made up not only in the sense of an applied, fake cosmetic but as an aesthetic, an artful fabrication. The aesthetic dimensions of blackface become clear only when Ned becomes Othello. To be sure, blackface takes on a minor significance when we see the second Othello (his make-up look is darker-looking – more like mud – and it is incompetently applied in order to show the difference between the two theatrical venues). Yet blackface only really assumes importance when Ned acts the part of Othello, making blackface a kind of passing, the equivalent of his female drag act. Similarly, the blackface of the earlier two Othellos is downplayed because they are marked off as part of a long-gone past, as is Ned's earlier drag act.

Yet the aesthetics of Ned's blackface Othello are related to a markedly awkward cinematic style in this generally classically cinematic film. The first image of Ned is a black and white engraving of a Restoration actress with Billy Crudup's face photoshopped into it. The fakery is accompanied by a slow tilt up from an intertitle giving Kynaston's name. The effect of fakery is registered in such a way that the power of digital cinema is affirmed. As the camera tilts upwards, we see that what looked like pixels surrounding the text make up a field that constitutes an engraving. The camera does not pull back to reveal the entire engraving as a whole, however, and, as it settles on Ned/Crudup's face in a kind of medium close-up, the accompanying prologue is written in an unusually small fontsize, making the text difficult to read on the DVD edition. A similar awkwardness obtains at the end of the film because the effect of Ned's Othello is inseparable from that of Maria's Desdemona. Just as the make-up of the three Othellos varies, so too does the make-up of the two Desdemonas. At the Cockpit, Maria debuts as Desdemona looking and acting as much like Kynaston's Desdemona as possible. When Maria appears for rehearsal, she is whiter than she was when Ned played her. Ned removes her make-up and her costume (her large white ruff in particular). His Othello – he has a lighter, brown face with black around the eyes and the cheeks, and sports a goatee – stands out as more artificial because he is paired with the much more contemporary and realistic looking Desdemona (little make-up, no wig, and hair down) played by Maria. The roles of Othello and Desdemona, that is, are not integrated into a seamless contemporary realism. Desdemona's contemporariness (her look, her acting, her feminist characterisation) makes Ned's lightened blackface Othello look all the more out of place.

Booty Call

Ned's success in blackface corresponds by the end of the film to a darkening or 'unwhitening' of Maria as Desdemona in order to suggest that, despite her anachronistic, feminist and supposedly more realistic interpretations, she fights because she is a woman. A Desdemona without make-up or wig who wears her hair down equals realism. To be sure, earlier in the film, light and dark, and white and black, work the opposite way: Ned's decline and Maria's rise are registered through the darkening of Ned and the whitening of Maria. After Ned is beaten, the camera focuses on his hand and fades to black. After an intertitle stating 'Six weeks later', the camera cuts to an artist's studio where Maria is being painted, flanked by two men in white wigs both made up with whiteface. Furthermore, the oil painting for which Maria is posing contrasts with the black-and-white postcards of engravings of Ned, one of which we see in the film's opening shot, and others we see later by his mirror and in a market through which he walks.

Yet the force of these contrasts between Ned and Maria is quickly muted. The artist's studio is a factory, with apprentices working on several other paintings in progress. Though Maria moves up the star image ladder (paintings of her are opposed to Ned's low-market, black-and-white postcards), she too has to heed the booty call and expose her breast, as Ned almost exposed his 'thingie' in Cockerell's tavern. To be taken seriously as an actress, Sir Charles states, she has to put bums on seats. Maria does not become the phallic woman. She believes she cannot act, and changes her mind only when she rehearses the death scene with Ned. Maria is also subject to a comparable desire for novelty. She is represented as the first woman to play a woman on stage, but, following a performance where the house was half-full at best, Samuel Pepys (Hugh Bonneville) tells her in her dressing room that he will not stay for the second performance. Maria plays in *King Lear* and, although her role is unidentified, one assumes it is Cordelia. All other women actresses in the film are in a similarly castrated position, regardless of their success. A series of dissolves of the star actresses is lit by two candles in the left foreground of the screen, while the dimly lit women, who are shot in medium close-ups from the waist up, fade in and out with, to the right, a black background. The other actresses perform the lead women in *Romeo and Juliet*, *Twelfth Night* and *Hamlet*. None has replaced Ned as Desdemona. We never see these star actresses reciting Shakespeare; instead, they simply receive applause. And, in the audition scene, only snippets of Shakespeare are heard as the women recite in preparation. The female Emilia (Madeleine Worrall) is granted no more lines than the male Emilia, who abandoned the theatre. Represented in the film as an orange-seller rather than the famous actress she also was, Nell Gwynn (Zoë Tapper) gains her power as Charles II's mistress. She whores herself when she goes down on Charles II to get him to pass a law prohibiting men from acting as women on the stage. Similarly, Mrs Barry has a lowbrow and newly successful patron, Mr Cockerell, as Maria does Ridley.

The lightening of Ned's Othello, and the darkening of Maria's white-face in their performance of the death scene, responds to the way in which whiteness fails to function in *Stage Beauty* as a stable signifier. The opening sequence of *Stage Beauty*, following the prologue, evinces a sexualisation of women taking place on both sides of the stage. A close-up of Cupid's very white backside is followed by a crane-shot up a background painting involving various classical, naked and also white mythological figures. After this painting is hauled up by stagehands to reveal a dark backstage area, an aristocratic man wanders through and pinches Emilia and then Maria on their rumps: they both slap his hand away. The other two theatres in the film expose women to similar male groping, unwanted or wanted. Cockerell gropes Maria's right breast before letting her play Desdemona in his tavern, and Charles II slides his hand down Nell's back and rests it on her bum after she finishes singing a Purcell aria in the court theatre.

Whiteness makes no difference in terms of a woman's exposure. Emilia is made up, while Maria is not in the first scene; Maria is not made up when Cockerell cops a feel; and Nell is very made up when singing for Charles II. Actresses and prostitutes are visually connected in two scenes. In one, Ned runs a gauntlet of auditioning would-be actresses, many of them heavily made up in whiteface, waiting to audition for Shakespeare roles for Betterton; in the other, which is shot subjectively with a steadicam to convey disorientation, Ned runs a gauntlet of prostitutes. Casting also ties actress and prostitute together. The uncredited women playing the would-be actresses waiting to audition are the same uncredited women who play the prostitutes accosting Ned. When the prostitute sequence with Ned dissolves into the montage of the women stars, visual links are similarly important.[18] Before the montage of the women stars begins, Pepys talks in voice-over as he identifies each actress and her Shakespeare role in turn. There is an awkwardness here as well since the montage suggests the passage of time while the voice-over takes place in real time.

White make-up creates confusion in the film because it is a marker of upper-class status as well as of prostitution. As Lady Meresvale pays Ned after they return to London from their tryst in the coach, Sir Charles propositions them all as 'ladies of the night' because their make-up is a 'universal' signifier marking them as sex workers. In the 'castration' scene when Ned is beaten, one of the ladies calls him 'bum boy', while one of the men conducting the beating, as if taking Othello's view of Desdemona, calls him 'the whore of the Moor of Venice'.

The film makes blackness and whiteness into unstable signifiers that expose, as it were, the political unconscious of its construction of Restoration theatre: the forces that both castrate and whore actors are revealed both in the labour of rehearsal and cosmetic preparation behind the scenes and in the work of prostitution (a putting of labour back into sex work).[19] Through an aesthetic of 'uglification' or self-mutilation, so to speak, *Stage Beauty* keeps the more graphic staging of *Othello* Ned desires separate from a pornographic staging arguably elicited by the play itself. *Stage Beauty* works against the eroticism commonly found in the play-within-the-film genre that runs from *Shakespeare in Love* to pornographic versions of Shakespeare in lust such as *Shakespeare Revealed* (dir. Ren Savant, 2001).[20] Hence, *Stage Beauty* shows actors with smeared faces taking their make-up off or putting it on – but never in the process of finishing and perfecting it (tarting themselves up). It is worth recalling that Ned only gets his name – 'stage beauty' – when he is most degraded, performing as the first transvestite stripper at the Cockpit.

The graphic and pornographic do not line up behind the clean and dirty, the white and black; rather, the successful *Othello* at the end of the film exemplifies a paradoxically degraded aesthetic as a response to a world where theatre, whoring and money are linked first to shit and then to boot-black.[21] Ned's blackface is composed not of burnt cork, as was usual, but of bootblack, which Sir Charles hands over to him, explaining that he has it with him because 'a scuff, sir, is a terrible thing'. The connection between bootblack and blackface follows from an earlier, apparently random sequence when we see Sir Charles being carried in his coach through the streets of London as fresh horse manure is being shovelled in medium close-up. The sequence ends as one of the men carrying the coach steps in the shit. Before the close shot of Ned's hand that concludes the beating episode, we see two successive medium close-ups of Lady Meresvale and we hear Sir Charles' voice as they step over Ned's prostrate and nearly unconscious body, now reduced to a shitty equivalent. Later, when Nell and Pepys locate Ned outside a tavern and implore him to teach Maria how to play Desdemona, the three of them walk through a number of white sheets hung out to dry: Ned steps in shit, complete with sound effect. His bootblack blackface Othello stands, as it were, in (w)horeshit.

Scuff Up Your Shakespeare

The death scene with Ned and Maria as Othello and Desdemona, and the final sequence of the film when Ned and Maria kiss backstage, perform what I have called the film's degraded, self-mutilated aesthetic of fakery. When Ned and Maria kiss, blackface is smeared on her face. The shots of her smudged countenance call up, if not allude to, the smudge on Maggie Smith's face left by Olivier in the Burge filmic *Othello*. Eyre's film participates in a long theatrical tradition where the blackface actor playing Othello smudges the actress playing Desdemona.[22] Whether or not Eyre knows the Burge film, *Stage Beauty* is clearly in dialogue with it.[23] Timothy J. Murray calls the shot a 'dirty still' that is a material trace of racism. It attests

> to the stains of blackness tainting the performance as well as the text of Shakespeare's tragedy. For *Othello*'s darkened stains read as material traces of nothing less than the Eurocentric horror of miscegenation, a horror often glossed over by critical overinvestment in the humanist theme of the enigma of moral darkness . . . at the expense of any commentary on Desdemona's desire for darkness.[24]

Murray reframes Stanley Cavell's account of cinema as inherently porno-graphic in terms of Lyotard's account of cinema as clean sutures versus the exclusion of cinematic dirt. Race becomes for Murray a metaphor for cinema's dirty pictures.[25] Lining up behind other critics who see Olivier's performance as racist, Murray writes: 'Olivier does more to maintain the cultural ideology of negritude, which inscribes resistance in the web of colonial fantasy, than to expose it to any sustained performance of ret-rospective critique'.[26]

While Murray's theoretical reframing of the *Othello* 'sloppy shot' as a dirty picture is extremely useful, his view of the smudge as a racial hiero-glyph strikes me as literal and monological.[27] The shot of Smith's smudged face not only signifies race through its excessiveness but also excessively signifies. And the shot cites not racial skin colour but the the-atricality of Olivier's performance of race, especially the fakeness of his performance. The shot also serves as a final reminder that the film records a stage production of the play rather than a cinematic realisation of it. Moreover, the smudge has a dark reddish rather than black hue and thereby picks up Maggie Smith's red hair, connecting Othello and Desdemona in an aesthetic manner also tied to her decay and death.

Eyre also engages a *Othello* performance tradition that involves a reverse smudging of white on black. Billie Whitelaw gives the following account, for example, of how her white pancake make-up smeared Olivier's Othello:

> Olivier was blacked up to he nines, of course. Only the part covered by his jockstrap wasn't. It took him about four hours to get himself buffed up. Jack, his dresser, put rich tawny-brown-black pancake on his body and buffed it up with silk so that he really shone. Olivier was a master of makeup and really looked magnificent . . . To make my own skin look 'white as alabaster', as the Bard says, I had alabaster makeup all over my body. Once, as I knelt down beside his feet, I put my hand on his knee. He glared down at me: there was a white mark on his black knee! Some of my white alabaster had come off on his beautiful shiny black makeup.[28]

Stage Beauty amplifies the excessive signification of race in previous *Othello*s in a number of ways: Ned wears a two-colour make-up (perhaps outing Olivier's two make-ups, Max Factor 2880 and Negro no. 2), and Desdemona goes from white make-up to none at all. The film plays up the black smudge by adding gestures of wiping off both Ned's blackface and the smudge on Maria, and it simultaneously extends dirt-iness into the film editing.[29] Unlike the shot of Olivier's smudge, which stands separate from the rest of Burge's clean film, *Stage Beauty* smudges the smudge, as it were, across other parts of the film. Though the rather faint mark on Maria's face is much harder to see than is the very visible smudge on Desdemona's face in the Burge *Othello*, the stain left upon her is highlighted in part because blackface is all that is left of Ned's Othello. His turban and multicoloured coat are gone. The smudge is also called attention to as both actors attempt to wipe off their make-up. Maria does so first, and her gesture is fraught. Why does she stop wiping? Did she think she could take the make-up off only to decide to wait? What does her gesture mean? She has already kissed Ned when he was made up as Othello, and she would have kissed him when he was made up as Desdemona, minus wig, after returning from his trip in the coach. So why bother with blackface make-up now? Ned's gesture makes more sense but it is not actually shot. The camera cuts away just as he touches her face with the curtain. Though the next shot shows Maria's unsmudged face, the edit is 'dirty' because the wiping gesture is omitted. The final eight shots of the film, a shot-reverse-shot sequence ending with a medium shot of the lovers in profile, are similarly dirty. A remarkable succession of eight continuity errors occurs as we see Ned from over Maria's shoulder with a curtain hanging from behind his head and down over his left shoulder and then, in the reverse shot, see Maria over Ned's left shoulder without the curtain hanging over where continuity demands it should be.

In addition to 'dirtying' his film and engaging with the theatrical tradition of smudged make-up, Eyre develops his damaged cinematic aesthetic by linking blackness to fakery through another theatrical performance tradition in which the actor playing Othello is said to threaten the life of the actress playing Desdemona. Ira Aldridge, for example, was accused of harming, possibly killing, his white Desdemonas, and the same fear has often been staged in numerous examples of the *Othello*-within-the-film sub-genre where actor and character merge, and the actor playing Othello attempts (and sometimes succeeds in) the murder of the actress playing Desdemona.[30] This scene occurs in *Stage Beauty* when, in the film's most sensational moment, Maria shouts out 'Help! He's killing . . . He's killing me!'. This coheres with Ned's earlier statement, recorded immediately after Charles II's dinner party, that he will see Maria play Desdemona because he is 'always interested in how [his] rivals die'. Similarly, just before he and Maria perform the death scene, he tells her, 'I blame you for my death', meaning the end of his performance as Desdemona.

The delivery of this arguably cheap moment of surprise – has he killed her or not? – and the dramatic pause it elicits, work to frame the death scene itself as a kind of posthumous performance or afterlife. The final death scene is presented as if it were thematically and dramatically discontinuous with Ned's drag version. That is, the final performance seems to give us the feminist interpretation and the more graphic performance Ned wanted. Yet various repetitions link it to earlier rehearsals and filmic shots. In many respects, Maria's Desdemona is not discontinuous at all. Her interpretation of the role in the first rehearsal with Ned is already feminist when she tells him that Desdemona 'doesn't kiss him'. Maria's feminist interpretation does not translate into a natural, realistic acting style, however. She is unable to perform the role on her own, though the pregnant actress, who returned to her mother's to have a baby, presumably could have done. In any case, Maria's Desdemona continues to mime Ned in order to extend the individual performance. After Maria revives and then dies again, the camera shows a close-up of her hand using the same gesture Ned used as Desdemona and repeated, as we have seen, after he is beaten. When Maria repeats it, the more realistic and the artificial (or theatrical) collapse into one another. Similarly, after Charles II interrupts the play, a close-up of her hand again repeats his gesture and her voice off-screen falsifies the play to announce, 'We still have one more scene to finish'. The continuities marked by repetitions between Maria and Ned's respective Desdemonas suggest that revival on the stage is bound to repeat and recall what have become defective goods (in this case, Ned's drag performance). Repetitions in the final backstage sequence operate similarly to connect and recall defects, dirt and darkness. For example, Maria wiping off Ned's make-up recalls Ned taking off her white make-up before they rehearse the death scene. Moreover, the curtain hanging over Ned's shoulder recalls the curtain from which Maria looks in the opening title sequence.

Yet it would be wrong to say that *Stage Beauty* is simply a dirty film. It is, rather, a smudged film that attempts to pass as clean. The smudges are evident but minor enough for us not to notice them or generally to overlook them. Eyre is not interested in filming an adaptation of Shakespeare, remarking that his filmed-for-television *King Lear* (1998) was not 'proper' cinema' because it was filmed theatre.[31] *Stage Beauty* is neither 'proper' Shakespeare nor 'proper' cinema. It is *faux* Shakespeare and a *faux* English film. *Stage Beauty* casts American actors with bad English accents; it uses an American playwright as screenwriter to adapt his play; it recreates a *faux* Restoration theatre and history. The opening, digitally-altered engraving of Kynaston is obviously unfaithful.[32] And, even before this fake engraving, there is the fake address of Qwerty films. For Eyre, it would appear, the real English Shakespeare cinema of Olivier has passed, just as the age of foreign film Shakespeare has passed. These two kinds of 'authentic' Shakespeare film can no longer be differentiated along racial lines, since the effects of 'glocalisation' and transnational cinema on Shakespeare are nowhere more evident than in the multiracial casts of Shakespeare films made in the UK and in UK Shakespeare made-for-television films and programmes such as *Macbeth on the Estate* (dir. Penny Woolcock, 1997), *Macbeth* (dir. Michael Bogdanov, 1998), *Twelfth Night* (dir. Tim Supple, 2003), *Second Generation* (dir. Jonathan Sen, 2003), *Indian Dream* (dir. Roger Goldby, 2003) and the ITV/PBS *Othello*. Registering the effects of globalisation in *Stage Beauty* as a *faux* English Shakespeare, Eyre oddly empties out *Othello*. Remarkably, *Stage Beauty* does not explain why Othello murders Desdemona, and the final rehearsal and performance of the play's death scene are valued not because the actors are faithful to Shakespeare but because they entertain anachronistic interpretations and introduce theatrical innovations. Even more remarkably, the plot of *Stage Beauty* is free of infidelity. There are no triangles, no adultery. The Duke of Buckingham stops sleeping with Ned after he decides to marry. Charles II has a mistress but no wife. There is no original to which one might be faithful. All that remains of Shakespeare is rehearsal, with effects limited to the new, surprise and so on. *Stage Beauty* acknowledges that the new theatrical effect is a leftover, inevitably recycling the old and becoming old itself. Hence, the film sets Shakespeare in a past whose actors are now largely forgotten, while the citation, rehearsals and revivals of Shakespeare constitute remnants rather than full restorations. Ned's self-appraisal – 'I wasn't good tonight . . . same old things' – could serve as a salient epitaph to the Shakespeare play in the UK/US romantic comedy film.

Notes

1. Laurence Olivier (1986), *On Acting*, London: Weidenfeld and Nicolson, p. 151.
2. See, for example, David Denby (2004), 'Playing Parts', *The New Yorker*, 11 October (http://www.newyorker.com/critics/cinema/?041011crci_cinema).
3. For further discussion of *Shakespeare in Love* as a post-colonial and/or transnational film, see Richard Burt (1998), *Unspeakable ShaXXXspeares: Queer Theory and American Kiddie Culture*, New York: St Martin's Press, p. xiii; Rebecca Murray, 'Interview with *Stage Beauty* Writer, Jeffrey Hatcher, On Adapting His Play, Casting Americans, and Combining Characters', http://movies.about.com/od/stagebeauty/a/stagejh101204.htm.
4. Romeo and Juliet are mentioned as characters once, and the title of the play is cited at the end of the trailer. The trailer also shows the balcony scene when Will woos Viola, and, at Wessex's ball, the narrator states that the film is a 'romantic comedy of errors'. The *Stage Beauty* trailer replies to the *Shakespeare in Love* trailer, too. Both trailers use the same section of Vivaldi's *Four Seasons*, and both are similarly structured, with the actors' names appearing close to the end.

5. Vincent Price plays a white Othello in *Have Gun/Will Travel* (Episode 54, 'The Moor's Revenge', dir. Andrew V. McLaglen, 1958), while a white Othello also appears in *Cheers* (Episode 26, 'Homicidal Ham', dir. James Burrows, 1983).

6. To be sure, *Othello* was a frequently revived play in the Restoration (Virginia Mason Vaughan (1994), *'Othello': A Contextual History*, Cambridge: Cambridge University Press, pp. 98–9). The film, however, does not aim to provide a historically accurate account of Restoration theatre. Kynaston played Cassio in one revival of *Othello* (Vaughan, '*Othello*', p. 98).

7. See Vaughan, '*Othello*', pp. 197–8 on controversies surrounding the casting of Othello in the wake of Paul Robeson's assumption of the role and in the context of the present taboo on white actors taking the part.

8. Katherine Eggert (2003), 'Sure Can Sing and Dance: Minstrelsy, the Star System, and the Post-Postcoloniality of Kenneth Branagh's *Love's Labour's Lost* and Trevor Nunn's *Twelfth Night*', in Richard Burt and Lynda E. Boose (eds), *Shakespeare, the Movie, II: Popularizing the Plays on Film, TV, Video, and DVD*, London and New York: Routledge, pp. 72–88.

9. I refer here to discussions of passing which is focused on blacks trying to pass as whites rather than the reverse. See Amy Robinson (1994), 'It Takes One to Know One: Passing and Communities of Common Interest', *Critical Inquiry*, 20.4 pp. 715–36. On Olivier's Othello as racist, see Bosley Crowthers (1966), 'Minstrel Show *Othello*: Radical Makeup Marks Olivier's Interpretation', *The New York Times*, 2 February (http://movies2.nytimes.com/mem/movies/review.html?title1=&title2=Othello%20%28Movie%29&reviewer=BOSLEY%20CROWTHER&pdate=19660202&v_id=105111); Barbara Hodgdon (2003), 'Race-ing *Othello*: Engendering White Out II', in Burt and Boose (eds), *Shakespeare, the Movie, II*, pp. 89–104; Timothy J. Murray (1993), *Like a Film: Ideological Fantasy on Screen, Camera and Canvas*, New York and London: Routledge, pp. 101–23; Patricia Tatspaugh (2001), 'The Tragedies of Love on Film', in Russell Jackson (ed.), *The Cambridge Companion to Shakespeare on Film*, Cambridge: Cambridge University Press, pp. 135–59.

10. The UK/US romantic comedy dates back at least as far as *The Tall Guy* (dir. Mel Smith, 1989) but was first successfully launched by *Four Weddings and a Funeral* (dir. Mike Newell, 1994) followed by *Notting Hill* (dir. Roger Michell, 1999). More recent examples include *Bridget Jones' Diary* (dir. Sharon Maguire, 2001), *Love Actually* (dir. Richard Curtis, 2003), *Wimbledon* (dir. Richard Loncraine, 2004), *Bridget Jones: The Edge of Reason* (dir. Beeban Kidron, 2004) and *The Wedding Date* (dir. Clare Kilner, 2005). *Fever Pitch* (dir. David Evans, 1997) was remade as *Fever Pitch* (dir. Bobby and Peter Farrelly, 2005). *The Tall Guy*, *Notting Hill* and *Love Actually* were all written by Richard Curtis, and Richard Loncraine also directed *Richard III* (1996). See also UK/US romantic melodramas such as *Sliding Doors* (dir. Peter Howitt, 1998), *Sylvia* (dir. Christine Jeffs, 2003), both starring Gwyneth Paltrow (in *Sylvia* she recites Shakespeare), and *Closer* (dir. Mike Nichols, 2004). The overt commercialism of *Love Actually* and *Wedding Date* (a remake of *Pretty Woman*) is also in evidence in the stripclub scenes in *Closer*.

11. Rick Altman (1999), *Film/Genre*, London: British Film Institute, pp. 17–18.

12. To be sure, yoking a Shakespeare play to romantic comedy is no guarantee of success. Consider the English film *Food of Love* (dir. Stephen Poliakoff, 1997), a film starring Richard Grant (who played Sir Andrew Aguecheek in Trevor Nunn's *Twelfth Night* and an actor who recites a passage from *Hamlet* at the end of *Withnail and I*, dir. Bruce Robinson, 1987) as a London bank manager and theatre teacher who reunites with his former university students to perform an amateur production of *Twelfth Night* as they did a decade earlier. The film flopped, received poor reviews, and has never been released on video or DVD.

13. The genre has not been recognised as such, as far as I am aware.
14. For other *Othello* scenes in films, see *Desdemona* (dir. August Blom, 1911); *Othello in Jonesville* (dir. Charles M. Seay, 1913) – the script was written by an English actor, with the film being released in England and France (Robert Hamilton Ball (1968), *Shakespeare on Silent Film*, London: George Allen and Unwin, pp. 163, 343); *Carnival* (dir. Harley Knoles, 1921); *Carnival: Venetian Nights* (dir. Herbert Wilcox, 1931); *Men Are Not Gods* (dir. Walter Reisch, 1936); *Paradise in Harlem* (dir. Joseph Seiden, 1939); *Serenade* (dir. Anthony Mann, 1956); *Have Gun/Will Travel* (Episode 54, 'The Moor's Revenge', dir. Andrew V. McLaglen, 1958); *Den Store Amatören* (dir. Hasse Ekman, 1958); *Saptapadi* (dir. Ajoy Kar, 1961); *Capriccio all'italiana* (dir. Mauro Bolognini, 1968); *The Flesh and Blood Show* (dir. Pete Walker, 1972); *Sanford and Son* (Episode 39, 'Lamont as Othello', dir. Peter Baldwin, 1973); *A Peleskei Nótárius* (dir. anon., 1975); *Zvezdi v kosite, salzi v ochite* (dir. Ivan Nitchev, 1977); *So Fine* (dir. Andrew Bergman, 1981); *Cheers* (Episode 26, 'Homicidal Ham', dir. James Burrows, 1983); *Une Histoire Inventée* (dir. André Forcier, 1990); *Don Tonin* ('Delitto al Teatro', dir. Fosco Gasperi, 1990); *True Identity* (dir. Charles Lane, 1991); *The Playboys* (dir. Gillies MacKinnon, 1992); *Orlando* (dir. Sally Potter, 1992); *Double Vision* (dir. Robert Knights, 1992); *Alcatraz Avenue* (dir. Tom Edgar, 2000); and *In Othello* (dir. Roysten Abel, 2003). For a related film involving *The Tempest*, see *Beginner's Luck* (dir. James Callis and Nick Cohen, 2001).
15. The connection between female impersonation and blackface might further link Hatcher's play and his script to American minstrelsy and African-American Shakespeare, though the precedents are contradictory. There were female impersonators in the minstrel shows, while Henry Brown's production of a version of *Richard III* at New York's African Theatre in 1821 cast all the parts with men in order to observe 'Elizabethan' customs (see Annemarie Bean, James V. Hatch and Brookes McNamara (1996), *Inside the Minstrel Mask: Readings in Nineteenth-Century Blackface Minstrelsy*, Middletown: Wesleyan University Press, pp. 245–56, 260).
16. Congratulations backstage are given to her first and delivered by Charles II. George Villiars, Duke of Buckingham (Ben Chaplin), writes 'bravo' on the mirror.
17. See Ruth Cowig (1979), 'Actors Black and Tawny in the Role of Othello – and their Critics', *Theatre Research International*, 4.2, pp. 133–46.
18. There is also an auditory link between the auditioning scene and the dissolve scene of the star actresses. The voices of women reciting lines are heard before the camera cuts to the actresses on the steps behind the theatre, and we hear snatches and repetitions of lines from *King Lear* and *Romeo and Juliet*.
19. The film's clearest figure of this repressed world is the stage manager and prompter (Derek Hutchinson). Though he is seen looking at the texts of *Othello* and *King Lear*, respectively during the performance of the death scene, the opening title sequence and the rehearsal of the 'carry scene', he never speaks a line from either play; similarly, the silent stagehand is seen glaring at Ned at several points in the film.
20. In *Kira at Night* (dir. Paul Thomas, 2003), the 'action' takes play in a building called the Shakespeare Art Centre, beneath which appears a sign indicating 'The Globe'. Posters of several of Shakespeare's plays, including *A Midsummer Night's Dream*, *Richard II* and *Hamlet* 'Improvised' are seen backstage, while Shakespeare's name, a painting of Shakespeare and scenes from the plays are visible as a *faux* version of the balcony scene is performed. Neither Shakespeare nor any of the plays mentioned are otherwise cited. This film is an example of a

literally on-the-wall Shakespeare where sex and Shakespeare's performance are wholly distinguished.

21. For a related set of concerns, see *The Libertine* (dir. Laurence Dunmore, 2004), a film that, like *Stage Beauty*, is based on a play (Stephen Jeffreys, 1994) and that shows a truly dirty London, in every sense of the word. At the start, Charles II (John Malkovich) states that he would like John Wilmot, the Earl of Rochester (Johnny Depp), to be what Shakespeare was to Queen Elizabeth: 'Elizabeth had her Shakespeare: you can be mine'.

22. On Othello's make-up, see Lois Potter (2002), *Shakespeare in Performance: 'Othello'*, Manchester and New York: Manchester University Press, pp. 29–30. On Gielgud and Olivier, see Murray, *Like a Film*, pp. 109–10.

23. There is a paratextual connection between the DVD edition of *Stage Beauty* and Burge's film version of *Othello*, which is famous for its use of a red rose. As the DVD menu loads, a rose appears on the left, only to dissolve into an image of Maria. Similarly, a large rose on the left serves as the background for the three DVD menu pages.

24. Murray, *Like a Film*, pp. 109–10.

25. Murray, *Like a Film*, pp. 104, 106–07.

26. Murray, *Like a Film*, p. 111.

27. Murray, *Like a Film*, p. 111.

28. Billie Whitelaw (1995), 'Billie Whitelaw . . . Who He?', *The Sunday Times*, 27 August, section 10, p. 13.

29. Olivier, *On Acting*, p. 158.

30. On Aldridge, see Herbert Marshall and Mildred Stock (1993), *Ira Aldridge: The Negro Tragedian*, Washington, DC: Howard University Press, pp. 269–70.

31. Christopher James (2004), 'Stage Duty: Richard Eyre tells Christopher James Why Filming the Bard is Hard', *The Times*, 4 September (http://www.timesonline.co.uk/article/0,,7943-1245801,00.html).

32. Eyre's interest in the US/UK axis in the theatre, especially Shakespearean theatre, is explored in Richard Eyre and Nicholas Wright (2001), *Changing Stages: A View of British and American Theatre in the Twentieth Century*, London: Alfred A. Knopf. Playwright and screenwriter Jeffrey Hatcher discusses casting American actors in Rebecca Murray, 'Interview with "Stage Beauty" Writer, Jeffrey Hatcher' (http://movies.about.com/od/stagebeauty/a/stagejh101204.htm).

Chapter 4

The Postnostalgic Renaissance: The 'Place' of Liverpool in Don Boyd's *My Kingdom*

Courtney Lehmann

One of the primary symptoms of late capitalism, as Fredric Jameson argues, is the rise of the 'nostalgia film', which projects on a collective level the confusion associated with the individual experience of post-modernity. This cinematic genre betrays a desire to escape the present via retreat into the past, even as its increasing failure to denote the past, by any means other than dead styles, conveys the more insidious problem of 'the waning of our historicity, of our lived possibility of experiencing history in some active way'.[1] Yet, at same time as Jameson was arguing his theme, this film genre was giving way to a sequel that signalled a crisis of historicity in an altogether different direction: the future. Combining the glossy elegance of traditional costume drama and the self-consciously unorthodox sensibilities of punk, the transitional nostalgia films of the early 1990s approached the concept of period dialectically and, in so doing, failed to provide adequate distance from a future that threatened to convert their imaginary dystopias into reality. Both genres tend to support neo-conservative conclusions through their strategic manufac-ture of 'nostalgia for the present', an affective paradox that generates complacency with the way things *are*.[2]

The Renaissance period and particularly Shakespearean film boom of the 1990s, which similarly fluctuated between the traditional nostalgia film and its hybrid descendant, moved somewhat belatedly in the direc-tion of the latter with the release of Baz Luhrmann's *William Shakespeare's 'Romeo + Juliet'* (1996). What I wish to explore here, though, is the arrival of a Renaissance-based film genre that, instead of lagging behind existing trends, is actually at the vanguard of a new one: the postnostalgia film. Rather than working to establish a sense of period which, ultimately, fails to offer an escape from historical inevitability, Don Boyd's *King Lear* spin-off, *My Kingdom* (2001), privileges place as a means of direct engagement with a present whose identity has been eroded by the centrifugal energies of globalisation, the paranoia of post-9/11 culture, an imploding cycle of neglect and, above all, the fear that the apocalypse has already arrived.

In this context, the appeal to the local becomes the site of an important intervention, particularly when this location is Liverpool, a place that has become synonymous with the spectre of long-term, cataclysmic decline. A city prone to lapse into nostalgia for its nineteenth-century glory as one of the world's pre-eminent ports, contemporary Liverpool is, simultan-eously, relentlessly oriented toward the future as one of the UK's priority urban rehabilitation sites. But residents of Liverpool remain sceptical of such 'rebirth' initiatives, typified in the city's bid to qualify as a European Capital of Culture by 2008 and a European Renaissance City by 2010. For Boyd, filming a Liverpool marked by local terrorism, internecine bloodshed, racism, poverty and moral depravity becomes a means to avenge the broken promises of urban renovation schemes that have wrested from Liverpudlians any opportunity to determine their own destiny. The film's representation of a war between family-based crime organisations is a far from subtle symptom of the demand for a return to local priorities, even as it betokens the impotence of local authorities to confront the real competition posed by a global market.

Luring its protagonists into the quest for a promised land that will clearly never materialise, *My Kingdom* sets a precedent for post-millennial filmmaking that is postnostalgic, for it implicitly recog-nises that the reparations of time in either direction, past or future, will not heal the present ravages of place. Through almost total nihilism, the film performs its own kind of urban 'renovation', parodying the regeneration schemes that have devolved into demolition and redlining, while simultaneously clearing space for new relationships to place that might yet prove democratic rather than neo-colonial.

I

'There's only three ways a poor lad can make it out of the back streets of Liverpool: show business, sport or crime,' announces Quick (Tom Bell), a customs officer in *My Kingdom*. Mourning a dying breed of citizen, he adds, 'Working-class heroes – tragic, really', and concludes by suggesting the current state of citizenship in Liverpool: ' "Humanity must perforce prey upon itself, / Like monsters of the deep" '.[3] This para-phrase of *King Lear* is delivered to Sandeman (Richard Harris), the Lear character, as he takes shelter with his grandson from a storm. Quick mimics the pseudo-sagacity of Edgar in this 'heath' scene, also serving throughout as a more menacing version of Lear's other devoted apostles, Kent and Gloucester. Like the loyal Kent, Quick assures Sandeman that he will continue to follow him 'all over the world', but only until he gathers enough evidence to commit this king of Liverpool's drug trade to a life in prison. Like Gloucester, however, Quick protects the old man from the far more dangerous predators who seek his life itself, stalling Sandeman's enemies when they are close to converging upon and killing him. Quick is subsequently blinded for his modest intervention and, more disturbingly, for his endorsement of an archaic belief system in which concepts of right and wrong exist and heroes may be distinguished from criminals. Until he loses his sight, then, Quick cannot see that the 'back streets' of Liverpool are everywhere, for they have become a state of mind in a city that has long since crossed over into what Giorgio Agamben calls the 'state of exception' – a society in which the predatorial instincts of global capitalism are universal – so that humanity must perforce consume or be consumed.[4] As with so many other blind prophets in Shakespeare, Quick's unenviable role is to guide Sandeman to this impasse, after which the world-weary customs officer stumbles along the rainswept railway until he arrives at a fork in the tracks, where he pauses to place his neck in the path of an approaching train.

II

Exploring the global endgame that *My Kingdom* localises in its vision of Liverpool as a city at war with itself, Michael Hardt and Antonio Negri trace the phenomenon of exceptionalism back to its imperial origins in the figure of the monarch, who once served as the singular embodiment of the 'sovereign exception', or, 'the notion that one who commands need not obey'.[5] The opening credit sequence represents Sandeman as the sole executor of this privilege, establishing him as the city's unofficial divine-right monarch in a dissolve that pictures Liverpool's spectacular Anglican cathedral fading into the palatial contours of his suburban home. Boasting one of the world's highest belltowers as well as one of the largest organs, the very architecture of the city's landmark resounds with the superlatives that characterise Sandeman himself. Indeed, if 'the desire to mark Liverpool's standing in the world economy came to be reflected in the built environment', then, like the cathedral that dominates the skyline, Sandeman's position of exceptionalism *vis-à-vis* the city's other subjects is also conveyed spatially – through the places which, at least at the start, he freely inhabits.[6] En route to a concert, for example, Sandeman sends his driver on a detour through one of the city's many slums; here, he sets his mermidons on a handful of men who, he states sanctimoniously, 'make the place look untidy'. The fact that no other explanation for the offence is forthcoming reinforces our impression that Sandeman *is* the law in Liverpool and, as Agamben concludes of the sovereign exception, 'the point of indistinction between violence and the law'.[7]

Subsequently, an intimidating, low-angle shot of the cathedral's soaring gold interior provides the backdrop for Sandeman's equally egregious exercise of power within the church itself, wherein he places calls to his multinational drug cartel from the front pew. 'Can you hear me now?' he shouts, acting as though his business, and not the religious celebration, were the main attraction. Convinced of his right to occupy any space with impunity, Sandeman exits the cathedral in the middle of the service and takes his wife, Mandy (Lynn Redgrave), on a shortcut home through the Granby-Toxteth ghetto. When a hooded black youth pulls a gun on Mandy and demands her purse, Sandeman does not even flinch, calmly asking the mugger: 'Do you have any idea who – I – am?' Sandeman's fatal misrecognition that the assailant *does not* know him is the first of many brutal indications that his personal monopoly on the sovereign exception has given way to an anonymous 'state of exception' in which vigilantism has devolved from a last resort into a reflex. Confidently guiding the mugger's gun away from Mandy and into his own eyes, Sandeman taunts: 'That's better . . . be sure you don't miss'. When the junkie fires two blanks, Sandeman laughs and instructs Mandy to give the pitiful punk her purse with a dismissive wave of his hand, glancing the tip of the gun in the process. This time it fires, point-blank, into Mandy's head and kills her instantly.

This is the primal scene of *My Kingdom*, signalling the formal end of Sandeman's sovereignty and ushering in a new rule of law, one that emerges as a particularly sinister variation on the theme of Liverpool's reputation for 'organised' lawlessness. Because of its geographical isolation as a port that faces away from continental Europe and towards Ireland, Liverpool has habitually enjoyed relative independence from the monarchy. In the absence of centralised authority, the city embraced models of localised sovereignty such as New York City's Tammany Hall, the powerful Irish-American boss system that kindled Liverpool's corresponding late nineteenth- and early twentieth-century tradition of 'boss' politics. Inspired by visions of renegade rule across the Atlantic, Liverpool historically defended its own posture of exceptionalism against the ongoing tide of Tory calls for reform by basing its sovereignty not on the hereditary privileges of Westminster but on the hard-won practices of working-class heroes. That Sandeman, an Irish *émigré* not to Manhattan but to Liverpool, has constructed his kingdom around this concept of rugged individualism is suggested by the film's introduction of the ageing patriarch hunched over a hand of solitaire. Moreover, the three American films that play in the background link the spirited independence of England's north-west to the outlaw orientation of the 'wild west': one screen depicts a Western; another, rebels on the run; and the last, an American flag. However, the implication that Sandeman's claim to sovereignty has long since expired is conveyed by the grainy quality of these old black-and-white movies, whose representations of rogue regimes no longer correspond to the exception but, rather, the rule in Liverpool.

In a culture wherein authority extends only as far as one's liquid assets, the buck stops for Sandeman when the family learns that his fortune, which has long been held in Mandy's name to avoid legal entanglements, has been transferred to the couple's youngest daughter, Jo (Emma Catherwood). Predictably, Jo wants nothing to do with the scandalous inheritance, and Sandeman retaliates by giving everything he has to Kath (Louise Lombard) and Tracy (Lorraine Pilkington): *King Lear* is here easily discernible. Yet there are deeper resonances between Shakespeare's king and *My Kingdom*'s Sandeman, both of whom register a unique form of historical trauma as representatives of a culture whose mode of economic production has violently outpaced its mechanisms of cognitive perception – what Jameson refers to, in a discussion of the velocity of postmodernism, as 'the incapacity of our minds . . . to map the great global multinational and decentred communicational network in which we find ourselves caught'.[8] In this context, nostalgia emerges as a source of perceptual deacceleration, functioning as a stop-gap mechanism that supplies the present with its missing grid of inclusiveness by arresting it within the familiar terms of the past.

In both *King Lear* and *My Kingdom*, the protagonists indulge in nostalgia as a means of coping with the vertiginous spaces of the present. Lear, for example, remains entrenched in an increasingly obsolete feudal system predicated on good lordship, servant loyalty, social fixity and benevolent astrological determinism. So, too, does Sandeman cling to an imaginary impression of Liverpool's Victorian and Edwardian splendour, polishing the filthy edges of his business with the faded glory of the British Empire, as though he were its lone torchbearer. Like Lear, then, Sandeman's social values are based on an outmoded economic system – here, the imperial or monopoly stage of capitalism alluded to in the title, *My Kingdom*. However, whereas Lear's dementia is ultimately indistinguishable from senility and, therefore, directly related to (the passing of) time, Sandeman's affliction is a consequence of the very space he occupies, a space, simply put, in which nostalgia has *no place*.

One formal consequence of the transition to late or global capitalism, as Jameson contends, is that 'our daily life, our psychic experience, our cultural languages [become] . . . dominated by categories of space rather than by categories of time'.[9] This privileging of space over time, and of surfaces over depth, extends beyond our apprehension of the present to our experience of the past, which is reduced to 'a vast collection of images' or simulacra that stand in for the 'real' content of a particular epoch.[10] In effect, within the perceptual schemes of global capitalism, time becomes a function of space, for the passage of time is rendered meaningful only insofar as it corresponds to the spread of capital into, and reflects the colonisation of, previously uncommodified territories. *My Kingdom* stages the extent to which time – indeed, an entire lifetime – is accessible only through stylistic connotation and other sources of commodification when, in the middle of Kath's toast to her dead mother, Tracy bursts into a cover of the Barry Manilow song 'Mandy'. Beginning with the third verse – 'Standing on the edge of time / Walked away when love was mine' – Tracy's hideous rendition evinces not a jot of the real Mandy Sandeman's history, other than the pure coincidence of her name with the eponymous heroine of a schmaltzy 1970s' ballad. Worse, in light of Manilow's more recent gravitation towards cabaret, 'Mandy' plays as pure camp: no matter how persuasive the performance, lines like 'Looking in her eyes, I see a memory / I never realised, how happy you made me / Oh Mandy', will only ever refer back to the made-up girlfriend of a gay balladeer.

As the reluctant applause of the audience suggests, such forays into historical time literally fall flat in the face of capitalism's self-reproductive agenda, giving rise to the perception that 'we now inhabit the synchronic rather than the diachronic'.[11] More important than the perceptual repercussions of the rise of global capitalism, however, are its lived consequences: as *My Kingdom* demonstrates via Sandeman's descent into homelessness, society increasingly comes to experience itself as an inherently displaced citizenry, a condition wherein private ownership becomes the only weapon to combat the experience of internal exile. This profoundly unnatural disaster is the source of the rising terrorism that characterises *My Kingdom*'s Liverpool, wherein social law mirrors the whims of the commodity form and everyone would be king.

III

It seems significant, then, that, prior to the onset of this war of attrition (which begins when Tracy lays claim to Mandy's car and Kath responds by blowing it up), Sandeman indulges in a nostalgic homage to Liverpool. Gazing out beyond the Mersey to the sea, he exclaims: 'Smell that . . . steam ships, iron shavings. I'm thinking about the past. This great city. Mine. I'm thinking about the first time I ever walked under a Liverpool sky.' The distinctly elegiac tone of Sandeman's recollection betrays the fear that this 'great city' and 'his city' no longer correspond to one another. Concerned that his respectability has declined in conjunction with Liverpool, Sandeman asks Mandy: 'Have I changed much since I got off the boat?' 'Yeah . . . You certainly have,' she replies, raising one eyebrow as though she were preparing him for the worst. But Mandy proceeds to deflect the question by qualifying her answer with reference to the city itself: 'You've changed *everything around you*.' On the one hand, Mandy's statement – that Liverpool has changed but he has not – suggests Sandeman's enduring modesty toward the vastly improved municipal infrastructure that has sprung from his entrepreneurial leadership. On the other hand, Mandy's response resonates as a backhanded compliment, implying that her husband's spaces are ahead of his (sense of) time, indeed, that his perception has failed to keep pace with accelerating flows of capital into and out of his urban environs.

In fact, even before the botched mugging provides painful proof that Liverpool's geography of disadvantage has subsumed its selective sites of urban renovation, the camera draws attention to the ways in which the spaces of the city have assumed a life of their own. Driving toward the cathedral, Sandeman informs Mandy that his work in Liverpool is done; but his effort to broach the future of his retirement is belied by images of present-day Liverpool that are profoundly *undone*, as scaffolded, burned and decimated buildings leer out of the pavement towards his car. That he sees only what he wants to see is implied in a shot of a building *façade* of mirror glass, an example of the flashy, futuristic architecture that characterises Paradise Street's newest commercial district. Through this architectural parable of uneven development, *My Kingdom* confronts the material inequities of the renovation scheme known as '*façadism*', in which the frame of an old building is converted into the structure of a new one, creating what is commonly called 'high-tech nostalgia'. As Michael Friedman, David Andrews and Michael Silk explain, the 'fundamental disconnection between the external appearance of the building and its underlying structure' is revisited in the relationship between city planners and the inner-city population, who promote 'the *façade* of an improved civic image . . . over citizen welfare'.[12] Catering to tourists and business travellers, such schemes ignore the real needs of those trapped in the poverty cycle, whose suffering is augmented by the constant diversion of revenue away from the low-income sector towards the maintenance of these 'islands of affluence' in 'a sea of urban decay and disinvestment'.[13]

Architectural *façadism* represents the mode of renovation that has been employed throughout much of Liverpool, particularly in the dock complexes, where a combination of heritage themes and high-tech amenities has led to lucrative returns for investors from the private sector, while failing to address the marginal-at-best existence of those living in and around such touristified zones. Mirroring the inconsistency of such city planning, Sandeman abruptly abandons the subject of his own plan for the future in favour of the past, indulging his sentimental memory of the day that he and Mandy first met. Appropriately, this lapse into nostalgia is complemented by receding shots of landmarks from Liverpool's past: *The Daily Post and Echo* building, the Roman Catholic cathedral and the glorious Anglican cathedral itself. But Sandeman's romantic impression of Liverpool – past and present – becomes untenable when, moments after his homage, the city's long-neglected 'back streets' rise up against his nostalgia and claim Mandy's life on behalf of their 'darker purpose' (I.i.34), which, as this brutal juxtaposition suggests, revolves around the revenge of space (and place) against time.

Sandeman's absorption in nostalgia emerges in part from his relation to the extradiegetic space that surrounds him, for the film's title brings to mind the association of Richard Harris with King Arthur in the nostalgia film *par excellence*: *Camelot* (dir. Joshua Logan, 1967). In fact, Sandeman's initial response to Mandy's murder is to forgo traditional nostalgia in favour of the production of what I term the 'Camelot effect', or, the attempt to conceal a regime change that has already taken place. Just as there is a correlation between the screen revival *Camelot* and the collective denial of Kennedy's death, so is there in *My Kingdom* a similar need to remain indefinitely in the present, despite the presence of trauma and tragedy. *My Kingdom* functions as a kind of 'sequel' to *Camelot* in which the character played by Richard Harris – unlike Arthur, Lear or Kennedy – is forced to survive the death of his sovereignty in order to acknowledge his complicity in the coronation of a far more ruthless sovereign power. At first, however, Sandeman denies his role in the cycle of addiction and abjection that precipitates Mandy's murder by asserting the existence of an elaborate conspiracy. A variation on the Camelot effect, Sandeman's recourse to conspiracy theory not only preserves the illusion of his authority but also augments it by singling him out as someone who is worthy of assassination, situating him within an epistemological construct overwhelmingly tied to Kennedy himself.

Conspiracy, which typically focuses on an assassination plot, is not to be confused with mere murder, for the former implicates an entire society in its intricate web of non-accidents, distinguishing the victim as a figure who is central to the social totality. Sandeman's insistence that the mugging was really a miscarried assassination plot serves precisely this function of raising his personal stock, as the media frenzy surrounding Mandy's funeral alone reveals. Yet more important than the status that such a narrative confers on its individual target is the cultural work it performs, for conspiracy theory serves as a means of shoring up an internally divided society by implicating everyone – and everything – in its network of hidden relations. The point not to be missed, however, is that the historical emergence of this genre in the 1960s stems less from an idiosyncratic fascination with the fall of the Kennedy dynasty than it does with the collective fear of the rise of a far less propitious – and distinctly faceless – sovereign, for this same period marks the point at which capitalism begins to acquire global form, inaugurating what Hardt and Negri ominously refer to as the 'self-rule of capital'.[14] As *My Kingdom* documents, decades after the transitional Camelot era, when the centrifugal forces of capitalism have achieved the status of a cultural or global 'dominant', the traditional consolations of conspiracy theory – the presumption of a world in which meaning, law and order ultimately exist – no longer apply. Hence, what Sandeman must come to terms with is the *new* totalising function of conspiracy in the age of global capitalism: once a theoretical construct, conspiracy has become an ontological imperative in a world in which space itself is an accomplice – a world, that is, in which there is no place 'outside' of capital.

Initially, Sandeman's conspiratorial surmise produces the desired effect by creating the impression that the entire city must answer to him. As his son-in-law, Dean (Paul McGann), reports, the quest to find Mandy's killer is city-wide: 'we've got men on every door of Liverpool'. Taking care to cover all his bases, Sandeman brings even scattered family members together under this umbrella of suspicion. When they protest at being frisked prior to entering the estate, the bodyguards reply: 'Boss' orders'. Once inside, however, Dean and Jug (Jimi Mistry), Sandeman's other son-in-law, share an irreverent laugh about the boss and his drones: 'I think this mugging's gone to their heads,' they chortle. 'What mugging?' Sandeman asks upon entering the room, as if to bait them with the fear

that the walls have ears. In an effort to build on the paranoia that augments conspiracy theory's explanatory power, Sandeman reprimands his
sons-in-law: 'Trust no one,' he exclaims. 'You are under commandment'.
But Jug retorts glibly, 'Man cannot live by commandments alone.' In this
brief exchange, *My Kingdom* delineates the distinction between traditional, Camelot-era conspiracy *theory* and the *practice* of conspiracy
under the self-rule of capitalism. Both are, of course, symptoms of an
interregnum, of a kingdom suddenly bereft of its king. However, whereas
conspiracy theory reflects a temporary 'state of nature' in which paranoia
and violence work together to organise the desire for the restoration of a
sovereign power, the practice of conspiracy itself refers to the more contemporary 'state of exception' in which civil war is the only viable model
of political 'order'. In other words, whereas chaos is a means to an end in
the state of nature because it creates the demand for law, in the state of
exception, the law functions only to prolong chaos, as a law which, in
Agamben's definition, 'is in force but does not signify.' [15] Entering into
league with its former adversary, *jouissance*, this law does not *signify* pro-
hibition but rather *enforces* enjoyment – precisely the menacing surplus
that Jug invokes when he claims that 'Man cannot live by commandments
alone' – and the hallmark of a culture whose sole structuring conspiracy
is mutually assured destruction.

That this paradoxical 'law' has long prevailed over Sandeman's commandment is evident in the formal introduction of his household
members, who are individuated only according to their preferred form
of illicit consumption. Watching Mandy's funeral procession through
binoculars, Quick informs us that Sandeman's eldest child, Kath, uses her
college degree to run a 'suck and fuck' salon, while his middle daughter,
Tracy, is a drug addict who launders money through her football fran-
chise. Although Kath and Tracy do not resemble each other physically,
their likeness is forged along the axis of enjoyment: both have insatiable
sex drives. Whereas Kath married her loser-husband Dean 'on the
rebound from some black snapper in London', Tracy 'loves to fuck' just
about anybody, despite being married to the sexy Sikh Jug, who is
described as 'the biggest heroin dealer in the north of England'. But it is
not until Quick introduces Jo that we recognise just how 'global' the state
of exception is: she is identified as the good daughter because she is
a *recovering* addict and prostitute, who took to the streets with the quad-
riplegic pimp known as 'the Chair' (Colin Salmon) in order to 'support
[a] smack habit the size of Kilimanjaro'.

Sandeman's insistent recourse to the stabilising logic of conspiracy
theory is a symptom of a shifting social infrastructure born of an

increasingly violent drive for 'renovation' through enjoyment, a drive which, as in Shakespeare's play, is aligned with the younger generation. This generational divide becomes particularly glaring during Mandy's funeral banquet, when Sandeman is informed that the murderer has been identified as Delroy (Otis Graham), the son of one of his oldest friends, Desmond (Oscar James). Out of respect for this friendship, Sandeman gives explicit instructions not to harm the boy, 'but', he adds, 'I must know who paid him'. Staunchly refusing to indulge this conspiracy theory, Dean replies with strained courtesy, 'Mr Sandeman, it was a *mugging*'. That everyone else in Liverpool is represented as being of the same opinion suggests the extent to which the state of exception has hardened into a mindset, producing a citizenry for whom random, 'man-made' violence has become entirely natural.

In this context, Sandeman's subsequent but seemingly arbitrary invocation of the distinctly organised violence of boxing, as well as the known boundaries of the nation-state, resonates as an extension of his Camelot-effect, for his appeal to 'England' assumes that the 'nation' *remains* a source of collective identification to which even Liverpudlians will defer. Accordingly, when Desmond arrives to beg for his son's life, Sandeman withholds his intent to pardon Delroy and exclaims to everyone within earshot, 'We boxed together. He boxed for England.' Proudly clapping Desmond on the back, Sandeman adds, 'He was the best.' Again linking Liverpool's past to the celebration of the British Empire, Sandeman evinces the city's historical reputation as a repository for prize fighters and African-born boxers in particular, who singlehandedly kept England in contention for international titles in the 1940s and 1950s, when there was a paucity of native boxing talent. However, like the defunct, postwar boxing partnership that Sandeman forged with Desmond, the partnership between the nation-state and monopoly-stage capitalism was, in this same era, already giving way to the unstable loyalties of global capitalism. Hence, in the very instant that Sandeman and Desmond are shown shaking hands in the banqueting hall, sealing their pact that Delroy 'will not be harmed', the camera cuts to a glimpse of the younger generation consuming its own in the kitchen below. Here, Delroy is not merely harmed but tortured by Jug, who strips him, dresses him in gold *lamé* underwear and mutilates him to death – a grotesque parody of the once sacrosanct national borders that Sandeman has just invoked. Indeed, as the blood runs across Delroy's lifeless black body, we see an emergent map of the world forming in which all barriers to the free circulation of commodities are eliminated, as well as a more specific allusion to the 'topography of exploitation' that is the price of entry into the global marketplace for many African countries, whose natural resources serve Western desires rather than indigenous needs.[16] The staging of this scene in a kitchen, a place explicitly tied to consumption, demonstrates how Sandeman's ongoing appeals to times past prove no match for the 'obscene importunings' of contemporary space, wherein, as Jug's butchery suggests, the table is set for humanity to prey upon itself.

These 'obscene importunings', described by Joan Copjec as audible to everyone but traceable to no-one, refer to the murmur of enjoyment that issues directly from the spaces of global capitalism.[17] *My Kingdom* invokes such spaces through its increasing compulsion to localise *jouissance* in the experience of otherness, manifested in phrases that link Kath's sex drive to 'some black snapper in London', Jug's heroin business to the scouse-infested 'north of England', and Jo's smack addiction to 'Mount Kilimanjaro'. But the most profound illustration of this phenomenon occurs in a scene in Kath's brothel, the archetypal space in which people are, in fact, consumed as things. Paraphrasing a line from the Beatles' song 'The Magical Mystery Tour', Kath's hostess shows a punter women who, she claims, will 'give you anything you want, from anything you see', tempting him to sample the merchandise. When the punter seems reluctant, Kath takes charge of the transaction, placing a call to another employee from whom she requests aperitifs, adding, 'And Yolanda, can you bring us the drinks?' 'Yolanda?' the punter gasps, with a mixture of disgust and intrigue. With smug satisfaction, Kath replies, 'Fresh from the Balkans.'

Kath's reply cuts to the chase of the conspiracy that *is* global capitalism, by demonstrating not only how enjoyment is uncannily endemic to space itself but, more importantly, how space (specifically, place of origin) returns to circumscribe enjoyment. For, in one respect, despite the fact that 'the Balkans' invokes a number of different countries in the former Soviet bloc, such details are of no concern to Yolanda's 'importers'. Rather, Yolanda is simply 'from the Balkans', a region so poor that its principal contribution to the global economy is indeed young girls, easy targets for the tightly organised gangs who trade and consume women's bodies with the impunity of their 'legitimate' corporate counterparts. But if the generalisation implicit in this attribution suggests the totalising trajectory of global capitalism – a world in which 'people' and 'things' become indistinguishable – then, in another respect, the regional specificity of the phrase 'fresh from the Balkans' points to the other 'truth of globalisation': the inevitability that, once this homogenising process has been accomplished, difference – the *balkanisation* of this commodified, worldwide flesh – is reimposed with a vengeance. Above and beyond the services that the local girls are called upon to deliver, then, Yolanda is further demeaned by her role as Kath's personal wait-ress. The implication is that she has experienced her fair share of upward mobility in being transported to Liverpool and, subsequently, like every other 'other' in *My Kingdom*, must be put back in her proper place.

Sandeman can only begin to comprehend his role in this broader conspiracy when he himself is rendered 'out of place'. Evicted from his own home by Kath and Tracy, Sandeman is forced to tour the Liverpool he never knew, left to beg in the streets with his mulatto grandson, Jamie (Reece Noi), presumably the product of Kath's appetite for black Londoners. In contrast to the film's early emphasis on Liverpool's shimmering nighttime waterfront, much of Sandeman's subsequent journey is cast in the menacing shadows of grey skies or eerie, artificial lighting, a change that connotes the film's ensuing exploration of what critics of *façadism* call 'the rot beneath the glitter' or the corrosive psychological scaffolding that underlies global capitalism's sleek surfaces.[18] Similarly, whereas early establishing shots support the impression of a navigable city, the 'heath' spaces through which Sandeman wanders are defined only by a pattern of escalating violence that leaves a trail of casualties scattered like so many breadcrumbs marking the (war)path of private ownership. Hence, perhaps the most insidious feature of the ongoing civil war that defines the state of exception is exceptionalism itself – the posture that prevents the First World from recognising, in its daily routines of savagery, the spectre of its Third World within, *especially* within, its cities. What makes *My Kingdom* an important contribution to the discourse on global capitalism is its refusal to represent the casualties of Liverpool's civil war as victims of an arbitrary violence. Rather, under the veneer of 'random violence' that the First World continues to find acceptable (provided it remains confined to the 'back streets'), *My Kingdom* exposes the real targets of this civil war in all their racial, gender, class and generational dimensions. By the end of the film, these victims include a black teenager (Delroy), a cancer-stricken senior (Quick), a mixed-race boy (Jamie), a Sikh *émigré* (Jug), a white, blue-collar criminal (Dean), several white women (Mandy, Kath, Tracy) and a dis-abled black man ('the Chair'), all representatives of oppressed groups within global capitalism, a system that will continue to prey on the weakest first, as long as it bases its strength on the constitutive scarcity of resources.

IV

As in *King Lear*, the heath scene in *My Kingdom* is the precondition for Sandeman's revelation that he has long served this system as its preferred *façade*, having endowed it with the dignity and decorum that has permitted its totalising agenda to extend from Liverpool to 'any city', as Quick explains. Set in the suburbs, the heath is a distinctly liminal space, represented as both a gateway into and out of Liverpool proper. Quite different from the open and unprotected plain on which Lear wanders, however, this heath, comprised of a diner and motel, is a locus of intense claustrophobia in which driving rain, close quarters and surveillance mechanisms all conspire to 'deprive us of setting', a gesture which, as Jameson observes, is emblematic of the extent to which there is no outside to, or hiding place from, the rapacious logic of consumption that governs the state of exception.[19] This effect is magnified by the giant billboard advertisement for 'Maiden Milk' that presides over this space. Replacing the Fool's witticisms, the billboard slogan – 'THE WHITE STUFF: Are You Made of It?' – becomes a singular messenger throughout the film's remainder, suggesting *My Kingdom*'s postnostalgic turn toward place-based marketing as the ultimate articulation of conspiracy in the age of global capitalism.

The first meaning of this slogan is revealed to Sandeman when Quick interrupts his self-pitying peroration to call his bluff as a 'working-class hero'. Eavesdropping, Quick listens as Sandeman, prompted by Jamie's question as to what he would like to eat, describes the life of martyrdom he lived on behalf of his daughters: 'Fed 'em . . . bred 'em . . . housed 'em I did . . . I worked and worked . . . if you have a tear, you can shed it now.' Before Jamie can do so, Quick interjects the lines with which we began: 'There's only three ways a poor lad can make it out of the back streets of Liverpool: showbusiness, sport or crime.' Then, in a softer tone, he adds with mock pity, eyeing Sandeman, 'Working-class heroes. Tragic, really.' Quick's purpose here is to expose Sandeman's highly selective memory as a sham and, consequently, to force him to confront the 'rot beneath the glitter' or, in this case, the glitter beneath the rot. For what lies beneath Sandeman's gritty yarn about his life as a plebeian 'hero' – replete with the memory of 'steam ships and iron shavings' – is a *white-collar criminal* who, as both Quick and the billboard suggest, is 'made of' the same 'white stuff' as all the other predators that are indigenous to the landscape of global capitalism. In other words, far from being the 'sovereign exception', Sandeman is the rule. Hence, for the last time, he attempts to rise above the madding crowd by resorting to his personal conspiracy theory, whispering to Quick, 'Who paid the black lad to shoot my wife, and to shoot me?', only to receive the reply: 'Nobody paid him. They didn't have to pay him. He was just like any other lad in the same boat in this city. Any city. Muggers. Thieves. Dealers. All chaos. It all comes back to *you.*' In this version of *King Lear*'s arraignment scene, it is Sandeman, not his daughters, who is on trial. When the guilty verdict is handed down by Quick, who tells him, 'I'm disappointed in you . . . I had you down for a nice old-fashioned gentleman: I thought you knew the difference between right and wrong,' Sandeman relinquishes his old-fashioned worldview once and for all. 'There is no law here,' he mutters, 'there are no rules anymore.' Quick's reply, which is uttered only seconds before he is abducted, blinded and left to die, is, simply, 'I want to stop the rot.'

Quick's words acquire deeper meaning for Sandeman when he directly encounters this rot, which precipitates his recognition that, wherever his journey takes him, he can never go home again. For, until this point, Sandeman has wandered the heath not as a genuinely homeless person but as a tourist, a figure whose travels are predicated on the certainty of safe return. Indeed, Sandeman's lifelong impression of Liverpool corresponds to this time-determined space of the 'tourist bubble', a place where the retroactive effects of nostalgia conspire to 'bind together the high points of global culture as framed by global capitalism' and, in so doing, reproduce the officially sanctioned image of the city featured in its place-based marketing campaigns.[20] But this tourist bubble bursts when, the morning after the storm, Jamie is murdered by thugs in search of Sandeman in a scene that alludes to scouser abuse of 'half-castes'.[21] Fishing from one of the retaining walls of the Mersey, Jamie is briefly left alone; when Sandeman returns to find his grandson's body washed up on a rocky spit below, he encounters the truth embedded in his longstanding fiction of Liverpool as a 'great city' of (un)equal opportunity. For this tableau is nothing other than a violently inverted image of Sandeman's romanticisation of the first time he took the ferry across the Mersey and walked under a Liverpool sky. The difference between his fate and Jamie's lies in the answer to the question: 'THE WHITE STUFF: Are You Made of It?'. For, in contemporary Liverpool, there are those who move of their own volition, like Sandeman, and those who get moved, like Jamie and Yolanda, both representatives of the 'half-castes' whom Homi Bhabha defines, appropriately, as 'the not quite/not white'.[22]

Such is the contemporary 'racism', defined not by differences of skin colour but by invisible structures of economic exclusion, that *My Kingdom* makes visible in its final juxtaposition of out-of-joint times and spaces. Framing Jamie's body in the extreme foreground, the camera pans out to reveal the Royal Liver building – ironically, the home of the city's oldest provider of life insurance and one of the UK's most profitable, incorporated 'friendly societies'. An elegant euphemism for a members-only organisation, a 'friendly society' is defined as much by its practice of exclusion as it is by solidarity. As this juxtaposition ultimately suggests, then, the gap that separates Jamie from the building on the other shore is much wider than the Mersey, for it is the ever-increasing economic divide that defines the 'members only' club, indeed, the advanced capitalist 'country' club, of globalisation. The film's postnostalgic turn thus lies in the cynical revelation that some things never change.

V

King Lear ends by evincing nostalgia for a future that will never arrive, as Lear entreats Cordelia to 'Come . . . away to prison. / We two alone will sing like birds i' the cage' (V.iii.8–9). *My Kingdom* begins with this happy family scenario, as the Sandemans gather to pose for their Christmas card, absurdly, in September. But this vision is steadily eroded as the family members turn upon each other, dying one by one, and Sandeman's only hope for the future – his desire, revealed to Mandy just before the fatal mugging, to get Jamie 'out of this place' – materialises only in the form of the boy's death, leaving the drug lord with the one certainty that this Christmas, whenever it arrives, will be a white Christmas indeed. Having glimpsed this future, Sandeman devises a revenge plot – an urban 'renovation' scheme that culminates in a blue-print of Liverpool as a place where survival is predicated exclusively on 'the white stuff' – where the trick, in other words, is not to beat but to *join* the conspiracy that is global capitalism. Herein lies the third and final meaning of the slogan for 'Maiden Milk', whose invocation of the street name for heroin, 'the white stuff', is the basis of Sandeman's epic double-cross, as well as an allusion to the drug trafficking that consti-tutes more than 8 per cent of global trade. In keeping with the milk metaphor that insinuates itself into the city's strategically placed advertisements, Sandeman initiates the rumour that cows are being used to smuggle an enormous shipment of drugs into Liverpool from Amsterdam. Significantly, the film never clarifies whether or not the farm animals actually contain the contraband, for the point of this ambiguity is to demonstrate the workings of commodity fetishism. Indeed, in and of themselves, the cows are of no value to Sandeman's urban-based enemies; rather, it is the cows' surplus value, the mystical 'white stuff' that exceeds their physical properties, which succeeds in getting everyone hooked on the desire to intercept the sacred cargo. Efficiently demonstrating the ways in which relations between people are not only constituted by but also, as the ensuing bloodbath makes plain, unblinkingly sacrificed to things, Sandeman's postnostalgic revenge plot performs the totalising function that his personal conspiracy could not, even as it parodies the participatory democracy that global capitalism advertises as its principal fringe benefit to those seeking membership in the club.

But if the cultural logic of late capitalism operates according to the principle that consumption will make you free, *My Kingdom* demystifies this notion in its concluding vision of commodity fetishism as the ultim-ate form of population control, making it clear that merely *consuming* the white stuff is not the same thing as being *made of* the white stuff. Exposing the contemporary forms racism assumes in a montage depict-ing multiple homicides, the film intercuts images of the Chair's men, all of them black, exchanging machine-gun fire with Dean's men, all of them white – their skinhead haircuts and Liverpool FC scarves serving as 'racial' markers of their dispensable social class. Subsequently, with Quick and Jamie already dead, representing both ends of the ageing spec-trum, Kath and Tracy are shown killing one another to insure this vision of generational implosion. The last to die is Jug, who is shot in the act of quoting Portia's famous line from *The Merchant of Venice*, 'The quality of mercy is not strained' (IV.i.179). Attempting to demonstrate his dis-tinctly English education, Jug cites a speech that has often been required reading for O' levels, a rite of passage into adulthood, if not proof of citi-zenship. When placed in the mouth of a post-colonial subject like Jug, however, this speech not only infantilises the speaker but also supports the fantasy that colonialism is an act of mercy towards 'the place' – and people – 'beneath', a reciprocal blessing between the giver and the taker. In this context, Jug's murder becomes a kind of 'mercy' killing based on his failure to assimilate, as he learns the hard way that quoting Shakespeare, the ultimate white stuff, may mean passing O' levels, but not passing for white.

The final recipient of this message in *My Kingdom* is the Chair, the figure whose confinement to a wheelchair mirrors the confinement of Liverpool's entire black community to the poorest of the city's thirty-three wards, Granby, out of which few black residents dare to venture. It is par-ticularly significant, then, that the scene of the Chair's arrest occurs on the outskirts of the city at the Grimwald Welcome Lodge, just off the M2 on the way into Liverpool. Literally paralysed, the Chair can only watch as the all-black cows pour out of the truck and are left free to roam the suburbs, while the all-white police squad closes in on him, guns drawn. Appropriately, the entire episode takes place in front of another billboard for 'Maiden Milk', an indication that the homogenisation process is at last complete. Strategically placed at the point of entry into and exit from Liverpool, the billboard thus performs its final gatekeeping function by welcoming the sole survivors, Jo and Sandeman, into the members-only club of this Renaissance city of the future, whose postnostalgic slogan may very well be: 'THE WHITE STUFF: Are You Made of It?'.

Notes

1. Fredric Jameson (1991), *Postmodernism, or, The Cultural Logic of Late Capitalism*, Durham: Duke University Press, p. 21.
2. See Jameson, *Postmodernism*, pp. 279–98.
3. *King Lear* (Conflated Text), in *The Norton Shakespeare*, Stephen Greenblatt, Walter Cohen, Jean E. Howard and Katharine Eisaman Maus (eds) (1997), New York: W. W. Norton, IV.ii.50–1. All further references to the plays are to this edition and appear in the text.
4. Giorgio Agamben (1998), *Homo Sacer: Sovereign Power and Bare Life*, Stanford: Stanford University Press, passim.
5. Michael Hardt and Antonio Negri (2004), *Multitude: War and Democracy in the Age of Empire*, New York: Penguin, p. 9.
6. Stuart Wilks-Heeg (2003), 'From World City to Pariah City? Liverpool and the Global Economy, 1850–2000', in Ronaldo Munck (ed.), *Reinventing the City? Liverpool in Comparative Perspective*, Liverpool: Liverpool University Press, p. 42.
7. Agamben, *Homo Sacer*, p. 32.
8. Jameson, *Postmodernism*, p. 44.
9. Jameson, *Postmodernism*, p. 16.
10. Jameson, *Postmodernism*, p. 18.
11. Jameson, *Postmodernism*, p. 16.
12. Michael Friedman, David Andrews and Michael Silk (2004), 'Sport and the Façade of Redevelopment in the Postindustrial City', *Sociology of Sport Journal*, 21, p. 127.
13. Dennis R. Judd, 'Constructing the Tourist City', in Dennis R. Judd and Susan S. Fainstein (eds) (1999), *The Tourist City*, New Haven: Yale University Press, p. 53; Friedman, Andrews and Silk, 'Sport', p. 130.
14. Hardt and Negri, *Multitude*, p. 157.
15. Agamben, *Homo Sacer*, p. 51.
16. Hardt and Negri, *Multitude*, p. 159.
17. Joan Copjec, 'The Phenomenal Nonphenomenal', in Joan Copjec (ed.) (1993), *Shades of Noir*, London and New York: Verso, p. 182.
18. Friedman, Andrews and Silk, 'Sport', pp. 129–32.
19. Fredric Jameson (1992), *The Geopolitical Aesthetic: Cinema and Space in the World System*, Bloomington: Indiana University Press, p. 56.
20. Dean MacCannell (1993), 'Democracy's Turn: On Homeless *Noir*', in Copjec (ed.), *Shades*, p. 295.
21. Diane Frost (2000), 'Ambiguous Identities', in Neville Kirk (ed.), *Northern Identities*, Aldershot: Ashgate, pp. 195–217.
22. Homi K. Bhabha (1994), *The Location of Culture*, New York: Routledge, p. 92.

Chapter 5

Our Shakespeares: British Television and the Strains of Multiculturalism

Susanne Greenhalgh and Robert Shaughnessy

As W. B. Worthen has argued, 'race' is a primary signifier in the increasingly globalised discourse of Shakespearean performance:

> Onstage and off, race and ethnicity signify differently within different national and cultural contexts; the challenge to Shakespearean 'whiteness', and to Shakespearean nationalism, is a crucial feature of Shakespearean performance in an era of extraordinary globalization of finance and capital, of expanded opportunities for travel and tourism, and of the replacement of eighteenth- and nineteenth-century models of political and industrial imperialism with economic relations characteristic of modernity, modernization, and postmodern capital.[1]

While these issues have received some discussion in writing on filmed Shakespeare, comparatively little attention has been paid to their significance for television treatments of Shakespearean works and derivatives. This essay examines shifting concepts of race and ethnicity in recent British television documentary and drama to show how these have both mediated and interrogated the social, cultural and therapeutic values of Shakespearean performance 'after multiculturalism'.

Interrogation of the 'force' which is frequently attributed to contemporary Shakespearean performance to articulate individual and communal identities reveals the extent to which Shakespeare retains a privileged status as a means to explore the complex relationships that exist between the local and the global, the urban and the rural, and the 'native' and the 'migrant', out of which emerge the shifting concepts of community and multiculturalism in twenty-first-century Britain.

In December 2004, Channel 4 Television screened Michael Waldman's documentary *My Shakespeare*.[2] It follows the black British actor Patterson Joseph, who, in his own words, 'has never directed anything, let alone Shakespeare', as he tries to put together an amateur production of *Romeo and Juliet* with a cast of mostly non-white young people in Harlesden, a neighbourhood in the North London borough of Brent. Harlesden is described by Joseph as a 'ghetto': it is an ethnically diverse area with a predominantly Asian and Afro-Caribbean population; its unemployment rate is nearly 10 per cent; a third of its school pupils leave with no formal qualifications; it is afflicted by high rates of both petty and serious crime; and over half of its households bring in less than one-third of the national average income. Brent, moreover, is home to one of the largest refugee and asylum-seeker populations in the UK, for over half of whom English is a second language. This context is suggested throughout the film by repeated shots of crumbling high rises, padlocked and shuttered shopfronts, pawnbrokers, and flyposters and billboards advertising instant cash loans and cheap international phone calls. If this seems, as Joseph says, 'one of the least likeliest places to have Shakespeare, to have this high art', the aim is to prove wrong the belief that 'people from Harlesden . . . are not going to be able to articulate strange English words, they're very limited, their imagination is small'.

If Joseph's commitment here is undoubtedly genuine (and, on the evidence of what transpires, not unfounded), the documentary's narrative technique is generic. The set-up, and the film's three-part structure (auditioning in the midst of local indifference, rehearsal and its tribulations, and eventual performance), adopt the industry-standard template of performance-related 'docusoaps', as well as referencing *Looking for Richard* (1996), particularly in Joseph's Al Pacino-style street interviews, where the Bard acts an agent of self-improvement, empowerment and enlightened pedagogy. Such a procedure also has an obvious predecessor in Penny Woolcock's documentary *Shakespeare on the Estate*, screened on BBC2 ten years previously.[3] This took Michael Bogdanov to Birmingham's Ladywood Estate, where he attempted to introduce the residents ('Asian youths, various representatives of the large black community, drunks, homeless, unemployed . . . Battered wives, thieves, drug addicts') to his distinctive version of a 'people's Shakespeare'.[4] Patterson Joseph, though inexperienced as a director, was born and raised in Harlesden, and this partly alleviates what has been described as the inherent tendency of the 'ethnographic' documentary to rely upon ' "us" (the documentary elite) . . . filming "them" (working people, the poor and underprivileged)': he is less of an outsider than Bogdanov in Ladywood.[5] Moreover, Waldman and Joseph are prepared to aim higher in terms of the anticipated output, the four-week rehearsal period culminating in a one-off performance in a 'West End Theatre' (actually RADA's Vanbrugh auditorium). In this respect, the project reflects the raised stakes of post-millennial reality television: part of the deal is the promise of instant celebrity.[6]

Once he is confronted with the magnitude of the task, and with truculent, under-confident and dilatory performers, a visibly stressed Joseph rapidly abandons the liberal-pedagogue role and adopts a more authoritarian posture: hopes of self-improvement are efficiently sidelined in the interest of getting the show on. The pressure of the (artificially?) tight deadline makes for good reality TV (Joseph's directorial inexperience lends an 'in at the deep end' element to the process), and the tears, the tantrums and the transformations that provide the standard stuff of backstage drama are all in evidence, as are the usual walkouts, the fear of public humiliation and failure, and the final, victory-from-the-jaws-of-defeat triumph of the performance itself. There are team-building sessions, which take the group out of the conflicted and dysfunctional space of the rehearsal room to go on location, in the interests of investing the performance with emotional depth and urgency. A street performance of II.i goes unnoticed ('Nobody cares about us; it's Harlesden. If only they did'), although, when Joseph gets his Romeo and Juliet to rehearse the tomb scene inside the chapel of rest at Kensal Green Cemetery, the results are much more newsworthy. With the final movement of *Carmina Burana* rumbling away on the soundtrack, Juliet is laid out on the slab. As the sun sets on the surrounding tombstones, ringed by candles, Romeo crouches over Juliet as he is coached through a performance of low-key naturalistic intensity that is perfectly pitched to a hovering camera that cuts from the lovers to the glowing statuary. Whilst this is the most 'authentic' and emotionally true piece of performance in the film, it is also the most heavily overdetermined and intertextualised most obviously with the tomb scene from Baz Luhrmann's *William Shakespeare's 'Romeo + Juliet'* (1996), the exemplar of globalised Shakespearean media performance. This tactic of quotation and pastiche from a film which is itself the paradigmatic repository of these techniques is in place from the opening, such as in the rooftop bling-bling prologue, delivered to ducking and diving steadicam by a combat-fatigued rapper. Luhrmann himself pops up throughout the documentary in person, dispensing aphoristic advice via videolink on this 'kind of cinematic interpretation', declaring that 'great storytelling is that which moves through time and geography'. Luhrmann haunts the documentary in the guise of memories of his own film, which is engaged both as an inspirational prototype and an anxiety of influence, his reflexive invocation of the 'cinematic' suggesting that it is this, rather than live theatre, that now defines the template for practice and the benchmark for achievement.

However, the sequence in which the group visit 'the shrine of all things Shakespeare', the Southwark Globe, gestures towards a different kind of relationship between the work of the documentary and the performance process. Briefly citing *Shakespeare in Love* (dir. John Madden, 1998) via a high-angled establishing shot of the stage, this episode shows the company visibly moved and excited by the experience of inhabiting the space ('it was made for us', cries Juliet), and a surge of Prokofiev's love theme suggests that the thrill of young love is for this theatre (and for theatre) itself. As the warm timbers of the Globe dissolve into the steel and concrete of a tower block on the 'infamous' Stonebridge Estate's Shakespeare Road, we may read a pointedly ironic juxtaposition of glamour and squalor, myth and reality, history and the present, even if the irony is qualified: a scratch rendition of the balcony scene, indifferently witnessed by local kids in hoodies, is shifted through blue filters to the plane of urban romance and linked to the Globe moment of ecstasy for Shakespeare by a reiteration of the Prokofiev theme. Romeo's upturned face is irradiated by the dappled light falling from the black steel mesh of the balcony; the streetlights turn to stars; and the everyday momentarily touches the sublime.

Considered as a British programme, *My Shakespeare* articulates a meritocratic optimism that is in keeping with the interventionist drift of government policy since 1997 (it is no coincidence that Harlesden is an area undergoing the government-backed Neighbourhood Renewal Scheme). What we also notice is that it is class, rather than race, that seems to be the key factor in these negotiations with Shakespeare: the participants speak not of racial discrimination and prejudice but of financial insecurity, educational underachievement, poor housing and facilities, and social marginalisation. In connection with this, the documentary's findings challenge easy suppositions about the significance of race within contemporary Shakespearean production, and the ways in which both of these interact with the transmission of cultural authority. First, there is no sense here of Shakespeare as an icon of privilege, or of exclusionary white culture, that demands to be contested or re-appropriated on behalf of subordinate groups: Shakespeare may be difficult and unfamiliar, but he is nonetheless there for the taking. Second, the Shakespeare that is on offer, and that seems to be accepted, is thoroughly 'straight' in a mainstream sense: contrary to the stipulations of much post-colonial criticism, he is not hybridised, transformed or adapted to the terms of the urban youth subcultures with which he seeks to connect. The rap prologue is a red herring: the Harlesden *Romeo and Juliet* is emphatically realist, text-centred and character-driven – typically English theatre, we might say.

Now You See It: Colour-blind and Colour-aware Casting in British Television Shakespeare

In a curious way, the utter normality of this *Romeo and Juliet* slightly undermines two of the basic, if unspoken, ethnographic premises of the film: that a non-white Shakespeare is worth documenting because it is somehow out of the ordinary, and that process and product can be framed so as to illustrate – or allegorise – contemporary race relations. The reality of early twenty-first-century Britain is that colour-blind casting and multicultural performance of Shakespeare are not just the everyday and unexceptional characteristics of amateur practice, from the primary school classroom upwards, but increasingly normative on the professional stage and screen. It is no longer news for black and Asian actors to be cast in major roles, not only in the obviously raced parts, but in traditionally white roles, and the major companies have made serious efforts in both their public profiling and their casting practices to promote diversity. The current dispensation, however, needs to be seen in historical perspective. As late as 1980, the National Theatre was still prepared to stage an *Othello* with Paul Scofield in blackface (as the RSC had done with Donald Sinden the previous year), and it was not until 1984 that the first black British actor was seen in the part on the twentieth-century London stage (Rudolph Walker, in David Thacker's Young Vic production). Although the American actor Gordon Heath, who played Othello in a production by Ken Tynan, also appeared in the role in a Tony Richardson production for the BBC in 1955, and the West Indian singer Cy Grant in extracts from the play in an ATV Schools programme in 1960, generally broadcasters, especially the BBC, were even more tardy than the theatre industry in creating Shakespearean opportunities for black performers. Given the aversion of Cedric Messina, its first producer, to the 'exotic' and 'anything too sensational', his commitment to period verisimilitude, his desire for productions that would 'stand the test of time', and the global ambitions of the series, it is no surprise that the BBC/Time Television Shakespeare featured very few non-white performers.[7] Rather more unexpected, though, was the decision by Jonathan Miller (despite his belief that with televised Shakespeare one should 'present the thing as naturally as you can') to cast a white actor (Anthony Hopkins) as Othello in the 1981 BBC version.[8] According to Rudolph Walker, 'the BBC bluntly refused to use any of the black actors in this country, saying that we were just not good enough'; Miller's response was that 'the play is about jealousy, not race'.[9] The 1981 season's *A Midsummer Night's Dream* did feature one example of colour-blind casting in Hugh Quarshie's Philostrate, but it did not set a precedent. Viewed in relation to the larger corporate culture of the BBC itself, this was, to say the least, anomalous.

Like many public-sector organisations, the BBC first began publicly to engage with the discourse of equal opportunities at the end of the 1970s, initially declaring that conditions of appointment and employment within the organisation were 'unaffected by such personal characteristics as sex, colour or race', but subsequently modifying this perhaps rather complacent assertion with the admission that 'special efforts' were being made 'to see that groups felt to suffer disadvantage . . . were given a reasonable chance of exercising their claims for consideration'.[10] During the 1980s, the Corporation increased its efforts to develop the diversity of both its workforce and its output.[11] By the mid-1990s, the BBC had introduced diversity targets; it also paid serious attention to the levels and kinds of ethnic representation in its programming, actively promoting black and Asian presenters and performers across its output, most notably in popular soaps which 'have successfully reflected multicultural Britain in new ways'.[12]

Most of the Shakespeare that appeared on British television during this period consisted of adaptations (or more or less straight filmed records) of acclaimed stage productions, their multicultural policies reflecting those of the producing companies rather than television *per se*: Deborah Warner's *Richard II* and Richard Eyre's *King Lear* for the Royal National Theatre, broadcast in 1997 and 1998 respectively; Gregory Doran's version of his RSC *Macbeth*, shown on Channel 4 in 2000; and Trevor Nunn's film of his acclaimed 1999 RNT *Merchant of Venice*, broadcast on New Year's Eve, 2001. This latter presents particularly complex interactions between race, ethnicity and the structuring of audience sympathies, in that its central ethnic and religious faultline lies between the Christian and Jewish characters, a division which Nunn sharpened by locating the play in a setting that merged Venice with early 1930s Weimar Berlin. Jewish ethnicity is realised in terms of cultural ritual and religious practice: as Shylock, Henry Goodman speaks in Yiddish to Jessica, reads the Torah and recites the *Shema* as he is about to carve up Antonio; the Christians are a poisonously louche, champagne-swilling bunch of predominantly white upper-class louts. Typically, when Jessica nervously relays Lancelot Gobbo's joke about there being 'no mercy for me in heaven because I am a Jew's daughter', Lorenzo is angered and embarrassed, and the clown is icily dismissed.[13] It is of some significance here that Gobbo is played by a black actor (Andrew French), as are Old Gobbo, Salerio, Morocco and the walk-on role of Leonardo; the casting is both strategic and, in terms of the production's moral economy, pointed. At one level, this creates an irony whereby the Christians' loathing of religious difference is matched by their apparent indifference to skin colour, as well as directly confronting the text's fears of miscegenation. Morocco (Chu Omambala) is a charming and stylish sword-wielding dandy in plus-fours who mesmerises Portia; when he chooses the wrong casket, both are in tears (the line 'Let all of his complexion choose me so' (II.vii.79) is cut). The key figure, however, is Lancelot Gobbo. As the only performer afforded the licence of sustained and regular direct address to camera, Gobbo sometimes acts as intermediary between the viewer and the world of the play, and more frequently as a silent, privileged witness to events, notably to Shylock's split with Jessica: as Shylock stands paralysed with anger and remorse, a reaction shot catches a single tear rolling down Gobbo's cheek. Yet he is ready enough to collude with the prejudices of his new employers: delivering his 'conscience' monologue as a stand-up microphone routine before a rowdy white audience, Gobbo solicits their attention by delivering his opening line, 'My master's a very Jew' (II.ii.93), with a spot of crude Semitic mimicry, but even he is lost for words, and shamed into silence, when Shylock, making an unscripted appearance, enters and catches him in the act. As the Jewish merchant stares at the black comedian in wounded, disbelieving silence, Gobbo looks, shamefaced, at the floor, keenly aware of his betrayal; the brief sequence also reinforces the sense that, in this production, Jewishness is visibly theatricalised in a way that blackness is not.

In Eyre's RNT *King Lear*, a black king of France and an Asian king of Burgundy do little beyond emphasising the whiteness of Lear's realm; in Doran's *Macbeth*, the First Witch is African but her partners are Geordie and Scots, and when they first encounter Macbeth and Banquo, the faces of witches and soldiers alike are blackened and smeared with grime and half-dried blood, a white skin/black masks effect that pushes the action into a dystopian post-national anywhere. If, in this production, the casting of a black actor as the Second Murderer can be properly described as colour-blind, Warner's painterly, Jarman-influenced *Richard II* is more pointed in its deployment of black actors in minor roles, namely Berkeley, Scroope, Fitzwater and Bagot. The latter is self-consciously picked out in the first ten seconds of the film being fondled by a white Bushy: together with its French queen and ambiguously-gendered king in the shape of Fiona Shaw, Richard's multiracial, cosmopolitan and sexually liberal court is sharply differentiated from Bolingbroke's aggressively masculine, exclusively Caucasian entourage of snobs and bullies (when Surrey calls Fitzwater a 'Dishonourable *boy*' during the gage scene, it is a racist taunt).[14] In the prison scene, Richard's final moment of human contact before he is murdered comes when an unidentified black hand clasps his (or hers?) reaching through the bars.[15]

The importance of national and cultural context in assessing specific modes of cross-racial and cross-cultural casting is illustrated by Peter Brook's film of his own production of *Hamlet* at the Bouffes du Nord in Paris for BBC4 in 2002.[16] Starring Adrian Lester in an acclaimed distillation of the play, it featured Brook's trademark multi-ethnic 'intercultural' casting together with a performance style and look infused with 'orientalist' elements, from the colours and styles of costumes to the pace and gestures of the actors. Here, it is difference within, and interaction between, cultural performance styles rather than skin colour that is the primary dynamic within a conception of Shakespeare as a universally accessible resource and repository of human truths. As such, Brook's *Hamlet* stands apart from other BBC4 productions, which capture the practices of different theatre companies, such as the two live transmissions of performances from Shakespeare's Globe, in which black actors also appeared, mostly in minor roles, anachronistically subsumed into the 'authenticity' of recreated early modern theatre. No less relevant is the National Youth Theatre's *The Merchant of Venice* abridged by Tom Stoppard (BBC4, 2005), in which the apparent racial and ethnic origins of the young actors were mapped onto the roles, so that Shylock was played as an Orthodox Jew and Morocco by an Afro-Caribbean: despite the presence of large numbers of black actors in the ensemble cast, all the main parts were played as white. In contrast, 'Shakespeare's Italian Job', one episode of BBC2's documentary series, *Theatre Biz*, which explored the economics of theatre production in the UK, documented the attempts of Malachi Bogdanov, son of the more famous Michael, to produce the next Reduced Shakespeare-style West End hit by melding plots and characters from the complete works with the narrative and roles of the 1969 British cult film *The Italian Job*.[17] At no point in the programme was it highlighted or commented upon that a black actor was cast in the role originally played by Michael Caine.

The diversity agenda also increasingly informed aspects of the BBC's made-for-television Shakespeare output as well as its performance recordings. In 1996, Anne Brogan produced *Shakespeare Shorts*, a nine-part mini-documentary series for BBC2's *English File* schools schedule made with the aim of making Shakespeare relevant to eleven to fourteen year-olds.[18] The series adopted a variety of often contradictory modes of multiculturalism in both interpretation and casting. *Julius Caesar* employed what appeared initially to be a 'colour-blind' approach, focused on the black actor, Patrick Robinson, investigating Mark Antony's reaction to the assassination of Caesar (also played by a black actor). However, the assassination scene was staged in a television studio with the political speeches presented as live broadcasts during a coup: at this point, the production evoked generalisations about the instability of African states that invited audiences to read the casting as raced, especially as the TV director was played as white. In the *Romeo and Juliet* episode, directed by Yvonne Brewster, founder of Talewa Theatre Company, on the other hand, an entirely Afro-Caribbean cast performed a version relocated to a temporally undefined era somewhere in the West Indies. This allowed Marcelle DuPrey, playing Juliet, to highlight not only the differences between society then and now, but also the similarities between Renaissance Italy and a patriarchally dominated Caribbean island culture, the values of which might still pervade a population relocated to Britain, creating conflict between first and second generations in black families. Perhaps most interesting of all from the perspective of colour-blind casting were the three programmes on *Macbeth*. The first of these, on the witches, was presented by the Asian actress Amita Dihri, and the third, on Lady Macbeth's madness, by Adjoa Andoh, an actress who is half Ghanaian. Other black and Asian actors appeared in minor roles, but the most intriguing element was the specially staged performance of the sleepwalking scene which, though set in medieval Scotland, complete with anachronistic tartans, featured a Chinese Asian actress as the woman attendant, alongside Macbeth and the Doctor played by white performers. Noteworthy in all these educational programmes was the fact that, despite the presence of actors from different ethnic backgrounds, the nature of the interpretations offered, as in the case of *My Shakespeare*, remained strikingly traditional, unlike, for instance, Woolcock's *Macbeth on the Estate* (1997), where 'the racial identities of the actors were . . . crucial' to introducing 'themes of race relations and incipient conflict' into the play.[19]

'What country, friends, is this?': *Twelfth Night* and *Indian Dream*

If the brief survey above reveals the extent to which race has featured only to be ignored, or read as reflecting the 'realism' of life in multicultural Britain, a different dynamic operates in the growing number of specifically Asian references, elements and actors, amounting almost to the emergence of a sub-genre at times. The year 2003 was particularly notable in this respect. Tim Supple's made-for-TV production of *Twelfth Night* was commissioned by Channel 4 Learning predominantly for the educational market with an avowed intention of its being 'multicultural'. It was first broadcast in January, with a cast featuring Zubin Varla as Feste and *Bend It Like Beckham* and *ER* star Parminder Nagra as Viola. Another Channel 4 commission, *Second Generation*, Jonathan Sen and Neil Biswas' two-part version of *King Lear* set in the entrepreneurial world of Asian manufacturing and music, was screened in September, and again starred Nagra in the Cordelia role, whilst the celebrated Asian underground composer, Nitin Sawhney, provided musical scores for both productions.[20] Avie Luthra's play *Indian Dream* aired in October. This scheduling ensured that the play resonated with another work by the same author, broadcast earlier the same month: his contribution to *The Canterbury Tales* series of contemporary and multicultural rewrites of Chaucer's stories, which retold *The Sea Captain's Tale* as a *film noir* influenced drama about gender and power, again set in the Indian business community – both dramas starred the actor Nitin Ganatra. All four productions explored themes of migration, and the conflicts to which it can give rise, within both the newly arrived and the established British Asian communities. Suddenly, as *The Sunday Times* put it, there was 'a new fashion for Asian programming', and it quoted a BBC producer as saying, 'For some reason, the white middle classes are eating up Asian culture like fish and chips'.[21] One of those reasons might have been because, as the BBC press release for *The Canterbury Tales* claimed, the series was not only concerned with the 'crossovers' between British and Asian cultures but also with 'issues that in some cases are as relevant to being British as they are to being Asian'. The view was made explicit by the adapter of *Twelfth Night*, Andrew Bannerman, who stated that the production sought to portray 'the Britain we all live in today' by tracing the story of how Viola and Sebastian 'assimilate' themselves into a new culture.[22] However, such perspectives, though important, ignore another aspect of these Shakespearean excursions into 'other' communities – the exploration of race and cultural relations and differences *within* groups too often subsumed into sameness by labels such as 'Asian' or 'Black'.

It is necessary therefore first to determine what 'Asian' refers to in a specific national or local context.[23] In a recent discussion of the current influence of Bollywood on British theatre, Jennifer Harvie has emphasised the 'fundamental hybridity of both Asian cultures and British cultures', which enables an 'impure' post-colonial form, imported or 'migrated' to Britain, to become the means for the 'Binglishing' of British identities: 'Bollywood in Britain . . . can shift the meanings of "British" away from culturally purist and exclusive definitions to more diverse ones'.[24] Evidence for the mainstreaming of these kinds of hybridities in British culture can be seen not only in productions such as Andrew Lloyd Webber's collaboration with Meera Syal, the musical *Bombay Dreams* (2002), but in post-millennial film adaptations of non-Shakespearean literary texts, such as Mira Nair's *Vanity Fair* (2004) and Gurinder Chadha's *Bride and Prejudice* (2004), as well as the still regularly broadcast BBC2 continuity ident (2003) featuring a typical Bollywood dance sequence. Despite the visual power and seductiveness of such images, it must be appreciated that not all British Asian-influenced drama is 'Bollywoodised'. Indeed, many second- and third-generation British Asians specifically resist being identified with this performance form. The journalist Yasmin Alibhai-Brown has drawn attention to the rejection by many young Asians of the 'traditional multiculturalism', based on a 'respectful' separation of cultural forms that have dominated British social and cultural policy for the last four decades. She argues that *all* Britain's communities need to escape from:

> the restrictions that multiculturalism and the way we think about it have imposed on the stories that we can tell about ourselves. We need to reimagine our collective culture with ties that bind, when the old multiculturalism debate is still looking inwards, erecting new barriers between groups in our own society, instead of enabling us to collectively benefit from our diversity.[25]

For Alibhai-Brown, author and performer of *Extravagant Strangers*, a play about the important role that Shakespeare played in her upbringing in Uganda, the Bard is a 'globally-inspired writer' who can appropriately mirror the 'global nation' she wishes Britain to become. In her view, the drawbacks of 'traditional multiculturalism' are summed up precisely in the ways in which it 'does not focus on the need to extend the appeal of Shakespeare to enable black and Asian children to feel this is part of their heritage and cannot see that white children need to see Benjamin Zephaniah as their poet too.'[26] Indeed, Alibhai-Brown stakes a claim for her community having an even greater intimacy with Shakespeare than that which is generally 'natural' to the white community, noting, in particular, the outcome of the clash of values implicit in the experience of migration and settlement, and conflicts between different communities of recently settled ethnic groups: 'We Asians are old Elizabethans. Romeo and Juliet happens every day in our communities . . . We are living his plays, not merely watching them.'[27] Comparison of the Supple *Twelfth Night* and Luthra's *Indian Dream* reveals the diversity of ways in which themes of cultural identity and ownership of British culture, as well as differences within and between migrant communities, are currently being explored by both white and Asian artists.

Although Supple's career trajectory echoes that of other successful British theatre directors, including a Cambridge education and experience as artistic director of the Young Vic, he was chosen to direct an explicitly multicultural *Twelfth Night* primarily on the basis of an established reputation for cross-cultural, Asian-inflected productions. He adapted and directed Salman Rushdie's *Haroun and the Sea of Stories* (RNT, 1999) and *Midnight's Children* for the RSC at the Barbican in 2003, both with predominantly Asian casts. His *Romeo and Juliet* (RNT, 2000), starring the *Twelfth Night* Orsino, Chiwetel Ejiofor, as Romeo, cast the Capulets as white and the Montagues as black, and in 2005 the director created a touring production of *A Midsummer Night's Dream* in India, built around traditional Indian performers, and included as part of the RSC's *International Complete Works of Shakespeare Festival* in 2006.

Although *Twelfth Night* has been identified with 'Bollywood *filmistyle*', these elements share the 'multiple, unstable, even volatile' qualities that Jennifer Harvie has identified as a recurring aspect of Bollywood in Britain.[28] One key to *Twelfth Night* is the casting of Asian actors as the twins, portrayed as asylum seekers from a violent homeland that is left unspecified and unlocalised, though both Pakistan and India are invoked in shorthand jump-shot images and sequences (for example, the twins' father appears to be a deposed military ruler rather than a merchant, and Viola's dress-code appears to be Hindu rather than Muslim). However, other racial trajectories are equally evident. If Olivia's household, with the exception of Sir Topas, the priest, is all white – including a Scottish Maria, and Fabian as an ex-boxer security guard of Italian descent – Orsino's is racially entirely Afro-Caribbean, with the exception of 'Cesario' and a white butler; meanwhile, Antonio is played as a fluent Urdu-speaker by a Cypriot actor, and the Sea Captain by a Turk. It is clear therefore that, at one level, the cast are indeed 'acting their skin colour' or accent, and that this *mélange* of identities is intended to be visible and compared one with the other. However, race or even ethnicity is by no means the production's chief framework for interpretation. Initial ideas – rejected on cost grounds – for setting the play included location filming in Soho's music business, with Orsino as a record producer; echoes of that remain in the portrayal of Feste as an Asian Underground musician whose CDs form part of the background music to the characters' dilemmas, and the basement den-cum-session room in which Belch and Aguecheek belt out their raucous versions of his hits. These popular 'fusion' music associations, juxtaposed with the presence of classical music in both households

(Olivia's chapel is also a music room complete with a grand piano once played by her brother, and the musical 'dying fall' that Orsino relishes comes from Pamina's love aria in *The Magic Flute*), also resonate intriguingly with the international celebrity culture which forms part of the background to the costume design concept and which crucially broadens out the racial and ethnic references. Orsino's playboy look is a conscious *homage* to that of the globally followed white footballer and fashion icon David Beckham, whose style has led him to be branded 'Britain's most famous black man'.[29] By contrast, in Olivia's household, the formally posed portraits of dead aristocratic males in Scottish Highland dress deliberately recall a long-favoured sartorial style of the British royal family, part of the invention of tradition through which a German dynasty made itself into the quintessence of Britishness. Olivia's mourning, moreover, is pervaded by memories of Princess Diana, from a black lace dress based on one worn by her to the jump-shot black and white images of the crashed car in which Olivia's brother had died, to the Paul Burrell-like obsequiousness of Michael Maloney's Malvolio.[30] If the cultural enigma that was Diana's international celebrity and mass mourning does indeed echo faintly within this production's evocation of the play's themes of loss and melancholy, it does so as a trope of change in the nature of British self-identity and in terms of the globalisation and hybridising of the nation's cultures.

The final visual twist is given by the setting and visual style created for the play. This seems partly designed to echo in contemporary terms what Supple believes to be the drama's original ideological context: the transition from a residual Catholic culture of ritual and festivity into a post-Reformation world in which Malvolio represents the emergent and soon-to-be dominant forces of Puritanism. Thus, Olivia's chapel is a shrine full of relics, photographs and old masterpiece paintings, just as the cellar where Belch and Aguecheek hang out is also a storeroom for the dead brother's possessions. The rest of her house, like Orsino's, reflects varieties of architectural modernity, although its sub-Barbara Hepworth and Henry Moore sculptures, together with Olivia's Bloomsbury-style wedding dress, seem to suggest an earlier, more outmoded version of modernism than Orsino's palace, the marble linearity of which recalls a feature on the latest retro modern style in an upscale international interiors magazine. In both cases, however, the visual recourse to trans-cultural modernism, of whatever era, obscures rather than reflects contemporary cultural and social changes equivalent to the sixteenth-century seismic shift from Catholicism to Protestantism. The grainy, hand-held 'documentary' sequences in violence-torn 'Messina', the asylum-seekers' boat, and the street markets of 'Illyria' also introduce a contradictory set of markers, apparently specific and intensely topical but actually serving to cast adrift any concrete sense of time and place. While these sequences certainly evoke themes of migration and assimilation – as when Viola disembarks from a fishing boat, her elaborate sari and gold bracelets setting her apart from the huddle of economic migrant fellow survivors watching, and as when Antonio and Sebastian break into subtitled Urdu in a meeting in an East End café – they also create a sense of *dislocation* rather than proximity set alongside the majority of studio-based scenes, which are dominated by the use of Hollywood-style blue-screen digital technology to create mesmerising panoramas of sunsets and seascapes. Such techni-coloured 'letterbox' screens may indeed recall aspects of Bollywood *filmi* style, but it is impossible to pin down their associations to so specific a cultural reference. Digital colouring and grading effects are used throughout the production, including the raw 'documentary' footage, so that, despite the apparent variety of visual styles employed, there is an overriding sense of the virtual, of placelessness. The film invites us to interrogate what kind of country we are witnessing, yet ultimately provides no satisfactory answer. If this is indeed a picture of 'the Britain we all live in today' – a society moving away from the safe parallel worlds of separate cultural, racial and ethnic identities enshrined in the formerly approved policies of multiculturalism into unknown territories of cultural fusion and cross-fertilisation – it is perhaps fitting that, after the outbreak of violence instigated by Belch and the rest (with its disturbing echoes of hostage-taking in the portrayal of Malvolio's imprisonment), the play's ending is subdued, with a sense of continuing melancholy and a tentative cross-racial kiss between Viola and Orsino. Though the presence of so many ethnicities in the production's casting certainly fulfils Channel 4's remit of demonstrating an empowering multiculturalism in action in Britain, at the level of subtext, the play's emotional timbre, conveyed by both music and visual style, hints at unresolved questions about losing, retaining or fabricating cultural identity, even as processes of cultural hybridity are embraced and embodied.

The kind of Shakespearean performance at the centre of Luthra's television play, *Indian Dream*, seems to stand at the opposite performance pole to both the streetwise urbanism of the Harlesden *Romeo and Juliet* and the ambivalently localised *Twelfth Night*. With its bucolic prettiness and virtually all-white cast, this is surely Shakespeare for 'local people' in the *League of Gentlemen* sense of the catchphrase.[31] However, if this too is a fiction about the fictionalising of Britishness, its meta-dramatic structure, like that of *My Shakespeare*, also enables interrogation of the metaphors and myths that inform the utopian ideal of Shakespeare as a paradigm for intercultural performance and understanding. The continuity announcement that preceded its first broadcast compared the narrative's hero to a 'Shakespeare Wallah', referencing the film that portrayed the declining status of Shakespeare performance by white actors in post-war, post-imperial India. One way to look at Luthra's play, then, is to argue that it deliberately reverses the tropes of cultural import and ownership with which the film, *Shakespeare Wallah* (dir. James Ivory, 1965), played, and which remain a source of covert anxiety in Supple's *Twelfth Night*.

The play was incorporated into the 'Big Dreams' Asian mini-season which ran for a few days in October 2003 on BBC2 and constitutes one of the 'themed' collections of programmes that have been popular on British television for a number of years, and which have also been a feature of much late twentieth-century Shakespeare scheduling. The thrust of the season was a celebration of 'Asian aspiration and achievement' and 'the dynamic impact that Asian communities have had on the UK', and it featured programmes ranging from *The Joy of Curry* to profiles of successful entrepreneurs, actors and politicians and examples of comic writing.[32] The season also showcased performances by many of the repertory of Asian actors working regularly in the UK media, causing *The Times* to comment that a season designed to show the breadth of Asian cultural life actually demonstrated the narrow stereotyping of a small pool of over-familiar faces.[33]

As was well publicised in press releases and interviews about his work, Luthra is a qualified psychiatrist who has worked with asylum-seekers and detainees, and the play came, to a degree, from his observations upon the dislocation and psychic damage that being so adversely labelled can precipitate. Speaking of the play as he envisaged it, Luthra called it 'Kafkaesque', but he detected elements of 'magic realism' in the treatment given by Roger Goldby, a director whose own short film on communication was nominated for an Oscar in 1997. Despite the darker undertones signalled in Luthra's own account of his original screenplay, *Indian Dream* was almost universally described by reviewers as 'lovely', 'charming', 'magical', a 'gentle fable that nevertheless manages to make a piquant political point'.[34] Originally entitled *The Village*, the play has a simple, almost fairytale-like narrative. An idealistic schoolteacher, Surender (played by *Coronation Street* actor Chris Bisson), on a cultural pilgrimage to England, loses his passport, and is sent to a detention centre from which he escapes to the 'most beautiful village in England'. A production of *A Midsummer Night's Dream* is underway, giving him the chance to audition as Puck in his favourite Shakespearean work. Although the production rules limit the cast to locals or their relatives, the visiting sister of the Indian GP, Rajiv (Nitin Ganatra), vouches for him as 'family', despite realising that Surender is a wanted man. He is embraced by the villagers, and welcomed into their pub and homes, especially that of Penny (Doon Mackichan), the play's director. However, Surender's instant popularity sparks off jealousy in Rajiv who, after six months, is still not assimilated into village life and, despite being a poor performer, longs to take part in the play too as a way of gaining acceptance. Envy finally leads Rajiv to expose the truth about his 'cousin's' identity, in the process unleashing an outburst from the play's producer against the threat posed by 'asylum seekers, paedophiles, terrorists', to which the cast gives silent assent. Surender makes a dignified farewell speech, leaving to give himself up to the authorities, while Rajiv takes over his coveted role of Puck, delivering the play's epilogue with tears in his eyes. But, as the drama turns full circle, ending as it began with Surender on a plane, it is revealed that Penny has left the village and its prejudices to join him.

Although Surender both beguiles and is beguiled by the village of Sedgton, it is unlikely that viewers will have been equally seduced by the wisteria-clad cottages and laughing children flitting in white dresses between the trees. Surender's first walk through its streets, past the churchyard, noting the minutiae of English everyday life that he has read about, such as milk bottles and Radio 3, is reminiscent of nothing so much as the opening shots of a *Midsomer Murders* episode, recalling its saturated colour values, attention to scenic and architectural detail, and frequent reliance on overtly theatrical casting and plotlines. It is clear from the start that all will not be as it seems in the rural idyll, that dark secrets will emerge in time. The sight of the banner for the production of the *Dream* introduces an even more powerful seduction, that of Shakespearean performance. Shakespeare is firstly marked out in predictable ways as an overarching cultural value, part of the 'great' English 'civilisation' that Rajiv so cultivates and claims to be part of when he says, 'We are English, not Indian', and which he sees reflected even in the trivialities of village life, such as the gnome-painting competition at the local fete. It might seem that Surender is perpetuating the same kind of imbibed colonialist values in his teaching back home, where he specialises in Shakespeare and directs regular productions of the plays. It might be tempting, then, to interpret the play chiefly in terms either of its post-colonialist discourses or of the 'loser' connotations which Richard Burt has argued inevitably shroud any teacherly enthusiasm for the 'Bard'.

But this is also a play about love: 'When the words are this good, how can you not know them by heart,' says Surender, as he delights in the opportunity to speak Shakespearean speeches in the land in which they were written. Sedgton may epitomise the fake 'olde worlde' half-timbered charm of the *clichéd* tourist experience, but it is not entirely a fake, even if it is not what it seems. And Shakespeare is the real thing, for Surender at least, glamorising everything with its magic for a while, in a way comparable to the enchantment experienced by the young people on the stage of the Globe in *My Shakespeare*. It is worth looking in more detail therefore at what kind of Shakespeare performance is represented and forms the object of such longing and possessiveness. To an even greater degree than Patterson's Luhrmann-inflected *Romeo and Juliet*, the production is small-scale and intensely localised on the surface. Yet, as was the case in the theatre culture for which Shakespeare's play was written, the village's performance is not entirely a local celebratory ritual, however linked to place and landscape it might at first appear. It is a competition entry, and its desired destination – and the justification for the £5,000 that has been spent on it – is the Edinburgh International Festival. This is highly ironic, in the light of the village's open dislike of 'bloody tourists' and its more hidden embrace of traditional multiculturalism, which keeps cultures in their 'native', 'proper' places, since the Festival is both one of the chief tourist and multicultural events in the British arts calendar, and one where the villagers themselves would be cultural tourists. As Penny cynically admits, the tokenism of having an Asian in their cast would be likely to go down well with those making the selection for this showcase of globalised exotica. Although we see little of the actual production beyond glimpses of rehearsal and backstage preparations, its visual features of set and costume and locale, and the juxtaposed performances of Surender and Rajiv, it is also possible to detect some 'intercultural' elements in its staging. The set consists of two pavilion-type structures linked by various railed walkways, which seem a cross between treehouses and Indonesian beach-huts. The costumes in Sedgton's production seem an eclectic *mélange*, with their blend of Victorian fairy elements, folkloric 'Green Man' leaves for Oberon, and wide-legged colourful and *appliquéd* garments for Puck and the fairy played by Rajiv, a cross between anglicised Chinese theatre costume, modern-day mummers, and village fete craft goods. If we are correct in seeing traces of 'orientalist' elements in this hodgepodge, this may suggest a 'mainstreaming' of theatrical exotica comparable to the embracing of colour-blind casting that we have already noted in talking about *My Shakespeare* and *Twelfth Night's* evocation of a 'black' David

Beckham: the kind of Britain where the made-up dish *tikka masala* becomes a local delicacy.

Surender and Rajiv's casting in the role of Puck also repays attention. It seems clear that they both implicitly take on aspects represented in Shakespeare's play by the changeling Indian boy. In Surender's case, his exoticism makes him a love-object, whereas, in Rajiv's case, it is his 'changeling' nature as an inhabitant and inheritor of two worlds that seems most to resonate. The cruel and troublesome aspects of Shakespeare's Puck, his 'shrewd and knavish' qualities, when attached to Surender, are shown to be only ever a figment of the xenophobic fears encapsulated in the police posters of the bearded troublemaker which he tears down or covers up with the advertisement for the play.[35] Surender is a 'merry wanderer of the night' (II.i.43), a 'goodfellow' (II.i.34), a bringer of mirth, and not just in the raucous atmosphere of the pub, where he can successfully pretend to enjoy best bitter. It is this aspect of Surender's charm that most riles Rajiv who, though he hates acting, claims to be good at comedy, a line that invokes the British television programmes most associated with Asians – the comedy sketch show *Goodness Gracious Me*, and its spin-off, *The Kumars at No. 42*. For Rajiv, as perhaps for the young people in Harlesden, theatrical performance, especially in Shakespeare, is a route to a feeling of truly belonging, a sense of cultural ownership that the material trappings he has acquired, such as the comfortable house, high-status profession and 4 × 4, seem unable to provide.

If the play crucially deals with the spectrum of ownership and belonging that can be experienced by Asian inheritors of English culture, the cross-racial romance between Penny and Surender presents the English perspective on migration and assimilation, most strikingly through the discourse of tourism and the photographs taken by each of them with the same camera. Hers are seen first, framed as decoration in her idyllic thatched cottage and mostly offering overtly nostalgic representations of the English pastoral idyll: a black-and-white portrait of an old groundsman on the village cricket field, a colour portrait of an Opheliaesque willow aslant a brook. But the image that Surender and the camera pay most attention to is, significantly, a close-up of a weathervane, again in black and white, hung over Penny's bed. Although we cannot tell whether the vane is pointing east or west, or neither, this shot is followed almost immediately by a sequence in which Surender describes a cloud he can see out of the bedroom window as an 'egg' from which grows a 'flower'. To this Penny adds the suggestion that the flower is an (English?) 'rose'. It is when Surender wants to take a photograph of the rose that

Penny lends him her camera so he can be a 'proper' tourist, capturing his own images of English life.

It is plain that the cloud-flower marking the beginning of the love affair between Penny and Surender is Luthra's equivalent of the 'little Western flower' (II.i.166) that redirects passion in *A Midsummer Night's Dream*. But it is less obvious how we should interpret the photography. By giving her camera to Surender, is Penny imposing her vision of a safe and homogenous England on him? Or do Surender's snapshots, in addition to the mirroring offered by the play and its outcome, allow Penny to see England in a new way, without the misty illusions of childhood? These illusions seem to be linked to the kind of emotional defensiveness represented by the actual moat near which she and Surender come close to making love. This, according to the play, has belonged to her family for generations, and resonates faintly with the moat evoked by Gaunt, in *Richard II*, at the point in his speech where the sea imagery transmutes into something much more local and domestic to become:

> as a moat defensive to a house
> Against the envy of less happier lands;
> This blessèd plot, this earth, this realm, this England.

(II.i.48–50)

England, the play gently suggests, no longer has need of such defences of separatism, which may also close the gates against personal self-fulfilment.

Although the play ends hopefully, there is no pretence that reaching the destination 'after multiculturalism' – of becoming, in Katherine Eggert's words, 'culturally fluid and culturally fluent' in the global world of 'postdiasporic transit, media, and flex (if not flux)' – will necessarily be an easy or always pleasant journey.[36] The main action is framed by two sequences of vomiting. On the plane to Britain, an Englishman is literally made ill by the smell of the Indian food that Surender generously shares with his fellow passengers, and which has previously stained his passport, causing him to wrap it in one of the plane's sick bags. The passport is subsequently lost when the sick bag is used by a passenger who can only respond blankly to Surender's comforting words, 'You are not alone'. In the last moments, it is Penny who feels ill, even though she is somewhat revived by Surender's kisses. Nonetheless, she, too, is sick, the last words of the film being her promise, 'It won't happen again'. Analysed in terms of C. L. Barber's theory of festive comedy, which, in its therapeutic bent, at least seems appropriate to Luthra's psychologically nuanced exploration, the play's comic action could be viewed as offering at least three 'clarifications' as a result of Surender's temporary

stay in the 'green world' of the village.[37] One is, of course, Penny's realisation that she need not be Mariana in the moated grange but can follow
her love across the world, that she, too, can be a tourist or even a
migrant. Another is the recognition by the villagers – and through them
the audience – of their own prejudices. The third is Rajiv's understanding, voiced through his performance of Puck's epilogue, that his love
affair with Englishness has led him to betray his 'kinsman'. His appeal –
'Give me your hands, if we be friends' (Epilogue, 15) – at one and the
same time articulates the larger purpose of Luthra's play, which is to offer
a diagnosis of the psychic damage done to both sides by the asylum
debate, and, perhaps more importantly, Rajiv's own awakening to his
need to find the best in himself, fully to become whatever it means to be
both 'English' and, as his sister says, 'Indian – sort of'.

That Strain Again: The Music of Multiculturalism

What is notable about many of the productions discussed here is the way
in which they make the emotional experience, rather than the politics, of
multiculturalism a main theme, nuances often conveyed through the use
of music. As we have already noted, popular Western classics, rather than
hip-hop or *bhangra*, dominate the soundtrack of *My Shakespeare*; similarly, a significant part of *Second Generation* unfolds in the Asian
popular-music world, and *Twelfth Night* was originally envisaged as
being set in the music industry. The soundtrack of *Indian Dream*, too, is
a 'fusion', although, like its director, the composer, Edmund Butt, is
English, and quintessentially so in that he received his musical training
at a choir school and at the Royal Academy of Music. The score blends
Indian harmonics, rhythms and instruments, particularly sitar and tabor,
with a range of Western classical influences, played mainly on piano and
strings. Throughout, these different strands intertwine, often in
predictable ways, so that 'Indian' music accompanies the bustle of an
intercontinental flight departure, while Western tunes are introduced first
on the radio, in an aria playing in the house of Peter, who will become
the spokesman for the villagers' threatened sense of themselves. It all
climaxes in the play scenes in which the famous Mendelssohn overture
is introduced and, at least momentarily, becomes a dominant. In a
discussion of Trevor Nunn's *Twelfth Night* (1996), Katherine Eggert
associates the film with a form of 'minstrelsy', one that is trapped within
the logic of 'post-post-coloniality', and is literally overshadowed by the
cultural imperialism of the American film musical and its progenitor, the
minstrel show. In his essay in this volume, Richard Burt also finds British

film portrayals of Shakespearean performance reduced to irrelevant (and racist) rehearsals that, in striving to achieve novelty, surprise and cultural authenticity, and in attempting to break free of 'mimicry', are either 'stained' by an irreducible racism or submerged beneath a symbolic system of whiteness. We would argue that concepts of minstrelsy and mimicry cease to be useful in relation to the television texts we have discussed, which are marked instead by tropes of a new kind of 'fusion' music, strains that, while capturing the tension that exists within the very idea of multiculturalism in Britain in the twenty-first century, illuminate harmonies as well as discords. By interrogating what is at stake, ethically and culturally, in performing Shakespeare today in multicultural Britain, these productions look forward, with varying degrees of trepidation and confidence, to a future 'after multiculturalism'.

Notes

1. W. B. Worthen (2003), *Shakespeare and the Force of Modern Performance*, Cambridge: Cambridge University Press, p. 121.
2. *My Shakespeare* (dir. Michael Waldman, 2004).
3. *Shakespeare on the Estate* (dir. Penny Woolcock, 1994).
4. Susanne Greenhalgh (2003), ' "Alas poor country!"': Documenting the Politics of Performance in Two British Television *Macbeth*s since the 1980s', in Pascale Aebsicher, Edward J. Esche and Nigel Wheale (eds), *Remaking Shakespeare: Performance Across Media, Cultures and Genres*, Basingstoke: Palgrave, p. 98.
5. Richard Kiborn and John Izod (1997), *An Introduction to Television Documentary: Confronting Reality*, Manchester: Manchester University Press, p. 46.
6. One of Waldman's previous high-profile projects for Channel 4, whose format *My Shakespeare* reworks on a smaller scale, was the series *Operatunity* (2003), in which amateur singers, taken under the wing of the English National Opera, were followed through the processes of audition, training and performance, culminating in a performance at the London Coliseum.
7. Cedric Messina (1979), 'The Shakespeare Plays', *Shakespeare Quarterly*, 30, p. 137.
8. Tim Hallinan (1981), 'Jonathan Miller on *The Shakespeare Plays*', *Shakespeare Quarterly*, 32, p. 134.
9. Lois Potter (2002), *Shakespeare in Performance: 'Othello'*, Manchester: Manchester University Press, p. 184.
10. *BBC Handbook 1980* (1980), London: BBC Publications, p. 68; *BBC Annual Report and Handbook 1981* (1981), London: BBC Publications, p. 69.
11. In 1987, for example, the Corporation registered 'a particular concern in the shortage of non-white journalists' and committed itself to an introduction of 'the work of black independent film makers' to editors and commissioners (*BBC Annual Report and Accounts 1986–87* (1987), London: BBC Publications, p. 25).
12. *BBC Annual Report and Accounts 2001/2002* (2002), London: BBC Publications, p. 13.

13. *The Merchant of Venice*, in *The Norton Shakespeare*, Stephen Greenblatt, Walter Cohen, Jean E. Howard and Katharine Eisaman Maus (eds) (1997), New York: W. W. Norton, III.v.27–8. All further references appear in the text.

14. *Richard II*, in *The Norton Shakespeare*, IV.i.56. All further references appear in the text.

15. Missing from this list are two of the most frequently discussed examples of recent colour-blind casting in the two British 'national theatres': the Nigerian actor David Oyelowo's acclaimed performance as Henry VI in Michael Boyd's 'This England' version of the *History Plays* (2000); and Nicholas Hytner's inaugural, anti-Iraq War production of *Henry V* at the RNT, starring Adrian Lester (2004). Although *Illuminations*, who produced the television adaptations of *Richard II* and *Macbeth*, had hoped to film the RSC's production, this proved economically unviable. Video clips of *Henry V* are available on the *Stageworks* website, and Oyelowo provided the digitally accessed commentary accompanying the BBC's 'Shakespea(Re)-Told' 2005 season of drama updates based on four of the best known plays.

16. *Peter Brook's 'Hamlet'* (dir. Peter Brook, 2002).

17. *The Italian Job* (dir. Peter Collinson, 1969).

18. *English File: Shakespeare Shorts* (prod. Anne Brogan, 1996).

19. Greenhalgh, ' "Alas poor country!" ', pp. 101–2.

20. *Second Generation* (dir. Jonathan Sen, 2003). Also in production that year was Big Cow's *From Bard to Verse* (dir. Neil McLennen), which, transmitted on BBC3, featured a range of black and Asian actors performing 'soundbite' speeches from the poetry and plays.

21. Sally Kinnes (2003), 'A race against time – Television', *The Sunday Times: Culture*, 31 August, p. 24.

22. *The Making of 'Twelfth Night': Twenty-First Century Bard* (dir. John Butterworth, 2003).

23. See Annabelle Sreberny (1999), *Include Me In*, London: Broadcasting Standards Commission/Independent Television Commission. This offers evidence on the ways in which British Asians identify themselves, and responses to the representations of those identities on British television.

24. Jennifer Harvie (2005), *Staging the UK*, Manchester: Manchester University Press, pp. 223–3, 256, 257.

25. Yasmin Alibhai-Brown (2005), *After Multiculturalism*, London: The Foreign Policy Centre, p. 3.

26. Alibhai-Brown, *After Multiculturalism*, p. 70.

27. Yasmin Alibhai-Brown (2005), 'The Drama of My Life', *The Independent*, 25 February.

28. *Twelfth Night* (dir. Tim Supple, 2003).

29. See the Channel 4 documentary *Black Like Beckham* (dir. Paul McKenzie, 2005).

30. Paul Burrell was Princess Diana's valet and has made a career on the minor celebrity circuit of presenting himself as keeper of her memory and secrets.

31. *The League of Gentlemen* is a black comedy BBC radio series set in the bizarre village of Royston Vesey. One of its key catchphrases emphasises 'local people' as opposed to any kind of incomer or stranger.

32. BBC Press Office (2003), 'Asian aspiration and achievement – Big Dreams on BBC Two', 22 July.

33. Joe Joseph (2003), 'The familiar faces in Avie Luthra's *Indian Dream* reflected just how small the pool of Asian actors is on British television', *The Times*, 23 October, p. 18.

34. Victoria Segal (2003), 'Pick of the day – Wednesday 22 October', *The Sunday Times: Culture*, 19 October, p. 72
35. *A Midsummer Night's Dream*, in *The Norton Shakespeare*, II.i.33. All further references appear in the text.
36. Katherine Eggert (2003), 'Sure Can Sing and Dance: Minstrelsy, the Star System, and the Post-Postcoloniality of Kenneth Branagh's *Love's Labour's Lost* and Trevor Nunn's *Twelfth Night*', in Richard Burt and Lynda E. Boose (eds), *Shakespeare, the Movie, II: Popularizing the Plays on Film, TV, Video, and DVD*, London and New York: Routledge, p. 84; Richard Burt (2003), 'Shakespeare and Asia in Postdiasporic Cinemas: Spin-Offs and Citations of the Plays from Bollywood to Hollywood', in Burt and Boose (eds), *Shakespeare, the Movie, II*, p. 269.
37. C. L. Barber (1972), *Shakespeare's Festive Comedy*, Princeton: Princeton University Press.

Chapter 6

Looking for Shylock: Stephen Greenblatt, Michael Radford and Al Pacino

Samuel Crowl

Several decades ago critics began exploring the resonant intertextual echoes between literary criticism and stage and screen productions of Shakespeare. These adventures led to some surprising discoveries, most importantly the way certain Shakespeare films had come to occupy the place of 'father' productions in the creative anxiety of influence driving modern stage versions of the plays.

At the present historical juncture, we find an interesting variation on this pattern in the ways in which the two major popular Shakespeares of the season – Stephen Greenblatt's best-selling biography *Will in the World* (2004) and Michael Radford's well reviewed film of *The Merchant of Venice* (2004) – talk to one another. Greenblatt's New Historicism was meant to rescue Shakespeare (and others) from the New Critics and the Jan Kott crowd (Shakespeare as 'Our Contemporary') by resituating him in his own age. Now Greenblatt publishes his major culminating work on Shakespeare and confesses that it was inspired by the recent, Academy-Award-winning film *Shakespeare in Love* (1998). Simultaneously, Michael Radford follows the former New Historicist-turned-biographer by specifically locating his *The Merchant of Venice* in the Venice of 1596 and rolling a historicist-inspired scroll over the film's opening frames, providing details of anti-Semitism and usury and sumptuary laws in Renaissance Venice.[1]

Interestingly, both Greenblatt and Radford, in their treatments of the play, attempt to historicise it but end up providing an essentialist's take on its troubling central character, Shylock. Equally interesting is the way in which the play and Pacino's performance of Shylock resist these moves. Ultimately, I find Radford's film more interesting than Greenblatt's analysis because of the tension it develops between Radford's contemporary conception of Shylock as a victim and Al Pacino's more complicated embodiment of the character. Pacino displays a remarkable technical mastery of the crisp, taut, repetitive invective (and sly irony) of Shylock's language and conspicuously avoids bending his portrayal to catch at modern sensibilities.

In 'Laughing at the Scaffold', his chapter on the character and play, Greenblatt makes a series of provocative (and slippery) moves to historicise Shylock. First, he gives us a quick sketch of Marlowe's radical life and sets him up as Shakespeare's principal theatrical rival. Then he segues into a treatment of Marlowe's *The Jew of Malta* and a brief history (with a nod to James Shapiro's massive work on the subject) of the forced exile of the Jews from England (1290) and Spain (1490). From there, as skillfully as a film director, he cuts to the Lopez affair and conveniently places Shakespeare in the crowd (a pure conjecture repeated so often as to make it appear a historical reality) at Lopez's execution. This allows him, in fine New Historicist fashion, to make fertile use of William Camden's eyewitness account of Lopez's final moment (and the crowd's reaction to it) on the scaffold where he declared that 'he loved the Queen as well as he loved Jesus Christ'. Camden reports that Lopez's words 'coming from a man of the Jewish profession moved no small laughter in the standersby'.[2]

The biographer latches on to that 'small laughter' and runs with it back to *The Merchant of Venice* where Shakespeare 'wanted, it seems, to excite laughter at a wicked Jew's discomfiture . . . and . . . wanted at the same time to call the laughter into question, to make the amusement excruciatingly uncomfortable'.[3] But, finally for Greenblatt, neither contextualising Shylock nor unlocking his ambiguities gets at his troubling power. For that, there is only the language of the humanist essentialist (and echoes of Harold Bloom): 'Shylock seems to have a stronger claim to attention, quite simply more life, than anyone else'; 'But the play would not count for much . . . were it not for the stupendous power of Shylock'; '[Shylock] is a soul under siege'; 'It is as if the ring [Leah's turquoise] were something more than a piece of the Jew's wealth, as if it were a piece of his heart'.[4]

Greenblatt's language here, particularly in the last two examples, resembles the way actors and directors, rather than literary theorists, tend to talk about dramatic characters. Greenblatt's structural strategy in 'Laughing at the Scaffold' (and it is representative of the whole) is the filmmaker's, cutting from one moment to another (Marlowe, Lopez's trial and execution, Shylock), flashing back (the exile of the Jews from England and Spain), and zooming in on his hero (Shakespeare) conveniently placed at the edge of the action absorbing it all. As Greenblatt borrows technique from the filmmaker, so Michael Radford raids some of the literary critic's historicising devices to structure his film and to create a Shylock understandable to a modern mass audience. Ultimately, however, the actor, Al Pacino, trumps both critic and filmmaker by creating a Shylock who transcends the sentimentality at the heart of both Greenblatt and Radford's designs.

Though Radford's film, released in late 2004, was the first major Shakespeare film of the new century, it followed a previous and little noted strain in the long history of Shakespeare on film. After Laurence Olivier and Orson Welles created the first truly successful Shakespeare films in the 1940s and 1950s, the genre became the almost exclusive property of actors and/or directors whose first experience with Shakespeare was in the theatre. Olivier, Welles, Peter Brook, Kenneth Branagh, Trevor Nunn, Adrian Noble and Ian McKellen all established their reputations as stage Shakespeareans before venturing into the world of film.[5] Even outsiders to the Anglo-American tradition, like the Russian Grigori Kozintsev and the Italian Franco Zeffirelli, directed Shakespeare on stage before making their famous Shakespeare films.

This dominant tradition was punctuated approximately once a decade by a Shakespearean film made by a director whose creative life was defined exclusively by film and who came to the Shakespearean material without the benefits and disadvantages of deep theatrical familiarity. This counter-tradition began in 1929, before Olivier and Welles, with the very first sound Shakespeare film, *The Taming of the Shrew*, directed by Sam Taylor. But its most important early manifestation was George Cukor's 1936 *Romeo and Juliet* made for MGM. Cukor is perhaps the most famous Hollywood insider ever to direct a Shakespeare film and he almost killed the form in childbirth. The more interesting films which followed included Joseph Mankiewicz's *Julius Caesar* (1953), Akira Kurosawa's *Throne of Blood* (1957) and *Ran* (1985), Roman Polanski's *Macbeth* (1971), and Michael Hoffman's *William Shakespeare's 'A Midsummer Night's Dream'* (1999).[6] All of these directors regarded themselves as filmmakers rather than Shakespeareans, and none had ever worked with Shakespeare on stage except Michael Hoffman, who acted and directed during his undergraduate years at Oxford. Some of these films are flawed by their reverence for their Shakespearean material; others by their sheer cinematic exuberance; while several are great film masterpieces. Michael Radford's *The Merchant of Venice* sits squarely within this tradition.

Radford was born in India and raised in the Middle East, a child of the last days of British colonialism. All of his best films – *1984* (1984), *White Mischief* (1987) and *Il Postino* (1994) – deal, in ways both tragic and benign, with the cultural outsider. In *1984*, Winston Smith finds himself an alien in his own society; in *White Mischief*, the decadence of the British colonial community in Kenya is exposed; and in *Il Postino*, the great Chilean poet, Pablo Neruda, plays a complicated cupid in the lives of a dispirited Italian postman and his beloved.

Radford brings both his personal and professional experience, in exploring the cultural territory where insider and outsider meet and clash, to his understanding of the tension between Christian and Jew in Venice at the heart of Shakespeare's play. The film, though set in 1596, is inevitably as much about our age as Shakespeare's. Radford, in the montages that frame the film, unavoidably brings his own cultural sensibilities to work on Shakespeare's material. The film is Venice-driven, which is to say that it is centred on Antonio and Shylock rather than on Belmont and Portia.

The opening montage follows the progress of a gondola ferrying an ascetic-looking friar holding a tall wooden cross through the canals of Venice. His plain, shorn figure is meant as a rebuke to Venice's lavish excess and a threat to the city's famed cosmopolitan tolerance. Reformation and Counter-Reformation energies are troubling the waters. Interspliced with his journey are flashcuts to the burning of Hebrew texts, crowds shouting anti-Semitic epithets, the friar delivering a fundamentalist harangue, cantors chanting prayers, a synagogue door being shut and bolted, and a long scroll explaining sixteenth-century usury and sumptuary laws (Jews were forced to wear red caps) in Venice.

The montage continues as the camera picks out Antonio (Jeremy Irons) moving through the crowd on the Rialto Bridge. When he is hailed by Shylock he spits on him and moves on to be greeted by Bassanio arriving, masked, in a gondola. The camera then follows Antonio to a mass being conducted by the friar, then cuts to Shylock at prayer in the synagogue (with Jessica watching with the other women in a gallery above), and finally to a group of masquers including Lorenzo, Gratiano, Salerio and Solanio observing father and daughter leave the services, thus defining quickly all of the principal Venetians in the narrative. Only then does Radford cut to Antonio's lodgings and the text's famous opening line: 'In sooth, I know not why I am so sad'.[7]

All of this flashes by in a minute or two and is Radford's version of Orson Welles' 'riderless horse': the visual device by which a film draws you into its landscape, narrative and mystery. The sequence establishes the major Venetian players and the crucial role religion will play in Radford's handling of Shakespeare's material. Antonio is linked not only with Shylock but also with the friar. He is represented as seeking out a religious extreme as a potential means of dealing with his sadness, here clearly figured as his inability to understand or accept his repressed desires for Bassanio. Unable to indulge or even admit those desires, he seeks to purge them by self-denial. Radford's Venice begins to look curiously like the contemporary world, where sexual licence, material excess and the anxieties of a global market have led to religious revival and sectarian intolerance.

The film's closing frame is briefer but equally pointed. We are in Belmont. The lovers are reconciled; the ring business has been concluded. It is dawn, and the camera, in long-shot, looks out over a lagoon where soon two tall figures standing in narrow boats (echoes of the gondola and friar in the opening montage) glide into the frame. Each is fishing with a bow and arrow. The camera's perspective is shared by a solitary figure – not Antonio as we might suppose, but a female gazing out at the exotic scene. The camera glances down at her right hand, and we see on her finger a stunning turquoise ring. The woman is Jessica (Zuleika Robinson); the ring is Shylock's ('I had it of Leah when I was a bachelor' (III.ii.101)); and the bittersweet irony is that she has not given it for any monkey. We know the ring, as only film can make us know such small details, because Radford includes a flashcut to it in the powerful moment when Shylock jumps to the conclusion that this turquoise is the ring Tubal reports that Jessica had exchanged for a monkey in Genoa. A reverse-angle shot ends the film with Jessica's beautiful, melancholy face caught in medium close-up as she ponders the consequences of her escape into a wilderness of Christians.

Between these opening and closing moments, Radford's film drives a hard bargain. The sun never shines in his Venice. The ghetto, where Bassanio and Antonio go to seek out Shylock, is cramped, teeming and distinguished by the lump (a pound?) of goat's meat Shylock is buying; only a few faint rays of light manage to penetrate the windows of Antonio's rooms; it is always night at Shylock's house, and Benoit Delhomme (Radford's cinematographer) shoots these (and many other Shylock scenes) through a cold, blue filter. The Rialto and Venice's narrow streets are packed, and Radford's camera repeatedly picks out the bare-breasted prostitutes who seem to linger in the doorways and windows of many cityscape shots. Radford refuses to provide us with any glimpses of the golden, dazzling Venice adored for centuries by painters, filmmakers and tourists.

Picking up on images in the text, Radford's Venetians are always feasting. Solanio (Gregor Fisher) and Salerio (John Sessions) are eating during the opening scene at Antonio's; the film takes us to the dinner at

Bassanio's where Shylock is a reluctant guest and, in a telling detail, we watch him play with his full glass of wine without ever lifting it to his lips; Bassanio and Gratiano are eating when the Gobbos arrive to make their pitch to join the Belmont expedition, and the camera is specially attentive to Old Gobbo's gift of a dish of doves; gustatory and sexual appetites are linked, and the film gets a surely unintended laugh when Solanio turns from nuzzling a whore's breast to ask Salerio, who is nibbling on another, 'Now, what news on the Rialto?' (III.i.1); and finally, the film negotiates the concluding ring exchange back in Belmont around a table loaded with fruit and wine for the just-returned travellers. Radford's film reads this abundance (as again our age might) as decadence rather than, as C. L. Barber suggests, a form of communal feasting and secular communion central to the festive pattern at work in the text.[8]

Radford creates this edgy, dark atmosphere to define a world that reflects a modern understanding of Shylock. Stephen Greenblatt, James Bulman and Miriam Gilbert (among many others) are right to insist that, however we try to balance the play's romance with its commerce, the caskets with the bond, New Testament mercy with Old Testament law, Shylock – though present in only five of nineteen scenes – is inescapably for us at the centre of the play.[9] And so he is in Radford's film. Shylock's story, from his being spat upon by Antonio in the opening frames to Jessica's fingering of his ring in its final image, is at the heart of the film's narrative.

What holds Radford's approach together and makes it work is Al Pacino's performance as Shylock. Not since Marlon Brando's Mark Antony fifty years ago has an American film actor given such an intelligent, subtle and accomplished performance of a major Shakespearean role in the movies. There are touches of some of Pacino's famed screen portrayals – from Serpico to Sonny Wortzik to Roy Cohn – in his Shylock, but, most importantly, there are strong traces of Michael Corleone buried deep beneath his beard and behind his eyes. Can any other actor capture so well the look of having been up all night?[10] Pacino's verbal technique is flawless. He works in a gruff register but hits sharply all of Shylock's famous consonants (ducats, rated, eat, bait, bond, fat, rat, hate, thrift) and plosives (pork, hip, ripe, spurn, pig, prick, pound). He can stretch a vowel (making urine rhyme with mine) and even discover little unexpected verbal jokes as when talking about water rats ('I mean pi-rats' (I.iii.20)) with Bassanio. Pacino's face is covered with a scruffy beard; his shoulders are stooped; he walks with a slight shuffle; he needs spectacles (perhaps more for effect than necessity) when checking the interest rates early on and rereading the bond in the trial scene. Pacino's Shylock carries the weight of his experience and tradition on his shoulders. Life is a burden relieved only by his daughter and his ducats.

His performance is intelligently linked by Radford with Irons' Antonio. Irons' tense and taut face ('love-battered' is Frank Kermode's acute formulation) perfectly expresses Antonio's story.[11] He gazes at Bassanio's face longingly, discovers a brilliant Shakespearean pun (delivered with a pleased little smile) when he assures him, 'My purse, my pers-on, my extremest means / Lie all unlocked to your occasions' (I.i.138–9), and poignantly responds to Bassanio's impulsive kiss (full on the lips) of thanks for underwriting the Belmont expedition.

We know from the outset 'Which is the merchant here, and which the Jew?' (IV.i.69), but the film makes us understand the natural confusion Shakespeare has built into the play's title. Shylock and Antonio share an unacknowledged secret: the ultimate commercial insider (Antonio) is displaced by his homosexuality as the ultimate killjoy outsider (Shylock) is replaced by a wounded essentialist: 'Hath not a Jew eyes? Hath not a Jew hands, organs, dimensions, senses, affections, passions?' (III.i.49–51). Pacino's delivery of these lines is the one moment (other than his eventual collapse at the trial scene) when his patience and resignation disintegrate. Radford shoots the scene with Pacino trapped on a narrow path between Salerio, Solanio and their whores and a canal. Salerio and Solanio's taunts about Jessica sting even more painfully because of the company they keep. Pacino's Shylock – torn between the pain of Jessica's loss and the joy of Antonio's mercantile collapse – lets it rip on 'To bait fish withal' (III.i.45), savours 'dimensions' and 'diseases', and comes close to losing control as he launches into a defence of his own humanity even as he puts that humanity at the service of revenge. Way back and deep down there is an echo here of Sonny Wortzik's hyperactive plea for tolerance as he paces out on the street trapped between the bank and the cops in *Dog Day Afternoon* (1975).

Radford shoots the scene through the blue filter I mentioned earlier, which comes progressively to define visually Shylock's remaining moments in the film. The camera cuts back and forth between Pacino and Fisher and Sessions with its tempo matching the building intensity of Shylock's outburst. Pacino regains control, without sacrificing his rage, with the arrival of Tubal (Allan Corduner). Again, Shylock is caught between Jessica's flight and Antonio's crash and, as the moment veers agonisingly between black comedy and pathos, Radford makes a stunning decision. He inserts a flashcut of Jessica's exchange of her father's turquoise ring for a monkey as lewdly imagined by Shylock. This exquisitely cinematic moment, where we see that ring along with

Shylock, sets up the film's final irony and forces us to rethink one of the crucial moments in the text.

The moment is even more effective because it complicates and enriches the core tension that gives the film its radical credentials. Radford treats Shylock sentimentally, Pacino does not, and the texture that tension generates provides the film's Venice scenes with their dark vitality. As I mentioned at the outset, Radford's opening montage shows Antonio spitting at Shylock and counters it with Shylock's piety; later, Radford's camera will follow the disconsolate Shylock, after his discovery of Jessica's flight, out into the rain, thus undercutting Solanio's comic report of the scene (' "O my ducats! O my daughter!" ' (II.viii.15)), here delivered in voice-over while our eyes absorb a more moving and tragic image; and finally, Radford cuts away from the reunion of Bassanio and Portia in Belmont to give us a final shot of a totally dispossessed Shylock, standing alone on a Venetian street shorn of his identifying red cap and with his hair in disarray, as Tubal and the other Jews enter the synagogue and bolt its door behind them. Each of these moments obviously reinforces our sympathy for Shylock and his victimisation by the Christians.

Pacino, however, makes no obvious moves in his performance to make his Shylock a victim. He is gruff from the outset; his dealings with Jessica are possessive and as matter-of-fact as those with Antonio and Bassanio; he is hard and adamant in the trial scene; and he inserts two extra 'mines' in 'The pound of flesh which I demand of him / Is dearly bought. 'Tis mine ['tis mine . . . 'tis mine], and I will have it' (IV.i.98–9). Pacino does give Shylock his dignity (there is no trace of the potential clown in his delivery of the character's famous repeated phrases), but he never backs off from exploring the nasty self-sufficiency of Shylock's desire for revenge (with wonderful echoes of Michael Corleone's hard heart at work here). Pacino finds the source of Shylock's bitterness not in his treatment by Antonio and his fellow Christians but in Jessica's elopement and betrayal. Pacino's Shylock is already steeled to protect himself from the Antonios and Bassanios of the world, but he has never imagined being torn from within. It is the ring report that stings and punishes. Pacino makes the only slip in his performance at this crucial moment when Radford allows him to insert an additional and absolutely unnecessary word when talking about the turquoise. Pacino says: 'I would not have given it [away] for a wilderness of monkeys' (III.i.101–2), thus hobbling the rhythm and bite of Shakespeare's line.

Because Radford's camera so obviously sympathises with the character, it gives Pacino the liberty to push against that image and to explore Shylock's own dark desires, and he threatens to run away with the picture. The use of the turquoise ring is Radford's way of regaining control. Pacino's Shylock jumps to conclusions about Jessica and the ring. Unlike Bassanio, she does not give it away; in fact, she wears it as a sign of her divided loyalties. Her melancholy thus ends the film as Antonio's began it, and the experience of Radford's *Merchant* has been to make us all understand why we are so sad.

The text, of course, provides an antidote to Venice and the bond plot: Belmont and Portia. Visually, Radford makes the contrast vivid. Venice is dark, dank and nasty. Belmont is a blaze of light located on the tip of a peninsula surrounded by water. Radford even gives us several long-shots of Portia's palace at night glowing like a little jewel in the dark. The palace interiors are warm and soft, distinguished by the slightly faded pastel colours of the Veronese frescoes that cover the walls and ceilings. This is a fairy-tale landscape compared to Venice's seedy, commercial grit. But, as Radford created an interesting tension between camera and character in his presentation of Shylock, he makes another experimental move in defining the relationship between Belmont and its princess.

Radford's Belmont is a star's setting (much as Titania's Hollywood bower in Hoffman's *Dream* was created specifically to contain Michelle Pfeiffer): it is made for a screen luminary like Paltrow or Kidman or Blanchett. But, instead of using an established film actress to balance Pacino's movie power, Radford makes the radical choice to cast a young American, Lynn Collins, in her first major film role. Collins has a handsome Renaissance face with wide eyes and a strong nose, and she is given a wonderful mane of strawberry-blonde hair framing her face in tumbling braids and curls like one of Botticelli's beauties. She handles the verse with skill (she played Ophelia at New York's Public Theatre, and Juliet for Peter Hall in Los Angeles) and has the ability to convey Portia's intelligence, especially in the trial scene, as well as her beauty. But she does not rivet our attention; she fails to make her intelligence (or her sadness) sexy. The camera does not function as her ally in the way that it does with Pacino and Irons (or even Zuleika Robinson). Her face does not absorb all the light in the frame, which is why her most successful moments come when she is disguised as Balthazar, with a wispy goatee and a scholar's cap pulled down tight over her curls.

In a production as tough and unflinching about the Venetian Christians as this one, Portia is crucial or the tale loses its delicate balance. She is the counterweight to Shylock, not just in the trial scene but throughout the unfolding of the narrative. Collins might have managed this in a stage production (as Geraldine James did when pitted against Dustin Hoffman in Peter Hall's 1989 production) but not on film, where the camera relentlessly presses in on the actor's face. Collins' beauty never dazzles, and her face rarely reveals the playful, ironic intelligence necessary to create the image of love's festive bounty as an alternative to Venice's harsh materialism. Radford, so careful in his handling of Shylock, does not help Collins by playing Morocco (David Harewood) and Aragon (Antonio Gil-Martinez) for broad laughs. He may have been driven to do so because of his failure to find any leavening comedy in either Young (Mackenzie Crook) or Old Gobbo (Ron Cook). Their hapless and hopeless routine makes even the unsatisfied long for Branagh's use of American comics for Shakespeare's clowns. Radford allows Harewood and his Moroccan retinue to infuse the scene with music hall and minstrel show schtict, but he does not have the courage to retain Portia's 'Let all of his complexion choose me so' (II.vii.79) in his screenplay.

Radford is more successful in casting against the golden-boy type by using Joseph Fiennes as Bassanio. Fiennes established himself as a romantic lead by playing an ink-stained author suffering from writer's block in John Madden's *Shakespeare in Love*. With his deep-set eyes and dark shadow of a beard, he is not a conventional leading man. In fact, his Bassanio – in appearance – is more appropriately matched with Irons' Antonio than with Collins' Portia. Radford seems to be working out a scheme here where the fair-skinned, generous Portia not only defeats the narrow and driven Shylock but redeems the relationship between Antonio and Bassanio and its unspoken subtext. Something like this is going on in the final exchange of rings where Portia specifically employs Antonio as the instrument through which the wedding ring is returned to Bassanio, thus creating a new role for him as secular priest rather than romantic rival or wealthy benefactor.

Portia's other major moment is, of course, the trial scene. Radford makes an interesting transposition of the text here by placing Lorenzo (Charlie Cox) and Jessica's exchange about moonlight and music (radically clipped) before, rather than after, the trial scene. It is another way of foregrounding Jessica and her melancholy links with her father as the film cuts directly from her 'I am never merry when I hear sweet music' (V.i.68) back to Venice and the beginning of Shylock's fall. For the trial, the crowd is packed in tight around Shylock, and Radford uses a hand-held camera to capture the claustrophobic intensity of the situation. The film recreates the atmosphere of the theatre-as-bear-baiting-pit here. The throng has to part first for Shylock's entrance into the tiny circle of space between the crowd and the Duke and the other Magnificoes and then again at the arrival of Balthazar. Radford intentionally allows the camera to be bumped and jostled once or twice by the spectators to increase the potentially explosive atmosphere, which is also heightened by Jocelyn Pook's music, scored here for mandolin and kettle drum. Several times he cuts to Tubal and other Jews in the crowd (those red hats an instant marker) for reaction shots. When Pacino refuses Portia's requests for surgeons to tend Antonio's wounds because – with spectacles pinched down on his nose – 'I cannot find it. 'Tis not in the bond' (IV.i.257), the camera cuts to Tubal who lowers his head in embarrassment for his friend. Collins does not play the moment as though her Portia is improvising the legal quibble she uses to ultimately trap Shylock. Radford has earlier provided a flashcut of Portia consulting with Doctor Bellario as they pore over law books, and one intuits that her defence of Antonio is being fully plotted at that point.

The trial scene is, of course, the climax of the Shylock plot and runs for twenty-five minutes in Radford's film. Here, he finally achieves the pay-off for casting Collins as Portia, as the two American outsiders (to the Shakespearean tradition and to the otherwise almost all-Anglo cast) square off against each other: the old film pro against the newcomer. They are even dressed alike in black tunics with just the touch of a white blouse peeking out at the neck. Even Shylock's cap is black rather than red: before the law, he regards himself as a citizen of the state rather than as a member of an alien minority. Collins plays the pert and nimble young doctor of Rome better than the golden girl of Belmont. Her delivery of Portia's most famous line makes it seem fresh and natural, the spontaneous response to the rapid-fire naturalistic exchanges that precede it, rather than the beginning of a well-worn Shakespearean set speech:

PORTIA:	Do you confess the bond?
ANTONIO:	I do.
PORTIA:	Then must the Jew be merciful.
SHYLOCK:	On what compulsion must I? Tell me that.
PORTIA:	The quality of mercy is not strained . . .

(IV.i.176–9)

Collins' matter-of-fact cadence (lightly hitting 'mercy' and 'strained') shoots the line back at Pacino's Shylock with a natural authority, and the battle between them is enjoined. Prior to this moment, Radford's camera cuts rapidly between Portia, Antonio and Shylock. Once Portia launches into her big courtroom speech, Radford's camera holds both Portia and Shylock in the frame in a tight two-shot. When Pacino's Shylock begins to sharpen his knife and to make his move on the bound, gagged (with a belt) and clearly terrified Antonio, and Portia begins her counter-offensive ('Tarry a little. There is something else' (IV.i.300)), the camera never captures them in the same frame again: now it is Christian against Jew, and Shylock is destroyed in the theatrical pit of Venetian justice. The camera focuses on Pacino's suddenly forlorn countenance as he slumps to his knees, curls his body in upon itself and rocks in agony clutching an amulet that hangs on a chain around his neck. When he finally rises, hoping to slink away like a wounded animal, he suffers the final indignity of having Gratiano rip his yarmulke from his head and toss it to the floor. Once Portia's triumph is secure, the camera, like the text, abandons Shylock for the victors: Collins wryly handles Balthazar's request for Bassanio's ring, nicely conveys her satisfaction when he refuses to part with it, and then skillfully swallows her disappointment when he changes his mind – at Antonio's urging – and sends Gratiano chasing after her, by gondola, to deliver it up.

Radford, like Mankiewicz, Polanski and Hoffman before him, comes to his Shakespearean material with fresh eyes and the experienced filmmaker's savvy about cutting, pace and rhythm. Earlier, he econom- ically cross-cuts between Portia's handling of Morocco and Aragon in Belmont and Bassanio's preparations for his wooing expedition. He effectively has Bassanio's ship departing in the rain on the night of Jessica's elopement with Lorenzo. This allows his camera to capture first Antonio standing alone in the rain on the wharf saying farewell to his young friend, and moments later Shylock wandering the same area in search of Jessica: merchant and moneylender are united in loss.

In a stunning cut (and rearrangement of the text), Radford flashes from Pacino's Shylock shuffling away from the camera into a chilly grey Venetian fog after the scene with Tubal, to Bassanio's galley approach- ing Belmont and Nerissa's excited report that 'A day in April never came so sweet' (II.ix.92). And in the trial scene Radford knows how to heighten cinematically and tighten the tension so that the audience jumps when Shylock makes his move to cut away Antonio's pound of flesh. These are the touches of the skilled film craftsman not often revealed by Shakespeareans-turned-filmmakers.

Radford's film, finally, leaves us not with the image of the dispossessed outsider or his troubled rival or the triumphant insider but with the haunting melancholy face of the character (Jessica) most in motion between the play's two worlds and at home in neither. This is the territory Radford's films investigate, and he has imaginatively mingled his own concerns with Shakespeare's to provide us with a tough and troubling version of The Merchant of Venice. Greenblatt closes his chapter – as Henry Irving did the play – with the trial scene, and not only the trial scene but also with a textual transposition that has the critic's interpretation culminate with Shylock 'inwardly' saying: 'I am a Jew. Hath not a Jew eyes?'[12] Radford's ending also takes us back to Shylock (in a way that Shakespeare's version, with Gratiano's tasteless bawdy, decidedly does not) in a more complicated and satisfying fashion. Jessica, with her ring and her melancholy, sends us back to Shylock and his mistaken assumptions and Pacino's forlorn expression as he is caught in a no-man's land shorn of his dignity, community and daughter.

Radford's 'ring business' is the device of an experienced filmmaker. It is small – like Marlon Brando's wicked little smile as he turns to the camera after finishing Mark Antony's funeral oration in Mankiewicz's *Julius Caesar* – but effective as a device or gesture that can only be registered, via the close-up, on film. Pacino's mature and restrained performance is filled with such telling details: his shuffling walk, his use of his glasses, his slightly ominous waving about of the package of goat's meat he carries with him when the bond is struck with Antonio, and the intense focus of his cold, beady eyes in the trial scene. Michael Gambon – along with Ian McKellen and Judi Dench, the greatest English classical actor of his generation – has said that his goal as a stage actor has been to combine his theatrical experience with the 'naturalism of the modern American wave. That influenced us tremendously – DeNiro, Pacino, Hoffman, John Malkovich. If you're steeped in theatrical acting, you take what those guys do, you mix and match them'.[13]

Pacino's performance of Shylock reveals that he can do his own mixing and matching. In Radford's astute film, Pacino goes looking for Shylock and finds him. The first Shakespearean film of the new century looks back to a little recognised twentieth-century tradition in the genre where mainstream film directors take on a single Shakespearean project even as it solidifies the more recent experiment, largely created by Kenneth Branagh, of mingling American and English stage and film actors in a cast. As with Cukor, Mankiewicz, Polanski and Hoffman, we are unlikely to have another Shakespeare film from Michael Radford, but the genre has been enriched by his *Merchant* and Pacino's Shylock.

Notes

1. I would like to thank all the members, particularly Thomas Cartelli, of Katherine Rowe's 2005 Shakespeare Association of America seminar on 'Shakespeare, Film and Theory' for their helpful responses to an earlier version of this essay. Richard Burt was quick to point out that the historical text-scroll used by Radford at the beginning of his film is an old movie device. I agree, but it has

not been used in a Shakespeare film since Laurence Olivier's *Richard III* in 1955, so I felt that Radford, like Greenblatt and the New Historicists, was returning to a former emphasis on historical context as an explicit assumption in his approach to filming Shakespeare's play.

2. Stephen Greenblatt (2004), *Will in the World*, New York: W. W. Norton, p. 277.
3. Greenblatt, *Will*, p. 278.
4. Greenblatt, *Will*, pp. 258, 271, 272, 285.
5. I include McKellen on this list as he was the driving creative force behind the film of *Richard III* even though it was directed by Richard Loncraine. McKellen had played the role in Richard Eyre's 1990 production of the play for the Royal National Theatre; he wrote the screenplay; he secured the funding; and he recruited Loncraine to direct the film after Eyre turned him down.
6. I do not include Oliver Parker in this list as his *Othello* (1995) was his first film and he had previously directed a stage production of the play, though with a cast entirely different from the one that appeared in the film.
7. *The Merchant of Venice*, in *The Norton Shakespeare*, Stephen Greenblatt, Walter Cohen, Jean E. Howard and Katharine Eisaman Maus (eds) (1997), New York: W. W. Norton, I.i.1. All further references appear in the text.
8. C. L. Barber (1959), *Shakespeare's Festive Comedy*, Princeton: Princeton University Press, pp. 163–91.
9. See James Bulman (1991), *Shakespeare in Performance: 'The Merchant of Venice'*, Manchester: Manchester University Press; and Miriam Gilbert (2002), *Shakespeare at Stratford: 'The Merchant of Venice'*, London: The Arden Shakespeare.
10. I am indebted to my friend and colleague Mark Halliday for this description of Pacino. The poets write all the good lines.
11. Frank Kermode (2005), 'Our Muddy Venture', *The London Review of Books*, 6 January, p. 17.
12. Greenblatt, *Will*, pp. 286–7.
13. Mel Gussow (2004), *Gambon: A Life in Acting*, London: Nick Hern Books, p. 15.

Chapter 7

Speaking Māori Shakespeare: *The Maori Merchant of Venice* and the Legacy of Colonisation

Catherine Silverstone

As Captain James Cook's ship the *Endeavour* entered New Zealand waters in 1769, so too did a copy of Shakespeare's *Collected Works*, included as part of the luggage of the ship's artist, Sydney Parkinson. In this chapter, I am concerned to explore the ways in which Don C. Selwyn's 2001 film *The Maori Merchant of Venice/Te Tangata Whai Rawa O Weniti* is shadowed by the processes of colonisation initiated by Cook's journey.[1] Strikingly, the film marks three firsts: it is the first full-length feature film to be shot in Māori, the first full-length Shakespeare film to be made in New Zealand, and the first full-length Māori Shakespeare film. Produced at the turn of the millennium, *The Maori Merchant* is, then, an engaging site from which to explore the effects of colonisation, especially in relation to *te reo* (Māori language) and culture. In the years following Cook's landfall, the European presence in New Zealand increased with the arrival of sealers, whalers, traders and missionaries, and in 1840 a treaty was signed between the British Crown and the Māori, the indigenous inhabitants of Aotearoa/New Zealand.[2] Although promised the benefits and rights of British citizenship and, hence, equality, in the 165 years since the signing of the Treaty of Waitangi/Te Tiriti o Waitangi, Māori have been affected, often adversely, by the settlement of New Zealand. These effects – present to a greater or lesser extent over the past century and a half – include the dispossession of land, a lower life expectancy and poorer health record than *Pākehā* (white New Zealanders of predominantly British and Irish origin), and lower educational achievement. Since the 1970s, there have been significant efforts by both Māori and the government to redress some of the systematic inequities that have been perpetuated since the signing of the Treaty/Tiriti, particularly with respect to the Crown's promise that Māori would maintain possession and authority over their *taonga* (treasures), such as lands, fisheries and, also, *te reo*. While recent census results and the 2001 *Survey of the Health of the*

Māori Language suggest that the situation is, in some respects, improving for Māori, New Zealand still bears the legacy of its colonial history, especially with respect to land, language and cultural dispossession of the Māori people.[3]

Through a reading of the film, a consideration of its representation in reviews, interviews and its own publicity materials, and an analysis of its relationships to political and cultural discourses, I want to examine the ways in which *The Maori Merchant* remembers and, paradoxically, on occasions elides aspects of New Zealand's colonial history. The film thus comes to stand as a monument to this history and traumatic aspects of its legacy. In this work I want to trace the various spectres that haunt the film and enable it to function, suggestively, as a repository both of memories and imagined futures. In so doing, I aim to interrogate some of the tensions that inhere in so-called 'intercultural' performances of Shakespeare, where Shakespeare's texts are produced in the context of 'local' performance traditions and cultures. Recent analyses of intercultural performances of Shakespeare, such as Ania Loomba's subtle reading of Kathakali productions of *Othello* and W. B. Worthen's wide-ranging analysis of the phenomenon, have sought to explore what Rustom Bharucha describes as the 'ethics of representation underlying any cross-cultural exchange' and the 'space in between' cultural polarities.[4] Such analyses, with which my work is aligned, move toward readings that seek to avoid Eurocentric understandings of 'other' performance traditions and that stress processes of exchange.

At first glance, *The Maori Merchant* invites consumption as a celebratory exemplar of the 'space in between'. It might thus be termed an intercultural hybrid which works to locate Shakespeare's narrative in a New Zealand context, meshing Western and Māori performance traditions into a singular cultural product. Drawing on the production strategies of Western cinema, the lush *mise-en-scène* oscillates between Venice/Weniti, shot at various Italian-inflected locations throughout Auckland, and Belmont/Peremona. The scenes in Venice/Weniti, where the actors wear ruffs and breeches, stand as homage to the play's early modern origins. Simultaneously, the images of bustling traders and visiting ships allude to New Zealand's colonial period; these scenes also reference Māori culture in the inclusion of *poi* dancers and flax artefacts. Peremona extends Venice/Weniti's range of references to Māori culture in the inclusion of the *tūrehu* (mist children) who are seen flying in the bush, the *tukutuku* panels (flax lattice) and *taiaha* (spears) which adorn the walls, the carving of Portia/Pohia's *tipuna* (ancestor), *moko* (facial tattoos), feather cloaks and *koru* (spirals). Peremona is also home to

Māori performance traditions, most clearly seen in the *karanga* (call of welcome) and *wero* (challenge) which are issued to the Prince of Morocco. As an aural accompaniment to the visual, the soundtrack merges Clive Cockburn's soaring orchestral compositions, performed by the New Zealand Symphony Orchestra, with Hirini Melbourne's compositions for traditional Māori instruments, which he and other musicians perform within the diegesis. The film, then, employs a range of cultural signifiers to produce a world that combines Māori cultural arte-facts, clothing and performance with Shakespeare, opera and Renaissance costumes. The modes of presentation and reception of this *mise-en-scène* are certainly celebratory; a release included in the press kit asserts that the 'design, costumes and music interweave Shakespearean elements with Maori arts in a rich, textured and modern way', and reviewer Sam Edwards praises the film for 'knitting different and often conflicting cultures and histories into a remarkable whole'.[5] In what follows I am concerned to interrogate the tensions that inhere in this celebratory 'cultural mix', especially with respect to the film's hybrid conceit *par excellence*: the translation of *The Merchant of Venice* into *te reo*.

Speaking (Māori) Shakespeare

The Maori Merchant is an adaptation of Pei Te Hurinui Jones' 1946 translation of Shakespeare's play into Māori.[6] Jones has been widely acclaimed as a bicultural pioneer, who sought to foster closer relations between Māori and *Pākehā*. In particular, he recorded the history of the Tainui *iwi* (tribe), translated Māori *waiata* (songs) into English, and translated Shakespeare into Māori (in addition to *The Merchant of Venice*, he also translated *Julius Caesar* and *Othello*). Delivered in *te reo*, the film's dialogue is accompanied by English subtitles which mix elements of Shakespeare's language with modern English. With the action unfolding over 158 minutes, the film offers a 'faithful' adaptation of Shakespeare's narrative through its rendering of the plot and the characters.[7] The translation might thus be posited as one that, in Jacques Derrida's words, 'performs its mission, honours its debt and does its job or its duty while inscribing in the receiving language the most *relevant* equivalent for an original'.[8] In the press kit and reviews, the project is framed repeatedly as honouring a twin debt by marrying Selwyn's 'passion for Shakespeare with his lifelong commitment to the revitalisation of the Maori language'.[9] Here, the debt is to be paid not only to the 'original' language of Shakespeare's English, but also (and, primarily) to the 'target' language of *te reo*. Indeed, the focus of Selwyn's long career has been to promote *te reo* and to create training opportunities for Māori in New Zealand's film and theatre industries. As part of this programme, he ran He Taonga I Tawhiti (Gifts From Afar) from 1984 to 1990, a film and television training course for Māori and Pacific Islanders; in 1992 Selwyn and Ruth Kaupua Panapa created He Taonga Films, *The Maori Merchant*'s production company, which has provided a platform for creating Māori film and television dramas.

Given He Taonga Films' focus on training Māori with the skills to tell stories about themselves, Selwyn acknowledges that making a film of Shakespeare's play provokes the response from both non-Māori and Māori that 'Maori shouldn't be doing Shakespeare'.[10] However, the media discourse surrounding the production works to naturalise this choice and to package it as part of a programme of both cultural recovery and development in the face of dispossession. The focus of this discourse is Jones' translation, which uses a poetic, rhetorical style of Māori known as *te reo kohatu*, where *kohatu* (stone) represents the language's ancient and enduring nature. This is in contrast to contemporary Māori language, which has undergone considerable change since the arrival of the British. Indeed, the language literally registers a history of colonisation through the number of slightly modified English words which have entered *te reo*, such as tiriti for treaty. As Scott Morrison, the film's Antonio/Anatonio, a Māori newsreader and part-time lecturer in Māori Education elaborates, Jones' translation is:

> a different kind of language. It's a language you don't hear that often. I believe our language initially belonged to the environment. It developed from the call of birds and the rustling of trees, and so when our ancestors spoke they used imagery and metaphor and simile and other devices in conjunction with the environment to describe their feelings. That kind of expertise is lost in the language now, where a lot of Maori speakers are just using the language to translate their English thought processes and that metaphoric language is lost.

Morrison continues, 'you can see by the way Shakespeare wrote and the way Pei Te Hurinui translated it, that the poetical element is back inside it, so I believe this film will really lift our language and people will get a lot out of it'.[11] Morrison also posits Jones' translation as a return to pre-colonial times, suggesting that the film 'captures the essence of how Maori language would have been spoken before the arrival of Europeans'.[12]

In an ironic paradox, Shakespeare – the emblem of the language which has linguistically colonised aspects of *te reo* – is the vehicle by which Māori are able to reclaim and develop their language. In effect,

Shakespeare becomes the means by which Māori are 'given' back their language, enabling a return to a prelapsarian world before an encounter with European colonisation. In this process, it is as if Shakespeare emerges somehow unscathed as the saviour of the Māori, sheered from associations with a well documented history of colonisation. But, by the same token, Selwyn asserts that the film enhances Shakespeare's plot, characters and setting by 'using Maori language and cultural elements as a vehicle to be able to express the dynamics that Shakespeare came up with'.[13] Here, Māori is credited with improving Shakespeare and releasing 'his' meanings. The film might thus be said to embody Walter Benjamin's thesis that 'in translation the original rises into a higher and purer linguistic air' and his claim that 'it is the task of the translator to release in his own language that pure language which is under the spell of another, to liberate the language imprisoned in a work in his re-creation of that work'.[14] The discourse surrounding the film thus works to blend *te reo* and Shakespeare's English into a seamless hybrid product which improves both languages, eliding any negative associations with a history of colonisation which Shakespeare might be seen to mark. Instead, it seems to propose what Derrida, drawing on Benjamin, might describe as a translation 'that manages to promise reconciliation', both of languages and, by association, cultures.[15] Indeed, Waihoroi Shortland, the film's Shylock/Hairoka, seems to suggest a kind of cultural reconciliation in his claim that Shakespeare's language is 'actually quite synonymous with whaikorero', which is traditional Māori oratory.[16]

The Maori Merchant – through its title and subtitles – also works, however, to undo this seamlessness, playing out a set of hierarchical power relationships between English and Māori, speech and writing. As Lawrence Venuti remarks, 'asymmetries, inequities, relations of domination and dependence exist in every act of translating', and, in New Zealand, these issues can be traced to the inequities produced by the mismatch in meaning between the English and Māori versions of the Treaty/Tiriti.[17] In particular, Māori understood that they ceded *kāwanatanga* (governance), rather than sovereignty, as the English version demanded. *The Maori Merchant* might, then, be seen as an attempt to displace the historical dominance of English instated with the signing of the Treaty/Tiriti. A consideration of the various translations which have led to the finished film helps to clarify these issues. First, Shakespeare's play was translated into classical Māori by Jones; second, Jones' translation was adapted into the screenplay by Selwyn; and third, the Māori voice-track was translated into 'modern' English subtitles, also by Selwyn. The finished product thus privileges Māori over English, with

Shakespeare's text positioned at several relations of difference to the text of *The Maori Merchant*.

The title reinforces this effort to instate the primacy of Māori, especially in relation to Shakespeare's text. In the majority of the media discourse, including He Taonga Films' website, the film is known primarily as *The Maori Merchant of Venice* rather than its Māori title, *Te Tangata Whai Rawa O Weniti*. The twin titles here flag the inability of translation to produce analogues, especially of names. Whereas the Māori title offers a translation of *The Merchant of Venice*, in the English title the word Maori is used to modify the title of Shakespeare's play, *The Merchant of Venice*. If a title, as Derrida suggests, 'names and guaran-tees the identity, the unity and the boundaries of the original work which it entitles', the reconfiguration of the title, both in Māori and as a modified English title, shifts the frame of reference for interpreting the film.[18] The use of the word Maori, which refers both to the Māori people and to *te reo*, effectively displaces the 'original' title of *The Merchant of Venice*. It also offers a succinct way of cannily differentiating the film from other *Merchant*s in the Shakespeare-on-screen marketplace by signalling its ethnic origins. Whereas Baz Luhrmann sought to exploit Shakespeare's cultural authority by naming his film *William Shakespeare's 'Romeo + Juliet'* (1996), the use of the word Māori to sup-plement the English title partially displaces the primacy of Shakespeare from the enterprise: the promise of the title is that Shakespeare's *Merchant* will be remade by Māori and in Māori. This process of dis-placement of English by Māori is further promised through the renam-ing of Shakespeare's characters with Māori names: Hairoka for Shylock, Pohia for Portia, Anatonio for Antonio, Patanio for Bassanio. This reas-signment is, however, fractured by the use of the more familiar Shakespearean names in the subtitles, while the Māori names are spoken by the actors.

This effect of fracture, or unravelling of the alleged seamlessness between spoken Māori and written English, occurs throughout the subtitles with respect to more than the title and the characters' names. Specifically, the brief prosaic nature of the subtitles, in contrast to the lengthy rhetorical speeches in Māori, exposes a series of differences between English and Māori. In this way, the film, as the viewer might expect, privileges speakers of *te reo*, excluding non-speakers from a 'fuller' account of the play's narrative. Here, the film works to counter language dispossession and to displace the primacy of English. But, because it uses a canonical English text and provides English subtitles, which, as supple-ments to the alleged 'fullness' of speech, always add to and threaten to exceed that to which they refer, the film cannot help but be traced, graphically, by the language of colonisation that litters the screen.

Te reo and the Future-to-come

Although Selwyn was aware of Jones' translation in the 1950s, it was not until 1990 that he staged the play as part of Auckland's Te Koanga Spring Festival of Maori Arts, and it took another ten years before funding was secured to produce it as a film. These temporal gaps sustain exploration as they offer a gloss on the history of language dispossession and cultural alienation. Following European contact, the oral language of the Māori began to be expressed in written form and, by 1820, the orthographic foundations of the language were articulated in Thomas Kendall's *A Grammar and Vocabulary of the Language of New Zealand*. As Samuel Lee notes in the preface to Kendall's text, this work was carried out with the aim 'of reducing the language . . . of New Zealand to the rules of Grammar, with a view to the furtherance of the Mission sent out to that country'.[19] Thus *te reo* was codified for the purposes of religious conversion, a key apparatus of colonisation, and also subjected to the rules of European grammars. As the British settlement of New Zealand expanded, *te reo* suffered a series of setbacks. Although the Native Schools Act of 1867 enabled the establishment of primary schools in Māori communities, the language of instruction tended to be in English. This can be read as part of a process of cultural domination on behalf of the new settlers, whereby English was established as the primary mode of communication. This pattern was to continue; even under the more inclusive education policies of the 1930s' labour government, the use of Māori began to decline. This situation was compounded further by the 'urban drift' of Māori into the cities during the 1950s and 1960s; consequently, Māori were further alienated from their language and culture, as highlighted in the 1960 Hunn Report.

In considering the possibility of staging the play, Selwyn remembers Jones saying, 'Kua tae mai te waa – the time will come'.[20] In a sense, Jones proposed a 'future-to-come', a future in which there would be sufficient numbers of Māori speakers to mount such a production. *The Maori Merchant*, spoken entirely in *te reo*, stands as testament to this future-present of cultural recovery. In part, this future has been produced as a response to Māori urban protest movements of the 1970s and to what is commonly termed the Māori cultural Renaissance. This saw a renewed interest in traditional Māori arts such as weaving and carving and also the creation of works that employed Western cultural forms,

such as Witi Ihimaera's short-story collection *Pounamu Pounamu* (1972)
and his novel *Tangi* (1973). Further, the government sought to address
its responsibilities under the Treaty/Tiriti, especially its obligation to
allow Māori to protect their *taonga* (treasures), of which *te reo* is one.
As such, *kōhanga reo* (language nests) were established in 1982, offering
Māori language immersion environments for preschool children, *kura
kaupapa* (schools) were created in 1985, and Māori was designated an
official language of New Zealand in 1987.

The actors' biographies included in the film's press kit stand as witness
to past dispossession and the possibilities for a future where *te reo* has
been encouraged to develop. Andy Sarich's (Tubal/Tupara) biography
notes that he 'grew up speaking the Maori language and was of the generation which was punished for speaking Maori at school and punished
for speaking English at home'.[21] Charting a shift from Sarich's
experience, several of the younger members of the cast noted that they
grew up in families fluent in *te reo*, attended *kōhanga reo* and *kura
kaupapa*, or learned Māori at university. That said, the fact that some
members of the cast noted that they are not fluent in *te reo*, or that they
did not grow up learning Māori, suggests that the utopian future-to-
come is, as the phrase suggests, yet to come. In this respect, it is interesting to note that the government's Māori Language Strategy consultation
document, *He Reo E Kōrerotia Ana – He Reo Ka Ora* [A Spoken
Language is a Living Language]: *A Shared Vision for the Future of Te
Reo Māori*, which was produced by Te Puni Kōkiri (the Ministry of
Māori Development), proposes 2028 as a target date by which:

> the Māori language will be widely spoken among Māori throughout New
> Zealand. In particular, the Māori language will be in common usage within
> Māori homes and communities. By 2028, non-Māori New Zealanders will
> have opportunities to learn and use the Māori language if they choose to.
> New Zealanders will recognise and appreciate the value of the Māori lan-
> guage within New Zealand society.[22]

The Maori Merchant, positioned halfway between the language initiatives which began in the 1970s and the future-to-come of 2028, can thus
be read as a cultural project which indexes the progress of the revival of
te reo at the cusp of the millennium.

Memorials and Responsibilities

Just as the proposed utopian future-to-come will be shadowed by the
traces of colonisation, so too is the present. In this way, *The Maori*

Merchant stands as an emblem of the future/past, condensing both what has gone before and what might be into the event of performance. Writing of justice in relation to accretions of the past and the future, Derrida argues that:

> no justice . . . seems possible or thinkable without the principle of some *responsibility*, beyond all living present, within that which disjoints the living present, before the ghosts of those who are not yet born or who are already dead, be they victims of wars, political or other kinds of violence, nationalist, racist, colonialist, sexist, or other kinds of exterminations, victims of the oppressions of capitalist imperialism or any of the forms of totalitarianism.

He goes on to suggest that it is not possible to ask questions of the future-to-come 'without this responsibility and this respect for justice concerning those who *are not there*, of those who are no longer or who are not yet *present and living*'.[23] *The Maori Merchant* might be said to model such a sense of responsibility to what has gone before and what might come in the context of justice for violations of the Treaty/Tiriti. This is most obviously borne out by an allegorical reading of Shakespeare's play in the context of New Zealand's race relations.

If one strand of *The Merchant of Venice* concerns the violation of a written bond which is then debated in court, an analogy might be made with the interpretation of the Treaty/Tiriti, especially following the government's creation of the Waitangi Tribunal in 1975 to investigate and redress land claims. The Tribunal initially had the power to consider breaches of the Treaty/Tiriti from 1975, but the Treaty Amendment Act of 1985 gave it the power to consider all breaches of the Treaty/Tiriti since it was signed in 1840. This has led to a number of high-profile compensation claims which have resulted in reparations being made to various *iwi*. The film's website and press kit certainly work to locate *The Merchant of Venice* in the context of New Zealand's cultural politics. Shylock's quest for justice is expressed as a desire for *utu*, which is translated as both 'revenge' and the less emotive 'payment' which it also entails. As such, Shylock's efforts to gain redress for the violation of his bond through the courts might be read as a neat reference to the processes of the Tribunal. Shakespeare's plot resonates further in relation to Tahupotiki Wiremu Ratana's successful spiritual and political mission, which was established in the 1920s. The Ratana movement located the Māori as God's 'Chosen People' in place of the Jews and interpreted the Old Testament as a parable for the displacement and suffering of the

Māori. Shortland makes this connection between Māori and Judaism explicit when he says:

> playing Shylock from a Maori perspective is the easiest role because you know something of what it is to hang onto your identity and to deal with prejudice, some of it overt, some of it not so overt, in the New Zealand sense anyway . . . I see him as acting on behalf of his people.[24]

The analogues between Shakespeare's play and the history of the Māori do, however, warp under the weight of further analysis to reinforce the oppression of the Māori. Indeed, the film's 'one-liner' tag, 'Revenge is not so sweet', taken to its logical conclusion in relation to New Zealand, would seem to suggest that the quest to honour the 'bond' of the Treaty/Tiriti cannot be fulfilled through the processes of the legal system. The film's courtroom scene certainly resonates in a New Zealand context in the ways I have suggested. It is, however, through extra-textual referents that the film most clearly references a sense of responsibility to the past and the future-to-come. This is most sharply articulated in the film's representation of I.iii, where Antonio/Anatonio makes his bond with Shylock/Hairoka.

As Bassanio/Patanio and Shylock/Hairoka begin their negotiations, the camera tracks their journey through a Venetian marketplace before Bassanio/Patanio introduces Antonio/Anatonio to Shylock/Hairoka in an artist's studio. As the scene progresses, through a sequence of slow-moving shots that highlight the division between the Christians and the Jew, the camera also captures scenes from the paintings that hug the perimeter of the studio. These images, painted by Māori artist Selwyn Muru, who is present as a painter in the diegesis, offer yet another instance of intercultural production. Thus, Muru uses the medium of painting to depict Māori history, which traditionally was recorded orally and through carving. More tellingly, the paintings offer a visual record of the conflict over land between Māori and *Pākehā* at Parihaka in the 1880s; coincidentally, in 2000/01, Wellington's City Gallery housed an exhibition entitled 'Parihaka: The Art of Passive Resistance', which explored the legacy of Parihaka in New Zealand art. While the Treaty/Tiriti gave the crown first option of buying land, the history of land purchase in New Zealand is enmeshed in narratives of land confiscation. The *pa* (village) at Parihaka, situated near Mount Taranaki, whose imposing shape is registered in Muru's paintings, attracted Māori who were drawn to the teachings of the prophets Te Whiti-o-Rongomai and Toho Kakahi. These prophets are remembered primarily for their campaigns of pacifism and passive resistance against *Pākehā* attempts to survey land. These programmes met, however, with an invasion of 644 troops and 1,000 settler volunteers on 5 November 1881, which resulted in the destruction of the *pa* and the arrest of the prophets. In the inclusion of paintings which depict this event, *The Maori Merchant* reiterates the memory of this traumatic event, emblematic of more widespread land dispossession and violence. It is, though, in the closing moments of this scene that the film works, most pointedly, to stand as witness to past events.

As Antonio/Anatonio and Bassanio/Patanio leave the studio, the paintings, which have occupied a peripheral position throughout most of the foregoing scene, are brought to the centre of the filmic gaze. Focusing on one painting, the camera pans up. At the bottom of the painting the spectator sees the word 'holocaust', distributed along the painting's vertical axis to read 'HO/LO/CA/UST'. As the camera reaches the top of the painting, the phonemes are again shown, rearranged horizontally to spell 'HOLOCAUST'. In this double iteration, the word 'holocaust' registers multiple meanings which spectators are forced to witness, their responses shaped by the particular circumstances of their cultural backgrounds. The dominant meaning that 'holocaust' carries is, of course, the genocide of 6 million Jews under the instruction of Nazi Germany. The insertion of the word thus provides a reminder of the way in which all productions of *The Merchant of Venice* after the holocaust are traced by this traumatic history. In a film that has resolutely insisted on the primacy of *te reo*, the insertion of an English word into the diegesis provides a sharp reminder of the linguistic colonisation that has created the need for the film in the first instance: literally, a linguistic holocaust is referenced. The dual iteration also signifies at the level of contemporary national politics.

In 1996, the Waitangi Tribunal released a report on land claims in the Taranaki region. In a paragraph buried near the end of the lengthy report, Chapter 12.3.3 states:

> as to quantum, the gravamen of our report has been to say that the Taranaki claims are likely to be the largest in the country. The graphic muru [confiscation] of most of Taranaki and the raupatu [conquest and marginalisation] without ending describe the holocaust of Taranaki history and the denigration of the founding peoples in a continuum from 1840 to the present.[25]

The report thus makes a connection between the effects of colonisation on the Māori and the way in which the term is more commonly associated with Hitler's programme of genocide. The term 'holocaust' was to resurface amidst much public controversy in 2000. In an address to the NZ Psychological Society Conference, Tariana Turia, an Associate

Minister of Te Puni Kōkiri, claimed that, while post-traumatic stress disorder was readily considered in relation to holocaust survivors and Vietnam veterans, 'what seems not to have received similar attention is the holocaust suffered by indigenous people including Maori as a result of colonial contact and behaviour'.[26] Turia's comments here, alongside her assertion in parliament that Māori child abuse could be linked to the effects of colonisation, were attacked. The New Zealand First leader Winston Peters dismissed Turia's claims as 'psychobabble', while National MP Roger Sowry asserted that it was 'the most off-the-planet speech by a politician in living memory'.[27] Further, a member of the Auckland Jewish Council commented that it was a pity that Turia 'reinforced the Waitangi Tribunal's use of the word'. Finally, prime minister Helen Clark issued the following edict: 'I know the [Waitangi] tribunal used it [holocaust] with respect to Taranaki. I do not agree with that and I do not want to see ministers using the term and causing offence again'. She went on to say: 'I don't accept that the word holocaust can be validly used about the New Zealand experience . . . I would not use that particular term, which has a specific and very tragic meaning'.[28] Subsequently, Turia made a speech in parliament that, while apologising for any offence caused, did not offer an official retraction of the term holocaust.[29]

The scene in the artist's studio was shot after Turia had been castigated, and Selwyn says that 'they couldn't resist' referring to it in film.[30] The inclusion of this textual referent, coupled with the images of Parihaka, offers a graphic (in a literal sense) representation of the dispossession of the Māori in the context of other histories of dispossession; indeed, the term has been used in relation to other indigenous peoples, such as David E. Stannard's analysis of the effects of colonisation on indigenous cultures in the Americas.[31] In banning the word (for government ministers at least), Clark limited the vocabulary available to account for cultural history, highlighting the way in which language can be used both to articulate and limit self-representation. In referencing the word 'holocaust', *The Maori Merchant* unshackles it from its ban and makes a case for the right to self-representation. As part of this programme of self-representation, Selwyn was keen to showcase *te reo* to the world via the international film festival circuit and DVD and video sales. In what follows, I want to explore the way in which Selwyn's vision of global distribution, and the images of Māori that his film offers, are imbricated in the politics of self-representation and mechanisms of globalisation, frequently associated with latter-day colonisation.

The Maori Merchant in Local/Global Marketplaces

The processes of globalisation are usually characterised as disseminating the homogenous cultural products of transnational corporations and destroying local markets and products. At the same time, these corporations are credited with the commodification of 'indigenous' products for resale in Western marketplaces as 'authentic' exotica. These processes are most striking in the sale of material items, such as wood-carvings, rugs and wall-hangings, but apply also to the sphere of performance. The Globe-to-Globe season at Shakespeare's Globe Theatre on London's Bankside illustrates this phenomenon. The Theatre's website states that Globe-to-Globe productions are intended as a celebration of 'the impact Shakespeare's plays have had worldwide'. The website also lists criteria for such productions, suggesting that they should be in 'a style true to the artistic, cultural and social traditions of the country of origin', use 'the language indigenous to the country of origin', be 'based on a plot true to the original Shakespearean story', employ 'live music in a manner integral to the staging', and incorporate 'a strong element of physicality'.[32] These productions have included *Umabatha, The Zulu Macbeth* from South Africa (1997, 2001), an Indian *Kathakali-King Lear* (1999), and Grupo Galpao's Brazilian *Romeu & Julieta* (2000). As the Globe's criteria and the media responses suggest, these productions function primarily as exoticised objects, an ethnic wonder-cabinet for the London stage. A similar phenomenon can be seen on the film festival circuit where the Sundance, Toronto and Cannes film festivals frequently laud films about cultures outside dominant Anglo-American cultural formations, such as the Inuit film *Atanarjuat (The Fast Runner)* (2000), or New Zealand's *Whale Rider* (2002).

The trade in this kind of intercultural performance rests on the notion of cultural authenticity. As Johannes Birringer notes, the global tourist economy 'generates the imperative to construct "authentic" indigenous local cultures for display and tourist consumption'.[33] New Zealand's tourist industry exploits just this notion of authenticity from the '100% Pure New Zealand' advertising campaign, where visitors are offered the 'real' New Zealand experience which in turn will enable them to 'rejuvenate' their spirits, to the participatory commodification of Māori culture with the promise that visitors can 'experience' Māori culture for themselves.[34] These sentiments reverberate in films such as Niki Caro's *Whale Rider* which, as Claire Murdoch argues, is 'fostered from an indigenous myth, washed (intentionally or not) in the gloss of its national and international arts-export ideology' in which cultural authenticity becomes 'one, totemic and inherently "meaningful" part of an appealing package'.[35] *Whale Rider*, the first recipient of a grant from the government's Film Production Fund, can, as Murdoch notes, be seen as a state-sponsored extension of Helen Clark's vision expressed in her speech 'Building Cultural Identity'. Here, film is credited with influencing 'the way we see ourselves and our country – and the way the rest of the world sees us too'.[36] Clark's use of 'we', 'ourselves' and 'us' raises a series of issues about identity and representation, especially in relation to representations of Māori culture. Indeed, *Whale Rider* was criticised for having a *Pākehā* director and production company, despite the fact that Caro had learnt *te reo* and had gained permission from the Ngati Konohi *iwi* to make the film on location in Whangara.

Filmed in *te reo* with an almost entirely Māori cast and director, *The Maori Merchant* seems, in contrast to *Whale Rider*, to exemplify Māori self-determination. However, it offers a perhaps unexpected take on the ethics and images of self-representation. A media release notes that 'contrary to what some expect, there are no piupius [traditional clothing] and no mokos [facial tattoos] in this vision of cross-cultural fertilisation'.[37] Similarly, as producer Ruth Kaupapa Panapa affirms, 'in this movie there are no tattoos, no leather jackets and no men in blue uniforms' or references to gang culture or the police.[38] Instead, *The Maori Merchant*, with its representation of Māori actors in Renaissance costumes, counterpoised against more familiar signifiers of Māori culture, seems to play with or parody the notion of cultural authenticity and 'exoticism'. In so doing, it offers a challenge to the pervasive association between Māori and violence propagated by Lee Tamahori's internationally successful *Once Were Warriors* (1994). As Kaupapa Panapa comments, 'we were sick and tired of seeing so much [Māori] violence in films. There is conflict in this film but it is not highlighted in a violent way'.[39] *The Maori Merchant* also challenges the other dominant vision of Māori available to international audiences: Jane Campion's representation of traditional Māori tribal life, which functions as a backdrop to a Western narrative of colonial romance in *The Piano* (1993). Unlike many indigenous films which are read as an analogue of the 'real' (which may or may not be the intention of the filmmakers), *The Maori Merchant* refuses this collapse. As Valerie Wayne suggests, the film's 'derivative narrative in a sense shields it from being taken as a direct representation of contemporary Māori experience'.[40] Instead, it proposes an alternative vision which celebrates images of Māori in a fantastical filmic diegesis. While articulating a right to self-representation, the film is, however, still implicated in processes that work to commodify Māori ethnic identity for consumption in Western entertainment markets.

Despite the fact that *The Maori Merchant* has yet to acquire sufficient commercial success to be commodified on a global scale as a piece of indigenous 'exotica', this narrative still infuses the film, played out on the bodies of the cast, crew and New Zealand landscape. Many of the cast were first-time actors, with backgrounds in teaching or Māori broadcasting. Others, though, had acted in a range of film and television productions, from the local soap opera *Shortland Street* to Hollywood-funded motion pictures, such as *Rapa Nui* (1994). Behind the camera, the production designer Guy Moana has worked on *Hercules, The Legendary Journeys* and *Xena: Warrior Princess*, and Selwyn was employed as a cultural advisor for *Rapa Nui*. Further, the 1990s saw a rise in the number of international film and television production companies shooting their films in New Zealand. This is due to New Zealand's relatively low production costs and an apparently infinitely malleable landscape, able to stand for J. R. R. Tolkien's Middle Earth and Japan in Tom Cruise's epic *The Last Samurai* (2003), not to mention the *faux* ancient worlds of *Xena* and *Hercules*. Alongside these developments in the 'local' film industry, Māori actors, like the New Zealand landscape, have found themselves commodified by Hollywood, variously playing Iraqis, Columbians, Easter Islanders and the entire clone army in *Star Wars* episodes two and three. It is as if Māori are able to function in the global filmic marketplace as blank ethnic signifiers, able to be substituted for any non-European nationality, almost invariably playing roles with negative character trajectories.

Although this process of commodification invites (and warrants) reading in terms of cultural imperialism, or latter-day colonisation, I am interested here in exploring how *The Maori Merchant* also offers a counter-narrative in which these processes of commodification and distribution are deployed as a means of attempting to redress some of the damage created by colonisation. *The Maori Merchant* was made primarily for an audience fluent in *te reo*, with the aim of recovering lost aspects of the Māori language, encouraging Māori to learn *te reo*, and, in the longer term, to become an educational resource. Using a slow-release strategy, the film toured around New Zealand and was screened at a series of charity premières to benefit the Pei Te Hurinui Jones Trust, formed to fund creative writing in *te reo*. In this way, He Taonga Films located *The Maori Merchant* as a performance event, designed to showcase it to maximum cultural effect and raise money to benefit Māori education. The film also screened on the newly launched Māori

Television channel in 2004. This channel is the latest addition to Māori broadcasting which, as the cast biographies note, has included *Te Karere*, the Māori language news programme, Ruia Mai, a Māori language radio production company, and *Marae*, a Māori magazine programme. The biographies and network screening stand as testament to the development of Māori (language) broadcasting, which has benefited from government support; indeed, the film was funded by Te Māngai Pāho, the crown entity that funds Māori broadcasting. The film also screened as part of the Inaugural Wairoa Maori Film Festival (2005) and can thus be seen as an integral part of the development of Māori filmmaking which this festival marked.

In addition to this local development agenda, Selwyn also sought to tap international markets to gain exposure for the Māori language. Indeed, it was Selwyn's intention 'to introduce the Maori language to the world through this'.[41] Alongside positive reviews in New Zealand and the Award of Best Actor for Shortland at the 2003 New Zealand Film Awards, the film won the Blockbuster Audience Award for Best Feature Film at the 2002 Louis Vuitton Hawaii International Film Festival, and was screened at the second Denver Indigenous Film and Arts Festival in 2005. Outside the festival circuit, screenings of the film at the 2003 meeting of the Shakespeare Association of America in Victoria, British Columbia and at a 2004 seminar on Māori Shakespeare at the International Centre for Writing and Translation at the University of California, Irvine proved popular; chapters on the film have also been included in this collection and in Sonia Massai's *World-Wide Shakespeares*.[42] As such, it would seem that the film has, indeed, managed to acquire a place in the niche (film and academic) markets of metropolitan centres. However, given that *The Maori Merchant* has received only limited international festival play and given that the much awaited multi-language subtitled DVD has yet to be released, Selwyn's dream of taking 'Maori language to the world' has yet to come to pass outside these relatively small markets.

Speaking Māori (Shakespeare)

The Maori Merchant might, then, be situated alongside productions of Shakespeare in New Zealand that have drawn attention to the politics of their location, particularly with respect to race relations and colonisation. These include Theatre at Large's *Manawa Taua/Savage Hearts* (1994), which rewrote *Othello* as part of a colonial fable, and the Court Theatre's *Othello* (2001), which set the play in the context of the 1860s' land wars. Taken together, these productions make a mockery of New Zealand actor and director Ian Mune's dismissal of the concept of 'New Zealand Shakespeare' with the words 'Not yet' at a 2000 panel discussion on 'Shakespeare in the Pacific'.[43] In the scenes set in Belmont/Peremona and in the artist's studio, coupled with the film's large cast of actors performing in the once profoundly endangered *te reo* and the celebratory mode in which it was produced and received, *The Maori Merchant* offers what Mark Houlahan describes as a 'luminous example' of just such a New Zealand Shakespeare.[44] In considering *The Maori Merchant*, I have suggested that this New Zealand (Māori) Shakespeare, while promoting an apparently seamless relation between Shakespeare and Māori, is, however, also traced by the effects of colonisation which it works to redress. *The Maori Merchant* thus functions as a spectre, always already reaching back and looking forward. As such, it stands as a monument to the trauma and on-going effects of what has gone before, and in its potential life as an educational resource and voice of *te reo* on national and global markets, offers a glimpse of the future-to-come. In keeping with Selwyn's goals to revitalise the Māori language, this is a future in which *te reo* is secure and, perhaps, one in which Shakespeare is secondary, rather than positioned as pivotal, to that security.[45]

Notes

1. *The Maori Merchant of Venice/Te Tangata Whai Rawa O Weniti*, directed by Don C. Selwyn (Auckland: He Taonga Films, 2001). The film was released in February 2002 in New Zealand. Long vowel sounds in Māori are denoted either by a macron or a double vowel; Maori can thus be expressed as 'Māori' or 'Maaori'. In this chapter, I have used macrons, except where they are absent from the texts I cite.
2. My analysis of New Zealand history is indebted to Michael King (2003), *The Penguin History of New Zealand*, Auckland: Penguin.
3. The Treaty/Tiriti is held in the National Archives in Wellington, and copies of the text, in English and Māori, can be located via http://www.waitangi-tribunal.govt.nz/about/treatyofwaitangi. See Statistics New Zealand for a detailed analysis of demographic trends relating to Māori and non-Māori New Zealanders (http://www.stats.govt.nz/default.htm). See also the *Survey of the Health of the Māori Language in 2001 (Part 1)*, available at http://www.tpk.govt.nz/publications/docs/survey_health_maori_lang01.pdf and *Survey of the Health of the Māori Language in 2001 (Part 2 – Appendices)*, available at http://www.tpk.govt.nz/publications/docs/survey_health_maori_lang_append.pdf, for details about developments in the Māori language and an indication of the work still to be conducted.
4. Rustom Bharucha (1993), *Theatre and the World: Performance and the Politics of Culture*, London: Routledge, pp. 4, 241. See Ania Loomba (1998), ' "Local-manufacture made-in-India Othello fellows": Issues of race, hybridity and location in post-colonial Shakespeares', in Ania Loomba and Martin Orkin (eds),

Post-Colonial Shakespeares, London: Routledge, pp. 143–63, and W. B. Worthen (2003), *Shakespeare and the Force of Modern Performance*, Cambridge: Cambridge University Press, pp. 117–68.

5. *The Maori Merchant of Venice* press kit, p. 3. The press kit can be downloaded from http://homepages.ihug.co.nz/~hetaonga/merchant/Media_Files/media_files.html, and all subsequent references will be to 'press kit'; Sam Edwards (2002), review of *The Maori Merchant of Venice/Te Tangata Whai Rawa O Weniti*, *Waikato Times*, 18 February.

6. Pei Te Hurinui [Jones] (1946), *Te Tangata Whai-Rawa O Weniti*, Palmerston North, New Zealand: H. L. Young.

7. MacDonald Jackson offers a summary of the film's narrative elisions and rearrangements and an acute list of errors in the subtitles in 'All our tribe', *Landfall*, 204 (2002), pp. 156–7.

8. Jacques Derrida (2001), 'What is a "relevant" translation?', *Critical Inquiry*, 27.2, p. 177.

9. Don Selwyn quoted in press kit, p. 38.

10. Selwyn quoted in Veronica Schmidt (2002), 'Te Bard', *Listener*, 2 February, p. 52.

11. Scott Morrison quoted in press kit, p. 17.

12. Morrison quoted in 'Shakespeare goes Maori', *BBC News*, 4 December 2001, available at http://news.bbc.co.uk/1/hi/entertainment/film/1691261.stm.

13. Press kit, pp. 8–9.

14. Walter Benjamin (1992), *Illuminations*, ed. Hannah Arendt, trans. Harry Zohn, London: Fontana-HarperCollins, pp. 75, 80.

15. Jacques Derrida (1985), *Difference in Translation*, trans. and ed. Joseph F. Graham, Ithaca: Cornell University Press, p. 191.

16. Waihoroi Shortland quoted in Margo White (2002), 'Shakespeare korero', *Metro*, March, p. 115.

17. Lawrence Venuti (1998), *The Scandals of Translation: Towards an Ethics of Difference*, London: Routledge, p. 4.

18. Jacques Derrida (1992), *Acts of Literature*, ed. Derek Attridge, New York: Routledge, p. 188.

19. Samuel Lee, preface to Thomas Kendall (1920), *A Grammar and Vocabulary of the Language of New Zealand*, London: Church Missionary Society, n.p.

20. Selwyn quoted in Peter Calder (2002), 'Footy to fairies – and way beyond', *The New Zealand Herald*, 16 February (http://www.nzherald.co.nz/index.cfm?ObjectID=939653).

21. Andy Sarich quoted in press kit, p. 28.

22. Te Puni Kōkiri (Ministry of Māori Development) (2003), *He Reo E Kōrerotia Ana – He Reo Ka Ora, A Shared Vision for the Future of Te Reo Māori*, March (http://www.tpk.govt.nz/publications/docs/korerotia_english.pdf), p. 6.

23. Jacques Derrida (1994), *Spectres of Marx: The State of the Debt, the Work of Mourning, and the New International*, trans. Peggy Kamuf, New York: Routledge, p. xix; Derrida's emphasis.

24. Shortland quoted in press kit, p. 13.

25. Waitangi Tribunal (1996), *The Taranaki Report – Kaupapa Tuatahi* (http://www.waitangi-tribunal.govt.nz/reports/niwest/wai143/wai143b.asp).

26. Tariana Turia quoted in 'What Tariana Turia said – in full', *The New Zealand Herald*, 31 August 2000 (http://www.nzherald.co.nz/index.cfm?ObjectID=149643).

27. Winston Peters and Roger Sowry quoted in Audrey Young (2002), 'Minister hammers colonial "holocaust"', *The New Zealand Herald*, 30 August (http://www.nzherald.co.nz/index.cfm?ObjectID=149518).

28. Wendy Ross and Helen Clark quoted in Audrey Young (2000), 'Holocaust apology puts minister in hot water', *The New Zealand Herald*, 6 September (http://www.nzherald.co.nz/index.cfm?ObjectID=150333).

29. 'Audio and transcript: Tariana Turia's apology', *The New Zealand Herald*, 6 September 2000 (http://www.nzherald.co.nz/index.cfm?ObjectID=150332).

30. Selwyn quoted in White, 'Shakespeare korero', p. 115.

31. David E. Stannard (1992), *American Holocaust: The Conquest of the New World*, New York: Oxford University Press.

32. http://www.shakespeares-globe.org/navigation/frameset.htm. Enter 'Globe-to-Globe' in the search panel and follow the links for 'Globe-to-Globe' and 'Artistic Criteria Globe-to-Globe Productions'.

33. Johannes Birringer (2000), *Performance on the Edge: Transformations of Culture*, London: Athlone, p. 164.

34. See http://www.newzealand.com/travel for links to the '100% Pure New Zealand' advertising campaign and Māori tourism.

35. Claire Murdoch (2003), 'Holy sea-cow', *Landfall*, 206, p. 103.

36. Helen Clark (2000), 'Building cultural identity', 18 May (http://www.beehive.govt.nz/ViewDocument.aspx?DocumentID=7442).

37. Press kit, p. 3.

38. Ruth Kaupapa Panapa quoted in Caitlin Sykes (2002), 'Manukau film-maker at forefront of industry', *Manukau Courier*, 7 March.

39. Kaupapa Panapa quoted in Sykes, 'Manukau film-maker'.

40. Valerie Wayne (2004), review of *Te Tangata Whai Rawa O Weniti/The Māori Merchant of Venice*, *The Contemporary Pacific*, 16.2, p. 428.

41. Selwyn quoted in Libby Middlebrook (2000), 'Language test for Shakespeare play', *The New Zealand Herald*, 24 November (http://www.nzherald.co.nz/index.cfm?ObjectID=161717).

42. Mark Houlahan (2005), 'Hekepia? The *Mana* of the Maori *Merchant*', in Sonia Massai (ed.), *World-Wide Shakespeares: Local Appropriations in Film and Performance*, London: Routledge, pp. 141–8.

43. Ian Mune quoted in Houlahan, 'Hekepia?', p. 148.

44. Houlahan, 'Hekepia?', p. 148.

45. A version of this chapter was presented at the 2005 meeting of the British Shakespeare Association in Newcastle-upon-Tyne. I am grateful for comments from audience members and my co-panellists Mark Thornton Burnett, Susanne Greenhalgh and Robert Shaughnessy, and also to Mark Houlahan, Judith Pryor, Julie Scanlon, Tory Young and Lindsey Moore.

Chapter 8

'Into a thousand parts divide one man': Dehumanised Metafiction and Fragmented Documentary in Peter Babakitis' *Henry V*

Sarah Hatchuel

Peter Babakitis' *Henry V* (2004) is the third English-language version of the play adapted for the cinema, coming after Laurence Olivier's 1944 and Kenneth Branagh's 1989 interpretations. Produced in the US, and distributed mainly through festivals and conventions rather than cinematic release, this post-millennium version of *Henry V* occupies a distinctive place in Shakespearean filmmaking in that it oscillates between two visual forms that are typical of the start of the twenty-first century – digital stylisation and docu-drama. Although these types of aesthetic would appear to be antithetically related, this essay argues that they come together in their fragmentation and dehumanisation of the filmic material. With the aid of computer-assisted techniques of digitalisation, Babakitis' film fragments time and space, creating different zones and dimensions, sometimes verging on the supernatural. The filmic material is transformed into a mixture of heterogeneous styles, isolating the character of Henry V within his own artificial dimension, within shots of his own and within colours of his own. Such an isolation of the main protagonist leads him to communicate less with the other characters in the narrative than with the film's audience. Henry's separation from the diegetic environment contributes to dehumanising him, since he is elaborated as an unreachable and indestructible leader. The digitalising techniques are complemented by a shooting/editing style strongly reminiscent of the genre of the docu-drama, since *Henry V* wavers between fiction and documentary and exploits such methods as reconstruction and re-enactment. This docu-drama influence again favours visual fragmentation, mainly through the journalistic film technique of fast jump-cuts and editorial discontinuity. Babakitis' adoption of the docu-drama style also results in a dehumanisation of the Chorus, whose part, transformed into the impersonal voice of an announcer, is ideologically implicated in the erasure of many of the play's ironic moments.

As it combines stylisation and docu-drama, Babakitis' *Henry V* appears as a synthesis of the two earlier cinematic versions. Olivier's *Henry V* is well known for the emphasis placed upon artifice and stylised metafiction. Opening at the Globe theatre in Shakespeare's time, the film introduces a framing device: the centrifugal experience of the cinema only begins when the Chorus refers to the departure of the English army. But these initial interpolations remain at some distance from the usual realism of cinema. The distorted perspectives, inspired by medieval illuminated manuscripts, point up the artificiality of the sets. Only the battle of Agincourt drives the viewer into realism. Alternation between theatrical, stylised and realistic modes of direction generates a self-consciousness about the media utilised both by the play and its subsequent adaptations. By contrast, Branagh's *Henry V* is famous for resorting to techniques that are particular to documentary, as the film aims to re-create the reality of medieval battles. During the retreat at Harfleur, the soldiers, running to escape from the horrors at the walls, are filmed with their backs towards the audience, as if followed by a reporter. The spectre of the war correspondent is conjured again when we join the Chorus just before the battle of Agincourt. He walks rapidly towards us along a palisade of wooden stakes, earnestly describing the enormous event about to take place. At the end of the battle, the corpses of the slaughtered boys are shown in one continuous shot, once more filmed as if by the hand-held camera of a journalist sent to cover the war. Babakitis' *Henry V* blends these two traditions, conflating the artifice of Olivier's metafiction and the authenticity of Branagh's documentary-like style.

Babakitis' adaptation is distinctive first in its extensive use of digital effects. Images are crafted numerically in forms and colours, which gives them the peculiar appearance of 'Penny Arcade' video games. This style is reminiscent of the digitally composed shots of Julie Taymor's *Titus* (2000), where surreal, nightmarish images of fire and body parts are repeatedly superimposed upon the characters of Tamora and Titus, creating shared memories of violence and murder. But, in Babakitis' *Henry V*, digital shots serve less to reveal the landscapes of the characters' minds than to develop the heterogeneity of the filmic material. The first speech of the Chorus is accompanied by graphic images successively displaying a skull, a medieval illuminated book, the agitated hoofs of horses viewed through red filters, and two castles (standing for the kingdoms of France and England) separated by a digitally shortened Channel and standing out against an artificial-looking, cloudy sky. From the beginning, the film thus mixes different kinds of images, moving rapidly from written words to picturesque worlds, from the symbol of death to energetic animal activity. The first sequence sets the scene for a film that has as its chief imaginative impetus notions of patchwork and heterogeneity. The sequences devoted to the siege of Harfleur and the battle of Agincourt both include digitally processed 'Penny-Arcade' shots in which splashes of saturated colour contrast with a predominantly greyish background. The combat is often discovered in slow motion, either through filters which change from warm to cold colours or via a dazzling effect created by an interaction between sunlight and the camera lens. With the aid of special effects, unusual viewpoints are facilitated, allowing for such arrestingly subjective shots as those that pursue the course of arrows through the air. Reality is mingled with the occult, as black-hooded figures of death are glimpsed hovering menacingly over the battlefield, recalling the powerful, *memento mori* image of the skull at the film's start. Through digitalisation, the film thus fragments space into different (time or colour) zones, supernaturally juxtaposing various dimensions and working on visual associations, whether literal or metaphorical.

In such a context, Henry V (Peter Babakitis) is dehumanised and 'digitalised'. He is often filmed in exaggerated close-ups and low-angle shots, through colour filters, with stylised slow motion or in front of numerically composed sets. During his infuriated speech before the three traitors, Henry's face is filmed in close-up, heavily lit from the side and standing out against a background in which the other nobles barely stir, as if the image had been frozen. The end of the speech reveals Henry speaking before a digital sky. In the background, the traitors' severed gory heads are held aloft on pikes, and a flag waves in slow motion. This effect is repeated towards the end of the film, when the King reads out the list of the dead soldiers. Henry is shot in profile against the sunlight; he speaks at a normal pace but, paradoxically, a flag flutters in slow motion behind him. It is as if the time were 'out of joint' and dislocated inside a single shot: Henry speaks in the normative, present tense, while his environment operates in a slower mode. Since Henry is often highlighted inside an alien setting, either artificially still, slow-motioned or digitally constructed, he appears to belong to a different dimension, to embody an autonomous and self-governing figure from another place and time zone. These effects convey the King's independent spirit, and also provide him with a powerful immunity against political vicissitude. For example, as he passes through the battlefield, hails of arrows fall around him; yet, magically, none makes contact with his form. The digital construction of the shot allows the audience to witness a small miracle – belonging to an alternative dimension, the King is able to avoid any wound or destruction in a here-and-now situation.

In fact, this version of Henry hardly interacts with his diegetic environment. He is constructed as generally located in a frame of his own, without other characters invading his space. The conversations he conducts with his men are filmed in shots/counter-shots, an editing decision that separates him constantly from his subjects. Even during the wooing scene, no viewpoint discovers Henry and Catherine together in the same frame. The audience is obliged to wait until the Princess is finally won to catch a one-shot glimpse of a shadow-graphed Henry and Catherine kissing in bed together. This spatial isolation of the King through cinematic editing is emphasised via a purposeful discontinuity in the colour composition of the shots/counter-shots. For instance, as Henry talks to the Herald, the shots of Montjoy are shown through blue filters, while the counter-shots of Henry remain in natural colours. A similar aesthetic discontinuity unfolds as Henry talks with the soldiers on the eve of the battle – Henry's own space is characterised by a nocturnal hue that is different from that of his soldiers. Diegesis is fragmented and contributes to the impression of a character-type marked by being reclusive and independent.

Henry may not interrelate with others, but he is the only character in the film to build a relationship with the audience. Because he regularly speaks his lines directly to camera, he is envisaged as oriented more towards the extradiegetic world than the diegetic. In Branagh's *Henry V*, the King delivers the line 'No king of England, if not king of France' in profile with a faraway look, as if lost in an ambitious dream, but Babakitis' monarch puts his crown firmly upon his head and looks at the spectators with a defiant determination.[1] By making the viewer self-conscious, the film deviates from the Hollywood ideology that attempts to conceal the very mechanism of artistic creation in classical realist films by forbidding the actor from looking at the camera. In Olivier and Branagh's versions, the Chorus is the only character granted permission to look at the camera in a Brechtian, alienating way. In both films, Henry remains a character wholly immersed in the diegetic world, never questioning or disclosing his status as an actor.[2] In Babakitis' adaptation, by contrast, the spectators are reminded of their own bodies and voyeuristic positions by the royal figure himself. Henry's gaze, which is directed at the camera, introduces a reversal that betrays and underlines the technical apparatus not only within the frame of the story, but also from inside the main dramatic action. Through the very disclosure of his acting status, the monarch clearly displays his histrionic and Machiavellian qualities.

If Babakitis revels in the stylisation and metafiction offered by new technologies and *avant-garde* cinema, he also aims at providing an impression of naturalism. In interview, he stated, 'I knew from the outset that I wanted an authentic approach to the battles in *Henry V*,' adding that the battle of Agincourt 'ought to look like CNN coverage of all the wars that go on today, with all the chaotic, unplanned shocks that appear in real documentary footage of the so-called "embedded" video journalists'.[3] The director's reflections are thus intimately related to the contextual underpinnings of the film's moment of production. Babakitis' cinematography, for instance, seems heavily influenced by media footage provided by 'embedded' commentators during the 2003 British and American invasion of Iraq. Notably, media treatment of the war involved hand-held cameras and jump-cut shooting, since journalists participated in the operations. In *Henry V*, accordingly, the final battle is turned into a chaos of soldiers, bowmen and horses via a *mise-en-scène* which uses a crowd of extras (apparently numerically magnified), and which purposefully confuses and disorganises editing and framing practice. Horrors of the battlefield are not concealed, but, rather, openly displayed in the form of bloody stabbings and ruthless beheadings. This desire to appropriate the aesthetic of the documentary in a fiction film betrays an attempt to capture a sense of the 'truth' of the originary historical moment. The rapid juxtaposition of shots covering the same action aims at communicating the impression of an ambiguous reality, and, here, the deployment of competing angles is essential. Babakitis' aesthetic thus aspires to apprehend history in all of its ambivalence and to elicit objective judgements on the parts of the spectators. According to William Guynn, the discursive form of the documentary, as opposed to that of fiction, encourages a greater spectatorial vigilance: viewers are in a position to summon up 'processes of awakened thought and controlled reasoning' when faced with facts that are presumed 'real'.[4] Experiencing a documentary as opposed to a fiction film, a spectator can no longer fantasise about the presence of the actors or the objects, since what is presented is a succession of events that have already taken place.[5] Babatikis' importation of this aesthetic may have been stimulated, therefore, by the desire to introduce into the imaginative representation of events a certain genuineness at the same time as his film activates a state of watchfulness, and a capacity for lucidity, in its audience.

One of the major differences between documentary and fiction is the existence (or lack) of a contract that is agreed between the audience and the filmic material. When we watch a fiction film, we know for a fact that what we see is only an illusion, yet still we suppress our knowledge. Such a denial of illusion, contractually settled upon between the film and its spectators, is one of fiction's essential components. The documentary can be defined, by contrast, as a cinematic genre which claims to operate without having recourse to this convention.[6] According to Roger Odin, the 'difference between a fiction film and a documentary is only a difference in terms of . . . a system of belief (or reading contract)'.[7] A reading that 'documentarises' can thus be applied to a fiction film, and a reading that 'fictionalises' can be applied to a documentary. In the case of a reading that fictionalises, the spectator will annex the filmic work to the realm of myth or pure fiction. In the case of a reading that 'documentarises', by contrast, the spectator will imagine a supposedly 'real' enunciative authority at work beyond the images. Each specific aesthetic, culturally linked to fiction or documentary, will contribute to guiding the spectators' general reading practice. By adopting the specific style of jump-cut editing and amateurish, raw footage suggestive of the journalistic representation of actual conflict, Babakitis' fiction film plays with the viewing contract that has been agreed with the spectators. We wonder what processes are at work when the aesthetics of documentary are deployed to figure events that are not real but only reconstructed. By attempting to present fiction as non-fiction, in fact, *Henry V* may engage in manipulation, a similar species of manipulation to that which is found in one of the most popular forms of television at the start of the twenty-first century – the 'docu-drama' or 'drama-documentary' (a TV drama based on actual occurrences and real people). This hybrid form blurs the boundaries between fiction and authentic footage. Although it is based on historical research, documentation and evidence, as is a documentary, the 'docu-drama' enlists the dramatic and narrative grammar of fiction film to mediate and appropriate the real world, whether present, past or anticipated.[8] For instance, in 2004, BBC2 broadcast a docu-drama entitled *Dunkirk*. According to the BBC website, the programme was intended to 'grip audiences with its historical relevance and . . . factual authenticity', for it retold 'the events of May 1940 from the perspective of the decision makers and the soldiers on the ground' and revealed 'the incredible race against time to save the Allied army trapped in France'. The BBC website also claims that 'all the characters are based on real people, and all the events actually happened'. *Dunkirk* is presented as 'the product of eighteen months of original research', which involved the exploration of 'every archive in Britain, France and Germany' and 'previously unseen and un-researched records'.[9] Via a blurring of codes, this kind of programme thus appears to argue that re-enactment and reconstruction may be as truthful and objective as the experience of reality itself.

The appropriation of the docu-drama style in *Henry V* is evident in the director's emphasis upon accurate reproduction. Writing on the military preparations for the film, Babakitis remarks:

> I turned to the Skirmishers to provide the hand-to-hand choreography, the Saint Sebastians for English longbow archery, who make their own gear, forge their own arrowheads and everything, including those amazing nine-foot great-bows, fired with the feet, and then, for the sieges, the Medieval Reenactment Society are experts at staging sieges at historical castles and the like, with hundreds of participants in full fifteenth-century gear . . . We found that we really needed the weight of the steel blades for the full-on Medieval European experience of banging and clanging; the exhausting, two-handed effort of wielding those massive horse-killer blades.[10]

Typically, the stress here is placed less upon acting than upon *re-enactment*. The concept of fiction seems to be abandoned in favour of an effort to reproduce the reality of medieval battle in every detail, from the accuracy of the difficult-to-manipulate weapons to the very physical sensations experienced during the fighting (with the need to hold the heavy swords with two hands). It is revealing, in this context, that the director elects to open the first scene of the film with a date that appears at the bottom of the screen – 1415. It is as if filmic diegesis is related from the start to a documented reconstruction of the past, to an attempt to offer a faithful historical experience.

But the same aesthetic that aims at producing authenticity can, paradoxically, expose film as an obviously constructed product. The exploitation of jump-cut images gives rise to another kind of spatial fragmentation, namely, discontinuous editing. Discontinuity is rarely found in classical realist cinema as it goes against the grain of a cinematic desire for 'transparency'. A 'transparent' film's only function is to tell a story while hiding its essential filmic nature. In the aesthetic of 'transparency', the passage from one shot to another, as well as camera movements inside those shots, are justified as much as possible by the narrative logic. The impression of continuity is facilitated via 'continuity cuts', which can be defined as each shot that, on either side of the cut, preserves elements of continuity. Continuity cuts can take the form of gazes (shots/counter-shots, for example), gestures (in 'action cutting', gestures begin in one shot and culminate in another) or movements ('matching cutting' involves a transition facilitated by the continuity of a character's movement). Camera moves are generally accompanying tracking shots, which follow characters or anticipate their physical progress. Editing, camera work and positional decisions, then, do not appear as relatively arbitrary acts of enunciation but as the logical, plausible and almost necessary effects of the diegetic world itself.[11] Film theorist André Bazin refers to 'invisible editing' to evoke this sense of transparency. For him, inside such a schema, 'the mind of the spectator quite naturally accepts the viewpoints of the director which are justified by the geography of the action or the shifting emphasis of dramatic interest'.[12] Consequently, while enunciative discourse still exists within this cinematic aesthetic, it finds itself concealed by (and placed beneath) narrative functions and operations. Babakitis' *Henry V*, by contrast, reveals an enunciative authority beyond the filmic work through highly visible editing that denies any sort of continuity between the shots of the Agincourt battle. The absence of logical, natural links between the shots gives rise to alienating effects, distancing spectators from the representation of events and presenting the film as a constructed, sutured piece. The cuts are made even more visible through the absence of melodic, extradiegetic music. In classical realist cinema, extradiegetic music has a healing, smoothing function, for it connects shots, makes editing less obvious and creates the impression of a continuous unfolding of the action. By reinforcing the hypnotic nature of cinema, extradiegetic music usually permits the spectator to ignore the frame, the technical construction and the filmic articulation, contributing to the concealment of enunciation within the fictional perspective. Music brings a dream-like aspect to images and allows for a potential suppression of disbelief on the spectator's part. The absence of a melodic tune during the battle sequences of *Henry V* reinforces, therefore, an impression of discontinuity: no melody is heard to allay the artificial, jump-cut effects, but only atonal music (sometimes eerie vocals) and the rattling noise of the military operations.

Such discontinuous editing affects the ways in which we perceive the characters. Since the performances of the actors are cut into pieces which seem to be connected by no internal rationale, the film creates divided, dehumanised personalities, which are split in space and time. This enhances the characters' histrionic rather than naturalistic qualities. King Henry goes through a corporeal dislocation, a cinematic anatomisation which turns him into a patchwork of body parts and emphasises his potentially monstrous qualities. For instance, at the end of the battle of Agincourt, an extreme close-up focuses on the King's left eye filling the screen. The fact that Peter Babakitis was performing on the San Francisco stage in the play *Frankenstein: A Modern Prometheus* during the course of the production may have influenced this anatomising aesthetic, this fragmentation of bodies through a speedy and discontinuous editing procedure. The aesthetic that turns Henry into a type of monster is accompanied by an attention to his calculations and mercilessness. As the director stated, 'I was attracted by this play because I thought it would be fascinating to get into the mind of this rather cold-blooded killer who believes he's doing God's work'.[13] The scene in which Henry declares that Bardolph, one of his former companions, is to be hanged for stealing from a church is relevant here. As in Branagh's film, a lingering shot, which illuminates Bardolph's slow death, reveals the execution of Henry's announcement. Yet, contrary to Branagh's *Henry V*, Babakitis' does not highlight the pain, effort and emotional distress involved in ordering the hanging. Whereas Branagh's film revels in close-ups of a King who vainly tries to conceal his tears (thus paradoxically creating empathy towards the executioner rather than the victim), Babakitis' fully concentrates upon Henry's cruelty and seemingly unperturbed conscience.

More importantly, the 'cold-blooded' dimension of Babakitis' perform-ance is revealed in the decision to retain one of the King's orders to execute the French prisoners during the battle of Agincourt. The execution of the prisoners is arguably the least glorious episode in the play, with Henry's premeditated decision to allow a large-scale slaughter of defenceless men making explicit his subscription to Machiavellianism. In the play, the King's order unfolds in a two-part arrangement.[14] It manifests itself first as a legitimate, military response to what takes place on the battlefield:

> But hark, what new alarum is this same?
> The French have reinforced their scattered men.
> Then every soldier kill his prisoners.
> Give the word through.
>
> (IV.vi.35–8)

This first order is directly linked to a pitiless strategy. Since the French are still powerful, the English soldiers cannot afford to look after the prisoners and avoid combat: Henry is thus represented as unemotionally deciding to transgress the codes of war. The order is then announced a second time, when the King discovers the slaughter of the boys:

> I was not angry since I came to France
> Until this instant . . .
> . . . we'll cut the throats of those we have,
> And not a man of them that we shall take
> Shall taste our mercy.
>
> (IV.vii.58–60)

This time, the order is related to a genuine and spontaneous expression of anger, a strategy of execution being formulated as a vengeful reaction to bloodshed. However, having already experienced the first utterance, an audience realises that the decision has been taken in 'cold blood' beforehand. The ways in which the two orders are performed and directed are highly revealing of the ideological positions that film production adopts. Crucially, the two screen adaptations that precede Babakitis' film erase Henry's murderous policies. Olivier's version removes the problematic lines so as not to damage the glorious image of a heroic and chivalrous monarch. Branagh, too, withdraws the orders, yet retains the scene in which Henry discovers the slaughtered boys. The monarch's distress and rage in Branagh's conception are directly motivated by the boys' deaths even though this does not result in an execution order decision. It is upon Montjoy, the herald, that the King's fury focuses, as the published screenplay reveals:

> HENRY pulls the herald from his horse, forcing him down on his knees. He screams at the unfortunate messenger.
> HENRY V
> *How now! What means this, herald?*[15]

Branagh elects to retain the spontaneous display of emotion linked to the discovery of the slaughter, but removes the two executing orders, thereby avoiding suggestions of calculating personality traits.[16] Thus, Branagh's film, instead of stressing the King's Machiavellianism, endorses a construction of a quasi-tragic figure who is made powerless by the battlefield's events. Paradoxically, the director justifies the decision to cut the controversial orders through a desire to finesse the role: 'to have [Henry] do that at that point was utterly inconsistent with the rest of what we were presenting as a troubled and ambiguous character,' he states.[17] Branagh's *Henry V*, in short, reverts to a tradition that endeavours to avoid tarnishing the monarch's image so as to facilitate a spotless self-presentation before Princess Catherine at the close.

Contrasting with Olivier and Branagh's versions, Babakitis' *Henry V* includes the first order to execute the prisoners, but leaves out the second. The film also cuts the scene in which Henry discovers the boys' corpses. This adaptation, accordingly, emphasises premeditation and pragmatism. As the order is given only in 'cold blood', the film omits suggestions of an emotional, revengeful motivation, placing itself in implicit opposition to Branagh's interpretation. While Branagh cuts lines of purposeful cruelty and leaves intact moments that provoke emotional reaction, Babakitis deletes the very scene in which the King is provoked to order the killing and focuses on the first, insensate command. Such an interpretation is of a piece with the director's strategy to reveal the 'truth' about the royal character, one that has often been bypassed. Babakitis' *Henry V* aims at challenging traditions, fleshing out concealed complications and achieving objectivity: it is thus consistent with an approach akin to investigative journalism.

Such a drive towards underscoring the genuine extends, as well, to the dehumanisation of the Chorus, who is transformed into an impersonal voice-over, lacking body and substance. The decision has several consequences, since the character of the Chorus, and his or her specific delivery of the lines, influence both idealistic and subversive assessments of the play. *Henry V* can be performed either as a glorious and heroic adventure, or as the narrative of an aspiring and politic King who cloaks an appetite for war beneath false piety.[18] This dichotomy of interpretation is inscribed within the ambivalence of the text itself. According to Stephen Greenblatt, 'The play registers every nuance of royal hypocrisy, ruthlessness, and bad faith, but it does so in the context of a celebration, a collective panegyric to "This star of England", the charismatic leader who purges the commonwealth of its incorrigibles and gorges the martial national stage'.[19] The play includes, therefore, an 'official' version of events for spectators willing to hear Henry's exploits and a parallel, more pernicious, construction that moves beyond surface meanings and dogma. The ironies in *Henry V*, however, can be performed in two opposing ways. They can be emphasised either by creating a discrepancy between the Chorus' laudatory announcements and the subsequent dramatic action (which might be seen as an interrogation of the 'official' script), or by playing the Chorus as a sarcastic type composed of wry reflections. In both cases, the performance of irony is intimately related to the Chorus' part and the ways in which it is interpreted. According to some critics, including Peter B. Erickson, the play traces its idealistic quality to the Chorus alone: '*Henry V* has often been considered official art geared to patriotic ideology – and, as such, either applauded or condemned,' he states, continuing, 'As I see it, this idea of patriotic ceremony applies primarily to the Chorus, and not to the play as a whole'.[20] For Sidney Shanker, similarly, the Chorus should deliver his lines as praise: 'The general purpose of the five Choruses is to give the play an exultant and fervent atmosphere of epic grandeur,' he argues.[21] According to Ralph Berry, the Chorus is also established to provide a heroic vision of Henry's undertakings: 'The Chorus exists to bring into being, and maintain, a glamorized reading of the action' is his formulation.[22] For all three critics, the Chorus presents an epic reading of the story, which is destined to have an affirmative effect. Subversion in the play, therefore, emerges from the gap between panegyric and the actions that follow hard upon each choric intervention. For instance, at the start of Act Two, the Chorus informs the audience that the army is already gathered at Southampton, ready to invade France. Yet this observation is immediately thrown into disarray by the next scene – the comical interlude at the Eastcheap tavern. Instead of a spotless English army prepared for a noble conflict, we are confronted with the petty fights of a divided, angry and crude plebeian sort. In the same way, the upbeat speech delivered by the Chorus to introduce the night scenes before the battle of Agincourt is destabilised by ensuing events. Incapable of diverting his men, Henry, disguised as a common soldier, receives only his subjects' criticism.[23]

Via the inscription of an 'official' representation of the monarch, the Chorus functions to construct a contrapuntal narrative that is in implicit competition with the dramatic action as it is performed. Such a critical line has been pursued by many theatre directors. Hence, the 1975 RSC production of *Henry V* featured a Chorus that, because it was directed towards the preservation of the royal image, the director, Terry Hands, termed 'the Official Version'.[24] However, another performance trend insists upon the exact opposite: the dramatic action is patriotic and transparent, while the Chorus is qualifying and ironic. Director Adrian Noble adopted such an approach in his 1984 RSC production, in which Henry and the Chorus appeared as structurally opposed. Henry, played by Kenneth Branagh, impersonated a juvenile, inexperienced and earnest monarch, while the Chorus, played by Ian McDiarmid, portrayed a blasé and cynical observer. In his second speech, McDiarmid's Chorus added a derisive touch to 'Now all the youth of England are on fire' (II.o.1), pointing up the cupidity of the English soldiers in a cynical enunciation of the line 'crowns imperial, crowns *and* coronets, / Promised to Harry and his followers' (II.o.1, 10–11). Moreover, the director cut the end of the speech, placing it after the pathetic discord of the tavern scene, with the effect that the Chorus' claim – 'The French, advised by good intelligence / Of this most *dreadful* preparation' (II.o.12–13) – becomes an ironic observation: the French do indeed have nothing to fear if the English army is composed of clowns. In fact, by displacing sections of the Chorus' speeches, Noble's production created a gap not so much between the narration and the action as between the action and a retrospectively ironic commentary. In the play of *Henry V*, showing is thus opposed to telling in both a formal and a meaningful way. While the dramatic action *shows* a version of what takes place, the Chorus frames each act by *telling* another version of events. It is via this peculiar construction (this oscillation between showing and telling) that irony arises, with the whole dramatic structure (the order in which the episodes appear) seeming to reveal the play's concealed dimensions. The more spectators are encouraged to establish connections between the various events, and in particular between the Chorus' narrative version and the play's dramatic action, the more the potential for irony might be appreciated.

In the two previous screen adaptations of *Henry V*, the performance of the Chorus is realised as essentially orthodox and idealistic. In Olivier's film, the Chorus, either on the stage of the Globe Theatre or in stylised, garish-coloured surroundings, delivers his lines with admiration and epic ebullience. In an early version of Branagh's screenplay for *Henry V*, the Chorus is imagined as very much in keeping with Adrian Noble's 1984 stage production concept, since an implicitly sarcastic orientation is apparent: 'Humorous eyes and his whole tone shot through with irony', it is stated.[25] An initial idea, then, was for the Chorus to have been realised contrapuntally. Yet the director ultimately rejected this interpretation, for, in the finished film, the action never contradicts the Chorus' narrative, and the Chorus never mocks the action. By reducing the length of the choric speeches, distributing them throughout the film, Branagh's *Henry V* dilutes the potential clash between the Chorus' lines and the King's actions while, in the same moment, encouraging the formation of links between key scenes. This is captured in the description accompanying the Chorus' first appearance: 'He welcomes us with the clarity and warmth of the great story-teller,' the published screenplay announces.[26] The threat of subversion is purposefully subdued to an immersion into fiction. As Chorus, Derek Jacobi eschews ironic counterpoint so as to suggest an allegiance to Henry and a favourable treatment of his behaviour. Furthermore, Henry's actions, and the Chorus' comments, are invariably consistent with each other: during the night-time tour of the camp, for instance, the camera reveals the monarch reassuring his soldiers, while the Chorus is constructed as merely adding rhythm and reinforcement. In this interpretation, alienation gives way to identification, with an empathically angled discourse promoting audience understanding and collusion.

Babakitis' *Henry V* is highly distinctive in its decision not to give a body to the Chorus' part. It is the first screen adaptation to replace the actor with an impersonal – and neutrally toned – voice-over. The disembodied address recalls the kind of voice that is typically found in documentaries, a voice that, similarly, lacks substance, wants representation and offers narrative and interpretive commentary. In the documentary, the voice-over functions to move the action forward by providing factual information, elaborating understandable images and generally encouraging consistency. Voice-overs introduce, explain, lead and teach: they occupy a secondary symbolic position, and a superior authority, which incarnate knowledge and contextualise forms, thereby creating an ideological frame and a series of hierarchical relations.[27] For William Guynn, the spectator 'can never contradict the voice-over. The reversibility of discourse seems impossible'.[28] Because the Chorus in Babakitis' film is no longer visibly manifested, the heroic and 'official' version of the play becomes more difficult to criticise: an ethereal voice symbolises the (illusory) stability of meaning and operates as a godlike authority that insists upon the passive reception of its pronouncements.[29] Throughout *Henry V*, the dramatic action only coheres with and corroborates the Chorus' brand of epic praise. As the voice-over positively delivers the 'Now all the youth of England are on fire' (II.o) speech, which comments on the build-up to the war, the images on screen actualise the uttered words, revealing soldiers preparing for their military campaign, trying out their bows, practising fighting and checking their armour and helmets. Even when the 'crowns and coronets' that are 'promised to Harry and his followers' (II.o.10–11) are mentioned, a shot focuses on money changing hands. The Chorus, then, illustrates literally and straightforwardly, and the ideology it promotes remains unchallenged. Consequently, the following scene, which features the riff-raff of Henry's army and their petty quarrels, loses contradictory potential, since the audience has already witnessed a sobriety of preparation underway elsewhere. The next choric speech, at the start of Act Three, is also realised via a *mise-en-scène* that asserts veracity. As the voice-over invokes the embarkation at Southampton, the screen images focus upon a digital forest of masts and sails reminiscent of the colourful maritime assembly of Olivier's film. Once on board, Henry – and his unregenerates – are glimpsed smiling broadly at the sea view. The whole sequence is shot in slow motion, which helps to emphasise the emotions on display and the sense of a lyrical pause. Once again, a discourse that may be perceived as laudatory is granted a potent visual accompaniment.

If the film cancels the ironies born from the differences between the Chorus' 'official' speech and the play's actions, it also wipes away the incongruities that inhabit Henry's soliloquies. For instance, the 'Upon the King' soliloquy (IV.i.218–72) is celebrated for alerting an audience to its ironic interstices. Irony is created, in particular, through a discrepancy between the King's discourse and the scene that we have just witnessed. Questioning royal ceremony and pomp, Henry envies even the slave who, in his opinion, is free of his own power-induced sleeplessness and anxiety:

Not all these, laid in bed majestical,
Can sleep so soundly as the wretched slave
Who with a body filled and vacant mind

Gets him to rest, crammed with distressful bread;
Never sees horrid night . . .

(IV.i.255–9)

Yet the audience of the play (or film) has just witnessed a scene in which three soldiers discuss their mutual fears and are unable to find peace. Shakespeare indicates, in fact, that both the sublime monarch and the ordinary man are unable to escape the taint of insomnia.[30] The director removes this irony from the Shakespearean text via the deployment of a specific *mise-en-scène*. At the very moment when Henry describes his inner turmoil and his subjects' tranquillity, the images on screen reveal a sleeping soldier whom the monarch gently tucks into his blanket in a composition that confirms, rather than calls into question, the speaker's reflections. In his film, Branagh, similarly, elected to flesh out Henry's lines with shots of soldiers asleep, thereby endorsing the King's rumination, as the published screenplay suggests: 'He is standing beside the sleeping figure of one of his men as he continues,' it is stated.[31] Like Branagh before him, Babakitis constructs a contrast between, on the one hand, the quiet sleep of mere soldiers and, on the other, Henry's tormented watch and accompanying, justified introspection. *Henry V* in Babakitis' hands subscribes to a filmic tradition that proves the King correct in his assumption that royal status brings heavy responsibility; paradoxically, moreover, this is an interpretation that legitimates the possession of previously denigrated ceremonial privileges.

Via a combination of digital stylisation and documentary-like naturalism that fragments and dehumanises in equal measure, Babakitis' *Henry V* points up complex ideological effects. On the one hand, the film visually attempts to capture a sense of the multi-faceted aspects of a historical event, using discontinuous filming and a multiplicity of representational angles as part of this endeavour. As far as textual decisions are concerned, the director does not balk at the inclusion of even the most unsettling monarchical pronouncements (such as the King's orders to hang Bardolph and to execute the French prisoners), pronouncements that cast Henry's claims to glory in an unflattering light. On the other hand, the disincarnated interventions of the Chorus eventually encourage a heroic reading which is difficult to reject entirely. The dramatic action is never performed so as to mount a challenge to, or to contradict, an 'official' recounting of history. On the contrary, the *mise-en-scène* asserts the 'truth' subscribed to by the Chorus and underwrites the personal beliefs expressed in Henry's soliloquies. Ultimately, the flag that recurrently flaps in slow motion becomes the most powerful symbol of a screen adaptation that, in attempting to demythologise nationalism and qualify royalty, succeeds only in promoting epic contemplation and imperial legitimacy.[32]

Notes

1. *Henry V*, ed. Gary Taylor (1994), Oxford: Oxford University Press, II.ii.190. All further references appear in the text.
2. However, Olivier's film begins and ends at the Globe Theatre in Shakespeare's time, thus showing Henry played by an Elizabethan actor and introducing the distancing device of *mise-en-abyme*. But this actor never actually looks at the camera directly.
3. See the official website for the film at http://www.henrythefifth.com/HenryVnews.html.
4. William Guynn (2001), *Un Cinéma de Non-Fiction: Le Documentaire Classique à l'Épreuve de la Théorie*, trans. Jean-Luc Lioult, preface by Roger Odin, Aix-en-Provence: Publications de l'Université de Provence, p. 193; my translation.
5. Guynn, *Cinéma*, p. 194.
6. See Patrick Baudry (1992), 'Terrains et territoires', *La Licorne*, 24, p. 9.
7. Roger Odin, preface to Guynn, *Cinéma*, p. 8; my translation.
8. See Burhan Wazir (2003), 'Docu-dramas set to storm the screens: Viewers lap up mix of fact and fiction', *The Observer*, 18 May (http://observer.guardian.co.uk/print/0,3858,4671489–102285,00.html).
9. See the BBC website at http://www.bbc.co.uk/pressoffice/pressreleases/stories/2003/12_december/04/bbc2_winter.shtml.
10. See http://www.henrythefifth.com/HenryVnews.html.
11. See Alain Bergala (1977), *Initiation à la Sémiologie du Récit en Images*, Paris: Ligue Française de l'Enseignement et de l'Education Permanente, p. 46.
12. André Bazin (1967), *What is Cinema?*, trans. Hugh Gray, Berkeley: University of California Press, p. 24.
13. See http://www.henrythefifth.com/HenryVnews.html.
14. See Norman Rabkin (1988), 'Either/Or: Responding to *Henry V*', in Harold Bloom (ed.), *William Shakespeare's 'Henry V': Modern Critical Interpretations*, New York: Chelsea House, p. 53.
15. Kenneth Branagh (1997), *William Shakespeare's 'Henry V': Screenplay and Introduction*, New York and London: Norton, p. 91.
16. In an early version of the screenplay, an allusion to the execution of the prisoners was retained. After discovering the murdered boys, Gower states: 'wherefore the king most worthily hath caused every soldier to cut his prisoner's throat'. See Kenneth Branagh Archive, Queen's University, Belfast, *'Henry V' by William Shakespeare: Adapted for the Screen by Kenneth Branagh*, unpublished screenplay (October 1988), p. 81. That Branagh eventually decided to cut the line as well is symptomatic of the director's desire to promote Henry's heroic status.
17. Gary Crowdus (1988), 'Sharing an Enthusiasm for Shakespeare: An Interview with Kenneth Branagh', *Cineaste*, 24.1, p. 39.
18. Writing in the ideological context of the 1940s, John Dover Wilson legitimates Henry's decision to go to war and compares his campaign against France with World War Two: 'The war against France is a righteous war; and seemed as much so to Shakespeare's public as war against the Nazis seems to us. Once this is realized a fog of suspicion and detraction is lifted from the play' (*Henry V*, ed. John Dover Wilson (1947), Cambridge: Cambridge University Press, p. xxiv).

George J. Becker shares this view when he states that 'Shakespeare's selection of historical materials, and the emphasis he gives them, is controlled by his central purpose: to give an heroic portrait of Henry V' (*Shakespeare's Histories*, New York: Frederick Ungar, 1977, p. 68).

As early as 1817, William Hazlitt denounced the cynicism and brutality of the monarch. For him, Shakespeare could question the meaning of war while simultaneously presenting a political satire. He writes that Henry V 'seemed to have no idea of any rule of right or wrong, but brute force glossed over with a little religious hypocrisy' (*Characters of Shakespeare's Plays*, London: Oxford University Press, 1949, p. 168). Such an unflattering construction of the character was a recurrent feature of nineteenth-century criticism.

19. Stephen Greenblatt (1994), 'Invisible Bullets', in Jonathan Dollimore and Alan Sinfield (eds), *Political Shakespeare: New Essays in Cultural Materialism*, Ithaca and London: Cornell University Press, p. 42.

20. Peter B. Erickson (1979–80), ' "The Fault/My Father Made": The Anxious Pursuit of Heroic Fame in Shakespeare's *Henry V*', *Modern Language Studies*, 10.1, p. 13.

21. Sidney Shanker (1975), *Shakespeare and the Uses of Ideology*, The Hague and Paris: Mouton, p. 71.

22. Ralph Berry (1978), *The Shakespearean Metaphor*, Basingstoke: Macmillan, p. 49.

23. Pauline Kiernan comments that 'when Henry comes on stage, we see no "cheerful semblance and sweet majesty", but a despondent king who does nothing to seek out his men. Instead of cheering their King, the soldiers either curse him or . . . call into question the justice of his war, and one of them challenges him to a fight' (*Shakespeare's Theory of Drama*, Cambridge: Cambridge University Press, 1996, pp. 147–8).

24. Ralph Berry (1977), *On Directing Shakespeare: Interviews with Contemporary Directors*, London: Croom Helm, pp. 49–58.

25. Kenneth Branagh Archive, Queen's University, Belfast, '*Henry V' by William Shakespeare: Adapted for the Screen by Kenneth Branagh*, unpublished screenplay (October 1988), p. 2.

26. Branagh, *William Shakespeare's 'Henry V'*, p. 1.

27. Guynn, *Cinéma*, p. 80.

28. Guynn, *Cinéma*, p. 138; my translation.

29. See C. R. Plantiga (1997), *Rhetoric and Representation in Non-Fiction Cinema*, Cambridge: Cambridge University Press, p. 167.

30. See Greenblatt, 'Invisible Bullets', p. 43.

31. Branagh, *William Shakespeare's 'Henry V'*, p. 74.

32. I am grateful to Dr Kevin De Ornellas and Dr Nathalie Vienne-Guerrin for reading this essay and for suggesting many constructive changes. I am also thankful to the editors for their astute and cogent copy-editing.

Chapter 9

Screening the McShakespeare in Post-Millennial Shakespeare Cinema

Carolyn Jess-Cooke

A scene in Billy Morrissette's *Scotland, PA* (2001) demonstrates one of the informing ideologies of post-millennial Shakespearean cinema. Detective Ernie McDuff (Christopher Walken) visits McBeth's fast-food diner, newly refashioned by Joe McBeth (James LeGros) and Pat McBeth (Maura Tierney) following the mysterious death of its previous owner, Norm Duncan (James Rebhorn), in a vat of sizzling French-fry oil. Quipping that the new proprietors of Duncan's burger-bar 'kill' their customers 'with all that greasy food', McDuff suggests the 'unnutritional' and, indeed, fatal quality of the fast-food industry as an establishment based on addictive repetition. 'Get 'em hooked,' he jibes, upon learning of the 'free fries' scheme launched by the McBeths to advertise their new culinary developments ('More, more!'). Drawing attention to the toxicity and inherently addictive ingredients of fast food, the scene can additionally be viewed as commenting upon the state of contemporary cinema culture with which Shakespeare is becoming complicit. Indeed, Morrissette's efforts at re-imagining *Macbeth* in a fast-food diner of *circa* 1975 are part of an increasing trend in Shakespearean cinema to reiterate the Bard not only according to the dynamics of popular culture, but also according to the relationships between globalisation, Shakespeare and a horizontally integrated Hollywood at the current moment.

This chapter argues that encounters with Shakespearean cinema in the twenty-first century inevitably involve the confrontation of fast-food ethics, cross-cultural uniformity and forms of repetition-compulsion that inhabit adaptation techniques after the rise of New Hollywood, and which contribute to the re-articulation of Shakespeare's plays in the light of a continually evolving post-global culture. Ten recent Shakespeare films respond to these notions from a variety of cultural positions: *Scotland, PA* (dir. Billy Morrissette, 2001), *Maqbool* (dir. Vishal Bharadwaj, 2003), *Macbeth: The Comedy* (dir. Allison L. LiCalsi, 2001), *Rave Macbeth* (dir.

Klaus Knoesel, 2001), *A Midsummer Night's Rave* (dir. Gil Cates, 2002), *'O'* (dir. Tim Blake Nelson, 2001), *The King Is Alive* (dir. Kristian Levring, 2001), *King of Texas* (dir. Uli Edel, 2002), *The Street King* (dir. James Gavin Bedford, 2002) and *Deliver Us from Eva* (dir. Gary Hardwick, 2003). Inspired by 'the McMovie', Harvey Greenberg's trope of unmitigated narrative damnation, this chapter constructs the 'McShakespeare' as a paradigm through which to observe the 'translocal' and sequential structures that are emerging in Shakespearean cinema.[1]

First, a word on Greenberg's trope. The McMovie denotes the 'grossly imitative' Hollywood 'rehashes' of the late twentieth century that subscribe to those franchising, commercialising and health-crushing activities of the king of conglomerates, McDonald's. As Greenberg puts it,

> Dogged imitation and allusion rather than experimentation, even within narrow genre confines, usually dictates the newest Vigilante Vengeance flick or Flash-in-the-pan-dance – in short, the latest McMovie. By now, McMovies have passed through several generations. Uninspiring prototypes have spun off sequels, which have birthed still drearier successors – a Barthesean chain of replication unfolding into ever-declining signification.[2]

The McMovie fundamentally draws attention to the ideological assertions and determining factors of a fast-food chain of film production. Its emphasis is on the 'schlock/exploitation circuit' of Hollywood rehashes and an acute, if not annihilating, analysis of film rip-offs that champion loose endings, weak, cartoonish characters, inconsistent screenplays, stale narratives, fast pacing, loud music and soundbite dialogue – designed, one thinks, to assert the tagline ethos of consumer advertising (departing from Dirty Harry's 'Go ahead, punk, make my day') in terms of the McDonald's 'I'm lovin' it' campaign. Likewise, the McShakespeare announces the processes of Bardic commodification in recent cinema, taking note of the McDonald's-inspired uniformity of meta-referential Shakespeare films and strikingly conventional off-shoots that march to the generic beat of the teen movie. Yet, like McDonald's, the McShakespeare also functions as a 'cultural experience'.[3] The McShakespeare is a scenario of multicultural traditions, identities, languages and ideologies through which the spectator can negotiate the cultural diversity of an increasingly global cinema and, indeed, a global homogeneity. Even the imperialistic tensions within the McShakespeare – most often between British 'high' culture and marginalised indigenous communities – provide discursively compelling perspectives on the Bard's filmic co-operation with the global economy.

The McShakespeare takes its primary cue from the McMovie's acknowledgement of the effects on cinema of 'McDonaldisation', a social development identified and analysed by George Ritzer.[4] Understood as 'a significant component of globalisation', McDonaldisation is defined as 'the process by which the principles of the fast-food restaurant are coming to dominate more and more sectors of American society as well as of the rest of the world', establishing McDonald's as 'an important cultural icon not only in the United States but increasingly throughout the world'.[5] Although McDonald's has yet to fund films, its relationship to cinema is first and foremost underscored by its alliance with the Disney Company, which began in the early 1980s when the McDonald's Happy Meal venture first included small toys based on characters from Disney films. In May 1996, a contract was signed that allowed McDonald's exclusive rights to produce fluffy toy figurines of Disney characters to accompany its Happy Meals. Such toys contributed enormously to the success of Happy Meals, which, by 2002, made up 20 per cent of the annual sales of McDonald's, totalling approximately $3.5 billion.[6] These 'movie mementoes', as I call them, cunningly trade on the popular desire to re-experience and interact with a film, an act described by Susan Bennett in terms of 'post-performance reception'.[7] In this connection, an observation by Steve McBeth, vice-president of consumer products for Disney, is significant: the policy of providing 'movie mementoes', he states, 'extends the entertainment experience for the child – it's a way of letting the fun of the movie continue'.[8] In other words, such 'movie mementos' are a small part of an escalating cultural specificity that is complicit with ideologies of repetition, continuation and interaction that in turn bake and fry an imperialistic dogma for the global palate. Due to begin a movie tie-in contract with DreamWorks Animation SKG (starting with a *Shrek 3* promotion) in 2007, McDonald's points to and perpetuates an important facet of global culture that Hollywood studios have capitalised on in the forms of the blockbuster, sequel, prequel, trilogy and remake: the desire to repeat, continue and interact with movie narratives. This desire to repeat – whether compulsively or otherwise – forms the critical framework of the McShakespeare.

In the McShakespeare, the Bard is used – like the golden arches – to localise cultural concerns within a global economy and, conversely, to signify the global within the local. The tension between the local and global is at the heart of the McShakespeare, largely in terms of the use of the plays to articulate experiences of displacement and to re-work social rituals, indigenous identities, traditions, languages and cultural codes for popular consumption. As Richard Burt observes, 'Shakespeare film adaptations significantly blur if not fully deconstruct distinctions between local and global, original and copy, pure and hybrid, indigenous and foreign, high and low, authentic and inauthentic, hermeneutic and post-hermeneutic, English and other languages'.[9] In contradistinction to Burt's comments, the McShakespeare suggests contemporary Shakespeare appropriation as a signifying practice instead of a point of textual origin. In the films considered in this chapter, Shakespeare serves less as an originating text or a cultural icon than as product placement, a secondary position of intertextual engagement that classifies, or legitimates, the often blatant registers of a McDonald's ideology.

The productions examined here depart from the plays' original titles and reinstate Shakespeare on the streets of LA, the Mumbai underground, the deserts of Texas and Namibia, fast-food diners, US high schools and in the middle of a rave. For the most part, Shakespeare's language is replaced with a contemporary vernacular or a different language altogether, requiring subtitles that transpose colloquial Hindi, for example, to American slang. There is something both exciting and unnerving about these levels of cultural activity, something not so much rotten in the state of cinematic Shakespeare as pointedly out of joint with categories of textual fidelity. It is the purpose of this chapter to consider if the processes of revisionism, hybridity, secondary identities, updated language and transnationality in twenty-first-century Shakespeare on film make inroads into new discursive territory for Shakespeare studies or, conversely, if these processes underline cultural engagement with Shakespeare as a marginalising textual practice that replaces the Bard with burger politics and blockbuster logic.

I

The primary imperative of the McShakespeare is predictability. As James L. Watson suggests of McDonaldisation, 'the key to McDonald's worldwide success is that people everywhere know what to expect when they pass through the Golden Arches'.[10] This does not mean that McDonald's serves the same food around the world: the real key to its success, as Watson acknowledges, is its incorporation of local cuisine – such as *teriyaki* burgers in Japan, the 'Maharaja Mac' in India and an absence of pork in Muslim communities – on the McDonald's menu.[11] A similar impetus informs the McShakespeare. Shakespeare is employed in the McShakespeare as a symbol of predictability and expectation. Whether the spectators of the McShakespeare have read the source text(s) or not, almost all twenty-first-century audiences will have been exposed to Shakespeare and his plays in one form or another. Yet the McShakespeare treatment of the 'local' is also very different from McDonaldisation: one does not have to travel to Mexico to experience Mexican culture in the McShakespeare. Moreover, the inherent predictability of the McShakespeare allows for a global dispersal of indigenous issues that otherwise might remain strictly local.

James Gavin Bedford's *The Street King* (2002) opens with a short sequence of graffiti artists spray-painting a version of the First Folio image of Shakespeare, soon adding a red bandana, goatee, bling (a gold crucifix earring), a beauty spot and sunglasses. On either side of the newly ethnicised Bard, the words *'plata'* and *'plomo'* are painted. Spanish for 'silver or lead' (and uttered twice through the film), the *'plata o plomo'* phrase is a direct reference to Pablo Emilio Escobar Gaviria, a Colombian drug lord who became the seventh richest man in the world by smuggling cocaine into the United States and other countries around the world. Suspected of bribing government officials, judges and other politicians, Gaviria's strategy was referred to as *plata o plomo*: a cash bribe or lead bullet. *Plata o plomo* bookends the film, returning at the end when Rikki (Jon Seda) is made to choose between the silver bullet of Juan Vallejo's (Mario López) gun or the money in the latter's hold-all. Rikki's obvious hero, Gaviria, is reinvented as Shakespeare, and it is indeed Gaviria, rather than Shakespeare, who provides the narrative's pivotal 'soundbite' vernacular. Shakespeare-as-Gaviria animates the film's engagement with, and contribution to, the McShakespeare as a framework within which the issues of drug addiction, ethnicity and crime franchising are discursively organised and represented as a troubling undercurrent of North American teenage life. In this production, Shakespeare serves as a *double* signifier, a dichotomous figure that iconises the *plata o plomo* ethos. More specifically, Shakespeare functions both as a cultural icon that unifies a linguistically, culturally and economically diverse global population and as a locally specific symbol of the problems faced by marginalised Hispanic communities in Southern California.

The film imagines Richard III as Rikki Ortega, who slays his way to the 'kingship' of a drug cartel in Los Angeles. Not so much 'untimely ripped', and definitely no hunchback, Rikki is a young, muscle-bound, cross-wearing Latino hunk who is haunted by his relocation to California at a young age when his mother could no longer afford to raise him. Throughout, Rikki not only engineers the deaths of his brothers and the love of Anita (Tonantzin Carmelo), but orchestrates a growing relationship between himself and *'mano'*, the spectator. Seda's Branagh-as-Iago-inspired performance is highly engaging, and the film's slant on some of the play's key moments – such as Rikki's quip 'Not bad for a first date', instead of Richard's soliloquy ('Was ever woman in this humour won?') – proves compelling for an audience familiar with both Shakespeare's text and other recent films of the play.[12] The film invokes Shakespeare's text *and* its avatars in an attempt to contextualise an inherently dualistic cultural identity. As Rikki tells us at the film's outset, the borderline in the middle of California (at Bakersfield) marks two disparate communities: north (*Norteño*), where the gang colour is red, and south (*La Eme*), where the gang colour is blue. The Bard's red bandana identifies him as *Norteño*. Specifically (and semiotically) located above the border, Shakespeare is nonetheless granted a 'second' identity – like Rikki – that is more broadly defined as 'local' Shakespeare. This process marks the 'deterritorialisation' of Shakespeare as a fluid, transnational cultural origin from which myriad global identities can be oriented and accessed. Yet the film's *'plata o plomo'*, or subject/other index of dichotomies, suggests the transition from Shakespeare's 'predictable' text to progressively evolving (and dissolving) cultural engagements, which embrace more than the mere guise of a bandana and shades. In other words, although the local can be signified, its subjectivity will always be displaced as long as its territory is mapped by a global, imperialistic icon.

II

While tensions between the local and global are of particular interest to the McShakespeare, the discursive geography of this paradigm hinges on placelessness. In Klaus Knoesel's *Rave Macbeth* (2001) and *A Midsummer Night's Rave* (dir. Gil Cates, 2002), cultural 'placelessness' is connoted by the rave within which Shakespeare's texts are situated. Rave culture exists as an urban environment wherein language barriers and social differences are erased by the structuring of a communal identity that is premised upon fantasy, technology and crowd logic.[13] As both films demonstrate, Shakespeare's occupation of the veritable 'no-man's-land' of the rave dislocates the Bard from an exclusive cultural positioning in the same moment as he is subversively placed 'in culture'.

The setting of the rave is intended to provide a culturally 'neutral' zone for a re-engagement with Shakespeare's work. In contrast to its 1980s' origins, twenty-first-century rave culture interrogates the effects of the global village on youth culture, striving to preserve its subversive *eidos* in the face of politically correct heterogeneity. As Diana Sandars puts it, 'by the late 1990s rave culture had evolved from an illegally organised activity enjoyed by a youth sub-culture, to an anti-authoritarian signifier of mainstream global youth cultures'.[14] In *Rave Macbeth* and *A Midsummer Night's Rave*, Shakespeare is posited as the 'mainstream' entity that, appropriated by a subculture, reinforces the 'anti-authoritarian' ideology of rave culture. Acknowledging Shakespearean cinema's main audience as teenage, these films stage *Macbeth* and *A Midsummer Night's Dream* in an explicitly 'youth culture' zone. *A Midsummer Night's Rave*, for example, draws its entire cast from a gamut of popular teen movies, such as *The Fast and the Furious* (dir. Rob Cohen, 2001), *American Pie* (dir. Paul Weitz, 1999), *Dazed and Confused* (dir. Richard Linklater, 1993), *Almost Famous* (dir. Cameron Crowe, 2000) and *Eight Legged Freaks* (dir. Ellory Elkayem, 2002), and two recent (teen) Shakespeare films, *'O'* (dir. Tim Blake Nelson, 2001) and *Ten Things I Hate About You* (dir. Gil Junger, 1999). Carrie Fisher also makes an appearance as Mia's mum, but more subtly conjures a brief reprisal of her role in *Star Wars*. Indebted to *Get Over It* (dir. Tommy O' Haver, 2001), the film's (loose) plot weaves together strands from a variety of Shakespeare's plays, mostly *A Midsummer Night's Dream*: Xander (Andrew Keegan) and Mia (Sunny Mabrey) are in love with each other, but it takes a rave and some green, glowing potion supplied by a Shakespeare-spouting British mystic named O. B. John (Jason Carter) – the film's nod to Oberon – for either to admit it. A tattooed Shylock named Doc (Terry Scannell) looms in the background seeking his stolen drug money, whilst Nick (Chad Lindberg), high on drugs, takes up Bottom's role as 'an ass' by donning a donkey costume at a daycare centre. Narrative-driven the film is not; nor is it ideologically subversive. Yet its effort to shove screen Shakespeare out of the front doors of the ubiquitous US high school and into an 'anti-authoritarian' setting – one that is both global and discursively 'placeless' – indicates a move away from a pedagogically entrenched Shakespeare towards a definitively 'in culture' location.

Whereas *A Midsummer Night's Rave* explores its characters' extra-rave activities by day, *Rave Macbeth* is set entirely in a rave over a period of one night. The film focuses on the attempts of Marcus (Michael Rosenbaum), aided by his girlfriend, Lidia (Nicki Lynn Aycox), to work his way to the top of a drug ring in a Munich nightclub, resulting in the death of Marcus' best friend, Troy (Jamie Elman), and Helena (Marguerite Moreau), Troy's girlfriend. The film is noteworthy as the first feature to be shot with the use of the Sony 24P-1080 digital camera. Similar to 35mm film cameras, this recently developed camera shoots at twenty-four frames per second, a cutting-edge characteristic that reduces post-production costs and enhances the clarity of night scenes. The production is shaped entirely by rave culture, incorporating dizzying shots of ravers up close and personal, as well as hallucinogenic superimpositions that force the spectator to share the drug-induced perspective of a rave participant. Like *A Midsummer Night's Rave*, Knoesel's camera cuts regularly to shots of celebrity DJs such as Mona Davis, Phil Fuldner, Tom Novy and DJ Tomkraft. A camera within an 'eye' logo permits the rave 'King', Hecate (Jeffrey Vanderbyl), to overview events. Shakespeare's text motivates the film's cultural engagements and some plot developments, yet the chief concern is the escalating commercialism of the rave scene, accompanied by a nostalgic urge to recapture the rave's glory days as a counter-culture community founded on 'peace, love, unity and respect' – the rave 'rules' that Marcus and Lidia break. As one of the film's producers, Seijin Ki, puts it, '[the club industry] is a much more cut-throat business now, and the gangster commercialism fits in with the story of *Macbeth* and its power struggles. Rave culture also has its own special hierarchy and supporters'.[15] Shakespeare is employed, then, to portray the effects of globalisation and commercialism on pop culture's last defence against heterogeneity and consensus: the cultural underground. Yet, at the same time – and in keeping with the paradoxes of the McShakespeare – the film betrays a temptation to endorse the commercial appeal of rave as a 'multi-million Euro youth industry', invoking rave-based productions such as *Blade* (the elaboration of 'blood [that] rains from heaven' in the form of red liquid streaming from overhead pipes is cribbed from *Blade*'s (dir. Stephen Norrington, 1998) opening scene) and *Groove* (dir. Greg Harrison, 2000) to ensure its popularity.

Yet it is arguable if the film's referentiality of rave is part of its effort to register the matrices between Shakespeare and popular culture and, in particular, those performative dynamics of the rave in postmodernity that find a corollary with early modern stage productions of the Bard. At one point the DJ invites Lidia and Marcus on stage where they are received by the crowd. This moment marks their ascension to the top of the rave 'hierarchy', which is defined by the ability both to interact with the crowd and to lead the process, or 'vibe', of rave interaction – much like a director negotiating cinema's interaction with Shakespeare. Shakespeare's cultural performance 'interacts' with rave culture in Knoesel's film not only in terms of the placelessness of the rave, but also in terms of the dialogue between the rave as a postmodern scenario of placeless culture and the 'traditional community-based pageantry' of early modern theatre, which involved 'a particularly vivid and engaging form of social participation' as well as 'conviviality and the expression of shared social meaning'.[16] Knoesel juxtaposes the convivial social participation of the rave with the recent tendencies in rave culture towards hierarchy and commercialism by staging and referencing *Macbeth*, signifying, therefore, the impact of globalisation as culturally regressive and the retention of 'high' culture as representable only within the spheres of the subversive.

III

Ritzer's McDonaldisation thesis largely ignores issues of race and gender, assuming, as Douglas Kellner points out, that the McDonald's ideology behind 'McDonaldisation' is race-less, sex-less, gender-less, and God-less.[17] In the McShakespeare, knowledge of diversity runs in concert with an ignorance about how to contend with 'multiperspectival' versions of Shakespeare.[18] This well-intentioned confusion informs Gary Hardwick's *Deliver Us from Eva* (2003), which reinvents *The Taming of the Shrew* as a black romantic comedy. The film's script, written by James Iver Mattson and B. E. Brauner, was an original composition with no intentional connection to Shakespeare's play. On the film's website, Hardwick recalls that the script 'reminded me of Shakespeare's *Taming of the Shrew*'.[19] Hardwick rewrote the script with an African-American cast in mind to 'make it different': different, it seems, from the last *Shrew* venture, Gil Junger's *Ten Things I Hate About You*, in which Hardwick's title character, Eva (Gabrielle Union), also had a role. The film is a timely effort to challenge the racial ideologies of popular romantic comedies, such as *Sweet Home Alabama* (dir. Andy Tennant, 2002), *Legally Blonde* (dir. Robert Luketic, 2001), *Love Actually* (dir. Richard Curtis, 2003), *How to Lose a Guy in Ten Days* (dir. Donald Petrie, 2003), *Two Weeks' Notice* (dir. Marc Lawrence, 2002) and *Wimbledon* (dir. Richard Loncraine, 2004), which noticeably play out the genre codes of box-office smashes such as *Four Weddings and a Funeral* (dir. Mike Newell, 1994) and *Pretty Woman* (dir. Garry Marshall, 1990) in terms of essentially white subjectivities. Of significance is the anticipation of a sea change: immediately following the film's release, the romantic comedy genre finally wandered into the global neighbourhood, where black, Hispanic, Indian and Asian identities and relationships emerge from the margins in features such as *Are We There Yet?* (dir. Brian Levant, 2005), *Hitch* (dir. Andy Tennant, 2005), *Shall We Dance?* (dir. Peter Chelsom, 2004), *Bride and Prejudice* (dir. Gurinder Chadha, 2004) and *Breakin' All The Rules* (dir. Daniel Taplitz, 2004).

Deliver Us from Eva imagines Shakespeare's shrewish Katherine as Eva Dandridge, a straight-talking, good-looking Los Angeles health inspector who keeps her three younger sisters – and their men – in check. At the brink of despair and divorce, the Dandridge sisters' partners conspire to get Eva out of their hair, homes and wives' heads by paying a straight-talking, good-looking meat packer named Ray (James Todd Smith) to 'distract' her. Inevitably, Eva sheds her uncompromising skin and reveals her soft centre. When Eva turns down a job promotion in Chicago to be with Ray, the Dandridge men stage his death. But Ray returns – on a white horse, no less – to save the day, and the newly reformed Eva stays out of her sisters' marriages and in Ray's buff arms.

In keeping with the 'battle of the sexes' scenario at the heart of black romantic comedy, the film plays out Eva's masculinity in pointed contrast to the men's castration anxiety. Timothy (Mel Jackson), husband to Kareenah Dandrige (Essence Atkins), is reduced to a self-proclaimed 'handy-man with a penis'. His desire to start a family is squashed once Eva's statistics of marital failure reach Kareenah's ears. Emasculated before his friends and ousted from fatherhood by Eva, Timothy imagines Eva taking a cleaver to his appendage and suggests Ike Turner – portrayed in *What's Love Got To Do With It?* (dir. Brian Gibson, 1993) as Tina Turner's mega-violent, rapist husband – as a possible 'love' candidate for Eva. When Eva and Ray proclaim their love, Timothy announces he's 'growing another penis' in Eva's absence. The suggestion is that Eva has not only replaced her sisters' dead parents (asking, at one point, 'Why don't you think of me as your mama right now?'), but additionally serves as the alpha (fe)male who fertilises the Dandridge homes with 'girl power'.

The Mars/Venus (or perhaps misogynist/feminist) struggle in the film is ostensibly about culture. As Eva puts it during a fight with Timothy, 'this is about women. Women who aspire to culture, and men who aspire to scratch themselves.' But the film is not about women; it is about black middle-class African-American women in the twenty-first century who assert their subjectivity on a white-dominated genre to underline difference and diversity as the catchwords of the post-millennial popular sphere. The film proposes to eschew homogeneity in the form of its departure from white-premised romantic comedies and in terms of an avid conflict between men and women. Yet, in the end, the conventions of the genre are fulfilled and balance is restored once Eva's masculinity is eschewed, suggesting that a 'multiperspectival' worldview unequivocally involves a struggle for power that cannot necessarily easily be resolved.

IV

The racial politics of the McShakespeare find surer footing in Tim Blake Nelson's 'O' (2001), a contemporary loose adaptation of *Othello* set at a fictional high school, Palmetto Grove Academy, in America's Deep South. 'O', or Odin James (Mekhi Phifer), is played as an award-winning teenage basketball player and the only black student at Palmetto Grove. As in Shakespeare's plot, 'O' succumbs to Hugo's (Josh Hartnett) lies and murders his girlfriend, Desi (Julia Stiles, daughter of the Dean), and his best friend, Michael Cassio (Andrew Keegan). The film's portraits of basketball culture, father-son/father-daughter relationships and high-school violence rather predictably list the genre codes of the teen movie, while Nelson's cast, fresh from appearances in *Ten Things I Hate About You* (Andrew Keegan) and Michael Almereyda's 2000 version of *Hamlet* (Julia Stiles), suggests a familiar territory for fans of teen Shakespeare films. More strikingly, the film's immediate familiarity lies in its evocation of the recent wave of high-school murders in North America. Although its contextual engagement with the Columbine High School massacre has been well noted, the film's announcement of Shakespeare's connection to this massacre and several others has gone unnoticed. In May 1998, a fifteen-year-old male, ostensibly inspired by Baz Luhrmann's *William Shakespeare's 'Romeo + Juliet'* (1996), shot and killed two co-students at Thurston high school in Oregon and wounded twenty-six others: police found the soundtrack to Luhrmann's film on continual repeat at the gunman's home.[20] In 2005, a seventeen-year-old male entered Red Lake High School in Minnesota during a Shakespeare on film class, shooting and killing seven co-students. The tragedy bore uncanny parallels to the Columbine massacre. A student, Cassie Bernall, was reading a book about Shakespeare; when the gunmen entered the library and asked her if she believed in God, she was promptly murdered. Similarly, a member of the Shakespeare on film class at Red Lake heard the gunman ask a student in the next classroom whether or not he believed in God before shooting him dead.

Although this parallel neither implicates the Bard in these murders nor solves problems of high-school aggressivity, what it does suggest is the involvement of Shakespearean cinema in the debate over the relationship between film and teen violence. Nelson's film does not attempt to run the gauntlet of this debate, but instead offers Shakespeare as a meaning system – an O-shaped lens, if you will – through which the complex encounters of contemporary high-school issues and teen violence can be perceived, in the same moment as it underlines the urgency for perception followed by action. As Barbara Hodgdon points out, the film portrays the high school as 'a microcosm of a larger culture that idolises sports heroes' and that is 'shot through with violence'.[21] Suffice it to say that, in the film's signifying practices, the letter 'O' is invested with multilateral referents: 'O' for *Othello*, 'O' for Odin, 'O' for OJ, 'O' for object, 'O' for Other.[22] Nelson's meticulous (and occasionally overwrought) contexts for the signified 'O' can be read in terms of a series of concentric circles, which moves from Shakespeare's play to the conceptual issues of objectivity and otherness at the heart of the film. Odin is objectified by Hugo, or rather persuaded to replace his own subjectivity with one that is duped, masterminded and ultimately rendered different. Likewise, Shakespeare is not the concern of the film but, rather, is pushed to the film's outer layer. Serving as an organising principle, Shakespeare unites the film's 'local' concerns with those of the global macrocosm. The local, in other words, signifies the global in this production. What Nelson seems to be suggesting is that, although teen violence has been afflicting high schools in the US of late, the 'kernel' of the problem is rooted in an unequivocally global system. As David Morley and Kevin Robins put it, the local is definitely relative to the global: 'the "local" should be seen as a fluid and relational space, constituted only in and through its relation to the global'.[23]

V

Not only the multiperspectival, but the 'multilocal' additionally informs the McShakespeare. Put differently, the McShakespeare is pertinent to the construction of a Shakespeare that belongs to many cultures at once. Shakespeare therefore not only becomes relevant to many disparate peoples but also iterates the importance of belonging, pointing, in the face of a persistently evolving global community, to the employment of text as a point of origin and identity, a substitute for a geographical location. In the absence of a motherland, the (paternal) force of the text seems to suffice. Allison L. LiCalsi's *Macbeth: The Comedy*, Billy Morrissette's *Scotland, PA* and Vishal Bharadwaj's *Maqbool* take up Shakespeare's 'Scottish play' and re-configure Scottish-ness as a somewhat quaint ideal of localisation through which a post-colonial imperative can be articulated. In imaginatively divergent ways, the multilocal is imagined throughout these productions in terms of hybridity, post-structuralism and sequelisation, whilst identity as a 'fixed' point of origin is thrown into question.

Allison L. LiCalsi's *Macbeth: The Comedy* (2001) is an independent film parody of *Macbeth* that was shot over a couple of days in New Jersey and New York. Couching Shakespeare's text within comic diatribes and sarcastic commentary (such as 'You'll have to excuse my father – ever since verse came into fashion he's been a bit confused'), the film invokes British comedy sitcoms such as *Blackadder* and *Monty Python* to contextualise its particular brand of wit and an anachronistic take on the Bard. The film advertises itself as 'the first gay and lesbian Shakespeare film parody', featuring Macbeth as a woman (Erika Burke) and adding into the mix a 'new' character, Lord Kilmarnock (Gary Brownlee).[24] Of central importance is the dislocation of Scotland from a geographical site and its relocation as a fragmented, commodified host of signifiers, including tartan, Scottish flags, bagpipes, shortbread, whisky and (one) 'genuine' Scottish accent. As other critics have argued, Scotland can represent the site of a historical homeland and a nostalgically configured cultural identity.[25] In turn, Scottishness is parodically reduced here to a collection of tourist toys, suggesting identity itself as a souvenir that may be transported between nations by the exile or diasporic subject. Arguably feeding upon the US frenzy for family history, the film underlines and pokes fun at the diluted 'Scottish-American' type who invokes Scottish citizenship through the use of a distant family name – or perhaps the prefix, 'Mac' – and who acquires a taste for tartan, flags and bagpipes. Yet beneath the film's comic glance at America's fascination with cultural origins and belonging, the evocation of Scottish identity, and the construction of Scotland as a conflation of histories and identities (an 'origin' that is only ever retrievable by the American subject as part of a 'multi-local' identity), suggest that the McShakespeare is premised upon a hunt for roots that are spread too far to recapture in full. Although LiCalsi's production imagines Scottishness as a hybridised identity that plays a vital part in constituting (a displaced) American pysche, Billy Morrissette's *Scotland, PA* (2001) reinvents the subject of the drama as a geographical site that is, as the film's title suggests, not Shakespeare's original bastion. Scotland, Pennsylvania, is pointedly the 'sequel' to Scotland, UK, a move that points up a cultural identity that is structured around sequelisation and 'afterwardness'. The film has a noticeably larger budget and more professional cast than LiCalsi's undertaking, and is motivated by the question: what if the McBeths were alive in 1975? Naturally, it seems, they would be a couple of married 'underachievers' flipping burgers in east-coast America. Shot in Nova Scotia (Latin for 'New Scotland'), *Scotland, PA* imaginatively switches the play's location to its colonial 'sequel', which was founded in the nineteenth century by Scottish immigrants and, as Mark Thornton Burnett notes, conjures the memory of Scotland in Morrissette's production.[26] 'Scotland' constitutes a purposeful gesture to the play's (national) locale, an after-life that serves as America's pseudo-Scotland. Birnam Wood appears as an actual forest park and as a fashion motif, captured by the pattern of black, leafless trees that adorns Pat's outfit. The witches in the play claim that 'Macbeth shall never vanquished be until / Great Birnam wood to high Dunsinane Hill / Shall come against him'; by contrast, Morrissette's film symbolically expresses this prediction by suggesting that Macbeth is vanquished by the *representation* of that territory, embodied (or adorned) by his wife.[27]

The film's treatment of geographical difference is construed in terms of national symbolism. Scotland is depicted not only via the film's title and its shooting location, but also through the tartan ovenglove Pat uses to hide her 'spotted' hand immediately before chopping it off with a cleaving knife. Deriving from the various indigenous tribes that arrived in Scotland from Ireland with their 'woollen cloths of different colours', tartan's numerous forms evoke specific Scottish groupings from as early as 500 BC and depict (somewhat loosely) national traditions and lineage.[28] Interestingly, Pat's ovenglove adorns the *MacBeth* (also known as the Stewart Brydone) tartan, which is composed of red, white, blue and green strands in a specific arrangement.[29] Of further note is the MacDuff tartan. The two colours of this tartan – red and green – festoon the McBeths' establishment (red letters and green roof) and, later, McDuff's (red/green letters and green roof).[30] The suggestion is that 'McBeth's' is the prophecy of McDuff's (less successful) enterprise, an anticipatory colonialist, and sequelised, endeavour. That is, the ethos of the Scottish tartan signals the film's preoccupation with national diversity and hybridity inside a sequelisation context.

Mac/McBeth's demise is further indicated by the film's engagement with representations and 'sequels', for Birnam Wood is initially shown when Mac, Banko (Timothy Corrigan), Jimmy (David Wike) and Kevin (Reed Rudy) go deer hunting, an obvious reference to *The Deer Hunter* (dir. Michael Cimino, 1978), which starred Christopher Walken in a leading role. In concert with Mac's descent into insanity and narcissistic vanity are the appearances of stuffed deer heads on the walls of his home. The gun he uses to kill deer and, finally, Banko, rests on a wall-mount beneath a stuffed stag, and the large horns on his car bonnet (which echo both ornaments of the 1970s and the headgear worn by Duncan (Erskine Sanford) in Orson Welles' *Macbeth* (1948)) allude to the act of deer hunting and, subsequently, Cimino's production. Mac's Christian name, 'Joe', references Ken Hughes' *Joe Macbeth* (1955), a *film noir* version of the play in which Macbeth/Joe (Paul Douglas) kills his way to the top of a criminal hierarchy. These intertextual, citational connections thus posit

Mac's death on the car-bonnet horns at the film's end as the fatalistic consequences of narcissism and, more importantly, excessive filmic allusion concomitant with the sequelisation phenomenon.

Perhaps the most forceful iteration of the McShakespeare's 'multilocal' dimensions is found in Vishal Bharadwaj's Bollywood version of Macbeth, *Maqbool* (2003), which points to the development of a global identity that celebrates the 'mobile, marginal, and hybrid nature' of a citizenship calling more than one location 'home'.[31] As one of the world's largest film industries, Bollywood is perpetuated and supported by a devoted indigenous fan base. As Faiza Hirji comments, 'roughly ten million people a day purchase tickets to see a Bollywood movie, and some of these will return repeatedly to view a favourite movie'.[32] Bollywood is the epitome of the 'multilocal', apparently resisting Hollywood's imperialistic system at the same time as the scores of different languages and identities in South Asia are ascribed to India's overtly monolithic filmic machine. And if Bollywood, through its name, concerns itself with conversations between East and West, *Maqbool* appears centred upon maintaining a 'balance' between carnivalesque 'multilocal' identities that compete for recognition and acknowledgement.

On occasion, such a 'balance' requires hybridity. This emerges initially in the form of the film's allusively conceived genre, which marries Shakespeare to an Islamic version of *The Godfather* (dir. Francis Ford Coppola, 1972) in the depiction of a latter-day Mumbai mafia. Triangulating the narrative, the film seeks to 'balance' Bollywood's cultural investitures in Islam, Hollywood and the global cultural mechanism represented by Shakespeare. Departing from *The Godfather*, *Maqbool* updates Duncan as a Don Corleone take-off (replete with Brando mumble) named Jahangir Khan and known as Abbaji (Pankaj Kapoor). Maqbool Miyan (Irrfan Khan) is Abbaji's right-hand man and surrogate mafia 'son'. When Abbaji's young mistress, Nimmi (Tabu), falls for Maqbool, a plot is swiftly put into action to remove the Don from his seat of authority. The *Godfather* reference is pointedly in keeping with a host of other Indian films that have revisited Coppola's classic (amongst them Mani Ratnam's Godfather-inspired *Nayakan* (1987), Feroz Khan's *Dharmatma* (1975), Balraj Deepak Vij's *Mumbai Godfather* (2005), Ram Gopal Varma's remake of *The Godfather, Sarkar* (2005), and Rajkumar Santoshi's *Family* (2005)): thus, *Maqbool*, the first Bollywood Shakespeare, constructs the text in a 'predictable' manner that in turn foregrounds a 'local' subject for Western audiences.

Although *Maqbool* can be read as a political venture for Bollywood's inclusion in the global economy, the film simultaneously rehearses the primary traditions and interests of Indian culture. Accordingly, Shakespeare's characters are given Muslim names, which at times creates problems in comparing the film to the play. The characters greet each other with 'Salaam' and 'Khuda Hafiz', honour prayer times, wear skull-caps and employ a dense Urdu vocabulary. Astrology – the Islamic equivalent of witchcraft – is the means by which Maqbool's rise and descent are predicted. Matching Bollywood's generic requirements, the director includes several song and dance numbers, which enforce the Hindu priorities of virginity, marriage and polarised gender roles. And while the Lady Macbeth character, Nimmi, forces Maqbool at gun point to call her 'my love', she never ventures near Lady Macbeth's aspirations to become unsexed. Nimmi ceases weeping only when Maqbool requites her romantic ideals, gives Maqbool an ultimatum ('It's me or Abbaji') in the context that servitude to the Don is preventing their love from blooming, and goes mad after giving birth. Despite the deployment of the gangster genre, then, the film's primary approach to *Macbeth* is at the level of the relationship between Macbeth and Lady Macbeth, which is configured here in terms of a Greek tragedy. At one point, Nimmi weeps in Maqbool's arms, forcing him (again) to tell her that their love is pure. Saturated with tones of blue, the film's use of colour further heightens the play's construction of desire. According to the *Natyashastra*, an ancient Indian dramaturgy text, the colour blue denotes eroticism. In this connection, the lust for dominion in the play serves the film's cultural purpose to warn of the dangers of 'impure' relations. And, of course, blue is also the signature hue of Islamic religion and culture.

Its indebtedness to Hollywood notwithstanding – particularly in relation to the ending, which is borrowed shot-for-shot from Luc Besson's *Léon* (1994) – Bharadwaj's film arguably enshrines the complexities of 'multilocalism' that inform the McShakespeare by placing a symbolic gloss upon the representation of multiple cultural identities. In particular, the film registers the pluralistic, or indeed hybrid, configurations of cultural identity at the current moment as strengthening, rather than eroding, Bollywood's cultural traditions and ideologies. Just as Shakespeare's text is replaced with a Hindi vernacular, so, too, the film suggests, is culture re-articulated and redefined as a result of global interaction. The allusions in *Maqbool* to Hollywood productions and Shakespeare may further be described as 'selective borrowing[s] from the West' that 'palliate the problems caused by the many competing cultures within India', insofar as 'multilocalism' is taken to involve the consciousness of global influences at every level of cultural exchange.[33] Or, to put it another way, the 'balance' of power is maintained in *Maqbool* by decisively invoking those foreign structures, identities and even films that underline differences within the indigenous community and without.

VI

David Morley's notion of 'reterritorialisation' finds a parallel in the McShakespeare's efforts to relocate Shakespeare to distant realms.[34] Two versions of *King Lear* – *King of Texas* (dir. Uli Edel, 2002) and *The King Is Alive* (dir. Kristian Levring, 2001) – evoke the McShakespeare's investments in contriving secondary 'spaces of belonging' that re-imagine the original homeland. Both films visit the concept of post-ness – most commonly introduced during the course of postmodernism – to answer with greater clarity the 'secondariness' of reterritorialisation. Notably, this concept brings to mind the 'inevitably derivative nature' of the McMovie, appearing in the McShakespeare not only in the form of textual post-ness, or the conceptualisation of 'coming after' a source text, but also in terms of the sequential logic of McDonaldisation. Earlier, this chapter referred to the McDonald's-Disney alliance that pivoted upon the idea of movie mementoes that exploit the spectatorial desire to re-experience and recall a film in the form of tie-ins. It is this kind of post-ness – driven by desire – that enlivens Edel and Levring's films, although here in the form of *politically motivated* desire. Both productions respond to the cultural environment of a historical juncture that is shaped in response to a previous era, employing the apocalyptic dimensions of Shakespeare's *Lear* to signal a dual point of closure and a moment of change. The compulsion to feel the past in the present (to repeat, re-experience and prevent the return of history) appears within these films as a cultural pathology at the same time as the 'reterritorialisation' of the past (for better and for worse) is constructed as a specifically twenty-first-century phenomenon.

The TV film, *King of Texas*, imagines *Lear* as a Western in post-Alamo Texas. The film stars Patrick Stewart as an aged ranch patriarch whose stern tactics spill over into his parenting skills when he demands confessions of love from his three daughters as payment for their inheritance, which represents one-third of his 200,000 acres of Texan soil. The film's opening shot is an extreme wide-angle of barren desert and two corpses hanging from the single bough of a leafless tree: starving Mexicans murdered by Lear for stealing one of his cows. Repentant Lear is not, continually admonishing those around him to 'remember the Alamo', making his tyranny and self-appointed 'king-ship' comparable, as Courtney Lehmann shows, to the 'post-9/11 imperialism' of the Bush administration.[35] In other words, the 'global' impact of a local event enforces an imperialistic dogma, which continually invokes and enflames all conceptions of the present as a post-temporal moment.

The film departs from the play's theme of divided land to portray a society, or nation, divided by land ownership. Within the macrocosmic historical context of the battle between Texan rebels and the Republic of Mexico at the Alamo mission in San Antonio, Texas, in 1836, Edel situates the Lear family and the deep-seated troubles that emerge in the wake of the decision to divide the ranch. When Lear asks his daughters for confessions of their love, Susannah (Marcia Gay Harden) does not hesitate to proclaim that 'there is no man in this country who can stand next to my father', even though she is represented standing next to her husband, Mr Tumlinson (Colm Meaney). Rebecca (Lauren Holly) informs Lear that she loves him 'like I love the sun', while Claudia (Julie Cox) 'has nothing to say' because she deems the whole scenario 'false'. Because Lear fails to see how much he is loved, seeking simultaneously to control the measure of love, Claudia refuses to supply on demand. It later emerges that Susannah and Rebecca's resentment towards Lear follows close on the heels of the death of their mother: 'you worked our mother to death. You never took no notice of Rebecca or me. Ever. All you cared about was your son. And after he died, all you cared about was Claudia', it is stated. While the film adumbrates several extra-textual back-stories to provide insight into each of the characters, it also symbolically underlines deeper contextual registers of post-ness. Typical is the convincing portrait of Lear, left at the end with only one child, as the embodiment of a single-boughed tree standing in the desert with its roots buried in the snake-invested earth. More significantly, when Lear is ousted from his own land at gunpoint by Susannah, he at first rejects Henry's (Roy Scheider) offer to take him in, telling him, 'I'm at home right where I am'. Lear's madness is suggested as a reaction to the displacement brought about by his daughters. His 'reterritorialisation' – relocated both physically from his home, legally as 'king' of Texas and emotionally as father of three daughters – is a microcosmic portrait of the migratory pathology inherent in America's origins. And his question – 'Who is it that can tell me who I am?' – is suggested in Edel's film as prompted by a displaced identity, a sense of self that, rooted in a particular place, must refigure a 'second' identity if, in the event of reterritorialisation, it is to survive.[36]

Such a narrative scenario is characteristic of Kristian Levring's *The King Is Alive*. The fourth production released under the banner of the 'Dogme 95' movement, Levring's film uses minimal filming equipment (the Dogme's 'Vow of Chastity' aimed at recreating the 'purity' of early cinema) to portray the story of ten coach passengers who are stranded in the middle of the Namibian desert when the engine breaks down. Waiting for help, and barely surviving on tins of carrots and stale water, the group is led in a performance of *King Lear* to pass the time. What transpires is the 'doubling' of identity: the collective creation of 'second', performed identities which relate to the emotional duress of displacement. Doubling, as Freud observes, is concomitant with denying death. As the film develops, however, the double becomes associated with *causing* or anticipating death, becoming 'the uncanny harbinger of death'.[37] Paul (Chris Walker) as Edmund finds a disturbing parallel between his new role and his biological/cultural one as Charles' (Bruce Calder) son. Gina dies twice: once as 'Cordelia' and finally as Gina. That Catherine 'doubles', to an extent, the role of Cordelia in the same moment as she murders Gina/Cordelia is further significant. Both Gina and Catherine are (unlikely) friends at the film's outset, and are candidates for the part of Cordelia and the role of Henry's daughter-figure. Catherine tells Gina (in French), 'I'm fed up with you sticking to my ass', and rejects Henry's offer of playing Cordelia. When Henry gives the role to Gina, Catherine can no longer live with her 'double' and ensures her quick demise.

In both productions, the effects of reterritorialisation engender specifically traumatic 'double' identities. This is not, however, to suggest reterritorialisation as a blurring of boundaries: rather, as David Morley emphasises, reterritorialisation involves 'borders and boundaries of various sorts . . . becoming more, rather than less, strongly marked'.[38] In the McShakespeare, these borders and boundaries embrace transitional modes of appropriation which are strongly classified and coded (as in genres, blatant allusions to other films and marketing strategies) and which, additionally, draw attention to seismic shifts inside multiple cultural identities. The effects of such dislocations are still being felt and are only partially open to representation at the current historical moment. The 'space of belonging' emphasised by reterritorialisation is captured in the interim in the form of predictable, recognisable and global 'texts' that instruct and guide spectators at a critical phase of post-ness and cultural uncertainty.

VII

Pinpointing the importance of scenarios of multiculturalism and globalisation in twenty-first Shakespearean cinema, I have argued that the McShakespeare constitutes a means of negotiating highly transitional and often uncertain modes of cultural activity and agency at the present juncture. As these films demonstrate, the McShakespeare can be regarded less as an attempt to re-engage with Shakespeare than as a repetition complex that is motivated and engineered by the global mechanisms of a horizontally integrated Hollywood or, at least, a Hollywood that has expanded from its original studio base to include media conglomerates, software companies and fast-food giants in its global output. Yet there is further evidence that the cultural discourses inherent in the McShakespeare – such as the effects of drug warfare, interrogations of globalisation, the centralisation of marginalised identities and re-articulations of 9/11 – are of particular significance for understanding what Shakespeare 'means' to popular culture in the twenty-first century. Although the McShakespeare is stridently concerned with the collapse of genres and cultural boundaries – registering, as Harvey Greenberg sees it, the cannibalistic consumption and regurgitation of prior narratives – Shakespeare films of the twenty-first century employ such variegated tactics to register deeper global and local contexts that acquire a voice solely through the Shakespearean textual affiliation.

Notes

1. Harvey Roy Greenberg (1993), *Screen Memories: Hollywood Cinema on the Psychoanalytic Couch*, New York: Columbia University Press, pp. 185–209.
2. Greenberg, *Screen Memories*, p. 199.
3. See James L. Watson (2002), 'Transnationalism, Localization, and Fast Foods in East Asia', in George Ritzer (ed.), *McDonaldization: The Reader*, London and Thousand Oaks: Pine Forge Press, pp. 228, 231.
4. George Ritzer, 'McDonaldization: Basics, Studies, Applications and Extensions', in Ritzer (ed.), *McDonaldization*, pp. 1–7.
5. Ritzer, 'Cross-Cultural Analysis, Social Movements and Social Change', in Ritzer (ed.), *McDonaldization*, p. 187; Ritzer, 'McDonaldization: Basics, Studies, Applications and Extensions', pp. 1–7.
6. Fara Warner (2005), *The Power of the Purse: How Smart Businesses Are Adapting to the World's Most Important Consumers – Women*, London: Pearson, pp. 10–15.
7. Susan Bennett (1997), *Theatre Audiences: A Theory of Production and Reception*, 2nd edn, London and New York: Routledge, p. 164.
8. James Twitchell (1992), *Carnival Culture: The Trashing of Taste in America*, New York: Columbia University Press, p. 142. Richard Maltby calls this experience 'commercial intertextuality' (*Hollywood Cinema*, 2nd edn, Oxford: Blackwell, 2003, p. 206).
9. Richard Burt (2003), 'Shakespeare, "Glo-cali-zation," race, and the small screens of post-popular culture', in Richard Burt and Lynda E. Boose (eds), *Shakespeare, the Movie, II: Popularizing the Plays on Film, TV, Video, and DVD*, London and New York: Routledge, pp. 15–16.
10. Watson, 'Transnationalism, Localization, and Fast Foods in East Asia', p. 228.
11. Watson, 'Transnationalism, Localization, and Fast Foods in East Asia', p. 229.

12. *Richard III*, in *The Norton Shakespeare*, Stephen Greenblatt, Walter Cohen, Jean E. Howard and Katharine Eisaman Maus (eds) (1997), New York: W. W. Norton, I.ii.216.
13. See also Ben Malbon (1998), 'The Club: Clubbing, Consumption, Identity and the Spatial Practices of Every-Night Life', in Tracey Skelton and Gill Valentine (eds), *Cool Places: Geographies of Youth Culture*, London and New York: Routledge, pp. 267, 271; Maria Pini (1997), 'Women and the early British rave scene', in Angela McRobbie (ed.), *Back to Reality? Social Experience and Cultural Studies*, Manchester and New York: Manchester University Press, p. 159.
14. Diana Sandars (2005), 'From the warehouse to the multiplex: Techno and rave culture's reconfiguration of late 1990s' sci-fi spectacle as musical performance', *Screening the Past*, July (http://www.latrobe.edu.au/screeningthepast/firstrelease/fr_18/DSfr18a.html).
15. 'HD feature *Rave Macbeth* makes its digital premiere at Cannes', *Sony Deutschland* (http://www.sonybiz.net/b2b/sony-business-de/35794-sony-deutschland-hd-feature-rave-macbeth-makes-its-digital-premiere-at-cannes-scene-to-screen-features-and-interviews.html).
16. Michael Bristol (1996), *Big-Time Shakespeare*, London and New York: Routledge, p. 34.
17. Douglas Kellner, 'Theorizing/Resisting McDonaldization: A Multiperspectivist Approach' (http://www.gseis.ucla.edu/faculty/kellner/essays/theorizingresistingmcdonaldization.pdf).
18. Kellner, 'Theorizing/Resisting McDonaldization: A Multiperspectivist Approach'.
19. http://www.deliverusfromeva.com/home_movie.html.
20. Peter Ritter (2001), 'Dis Bard: O forces Shakespeare to concede to Gore', *City Pages*, 29 August (http://citypages.com/databank/22/1082/article9788.asp).
21. Barbara Hodgdon (2003), 'Race-ing *Othello*, re-engendering white-out, II', in Burt and Boose (eds), *Shakespeare, the Movie, II*, p. 99.
22. *The One*, the film's European DVD title, self-consciously alludes to *The Matrix* (dir. Larry and Andy Wachowski, 1999).
23. David Morley and Kevin Robins (1997), *Space of Identity*, London and New York: Routledge, p. 17.
24. See the *Tristan Films* website (http://www.tristanfilms.net/macbeth/macbeth.html).
25. Mark Thornton Burnett (2004), 'Local *Macbeth*/global Shakespeare: Scotland's screen destiny', in Willy Maley and Andrew Murphy (eds), *Shakespeare and Scotland*, Manchester: Manchester University Press, pp. 189–206; Courtney Lehmann (2003), 'Out damned Scot: Dislocating *Macbeth* in transnational film and media culture', in Burt and Boose (eds), *Shakespeare, the Movie, II*, pp. 231–51.
26. Mark Thornton Burnett (2005), 'Writing Shakespeare in the Global Economy', *Shakespeare Survey*, 58, p. 194.
27. *Macbeth*, in *The Norton Shakespeare*, IV.i.108–10.
28. See *The Scottish Tartans Society Website* (http://www.scottish-tartans-society.co.uk); James Grant (1992), *Scottish Tartans in Full Colour*, New York: Dover Publications; Iain Zaczek (2000), *Clans and Tartans of Scotland*, New York: Barnes & Noble Books.
29. See *The Scottish Tartans Society Website* (http://www.scottish-tartans-society.co.uk); *Tartans of Scotland* (http://www.tartans.scotland.net/tartan_info.cfm?tartan_id=1975).
30. 'Tartan no. 1453', *The Scottish Tartans Society Website* (http://www.scottish-tartans-society.co.uk).

31. Hau Ling Cheng (2005), 'Constructing a Transnational, Multilocal Sense of Belonging: An Analysis of *Ming Pao* (West Canadian Edition)', *Journal of Communication Inquiry*, 29.2, p. 8.
32. Faiza Hirji (2005), 'When Local Meets Lucre: Commerce, Culture and Imperialism in Bollywood Cinema', *Global Media Journal*, 4.7 (available at http://lass.calumet.purdue.edu/cca/gmj/Fall2005/graduate/Hirji-%20Refereed.htm).
33. Hirji, 'When Local Meets Lucre'.
34. David Morley (2001), 'Belongings: Place, Space and Identity in a Mediated World', *European Journal of Cultural Studies*, 4.4, p. 428.
35. Courtney Lehmann, 'The Passion of the W: Provincializing Shakespeare, Globalizing Manifest Density, from *King Lear* to Sacred Cow(boy)s' (http://www.clemson.edu/caah/shakespr/pastfestivals/LehmannLecture.pdf).
36. *The Tragedy of King Lear*, in *The Norton Shakespeare*, I.iv.195.
37. Sigmund Freud, 'The Uncanny', in James Strachey (ed.) (1953–74), *The Standard Edition of the Complete Psychological Works of Sigmund Freud*, 22 vols, London: Hogarth, XVII, p. 235.
38. Morley, 'Belongings', p. 428.

Chapter 10

Shakespeare and the Singletons, or, Beatrice Meets Bridget Jones: Post-Feminism, Popular Culture and 'Shakespea(Re)-Told'

Ramona Wray

'Shakespea(Re)-Told' was launched by the BBC in late 2005 as part of a concerted drive to re-animate the relevancies of the Bard for a range of early twenty-first-century listeners and audiences.[1] Consisting of a variety of 'tellings' of Shakespeare, from radio broadcasts and cartoons to documentaries and screen adaptations, the season promised, in Daniel Fischlin and Mark Fortier's words, not so much to honour Shakespeare's 'unsurpassed originality, the sanctity of his texts, and the cultural taboo on presuming to alter them' as, rather, to illuminate the extent to which, from their inception, the works 'have been both the product and the source of an ongoing explosion of recreation'.[2] Indeed, a 'mockumentary', *Shakespeare's Happy Endings*, screened to accompany the season illustrated precisely this phenomenon: beyond the parodic diversions lay a more sober recasting of the means whereby Shakespeare, and his works, had been appropriated in seventeenth-, eighteenth- and nineteenth-century theatrical practice in particular and popular culture in general.[3]

The 'Shakespea(Re)-Told' season prioritised television adaptations, 'spin-offs' that translated into a modern vernacular the Shakespearean parlance while simultaneously retaining the dramas' structural schemes. Of the four 're-tellings' commissioned (in order of transmission *Much Ado About Nothing*, *Macbeth*, *The Taming of the Shrew* and *A Midsummer Night's Dream*), *Much Ado About Nothing* and *The Taming of the Shrew* stood out as notably daring and distinctive choices. Infrequently filmed and/or televised, *Much Ado About Nothing* and *The Taming of the Shrew* present obvious updating problems, especially in relation to the treatment of women, sexuality and the place of romance. Arresting in this connection is the fact that, while *Macbeth* and *A Midsummer Night's Dream* were both uniquely individual as far as their thematic organisation and aesthetic delivery were concerned, *Much Ado* and *Taming* employed a similar situational idiom and conceptual frame-work, despite being produced by different creative writing teams. Because these two appropriations are accorded the same species of 'makeover', a contemporary purchase for Shakespearean comedy is suggested, one that is capable of accommodating the genre's seeming intransigence and resist-ant ideologies. Jointly foregrounding identical popular television genres, character types and contemporary media debate, *Much Ado* and *Taming* demonstrate an assured sense of modern equivalents for Shakespearean comedy and a considered awareness of the ways in which post-feminist understandings of gender and genre push into productive proximity early modern constructions of 'woman' and twenty-first-century reflections upon love, marriage and heterosexual relations.

I

Distinctive about the 're-telling' of *Much Ado* and *Taming* is the priori-tisation of romantic comedy dimensions inside an affluent English setting. Hand-in-hand with the evocations of history and tradition embodied in Shakespeare goes *Much Ado*'s investment in all things English, including Anglican churches, windy seaside promenades and historic country hotels. Similarly, *Taming* makes extensive use of estab-lishing shots of derelict stately homes, Big Ben and leafy London parks, and pauses over images of bandstands and eccentric Etonians, in order to underscore stereotypical national associations and an English heart-land unchanging in the face of the trappings of globalisation. Emerging from these emphases is the privileging in both *Much Ado* and *Taming* of two fully-fledged weddings. Here, the plays (in which marriages take place off-stage or are a matter of report) are departed from, with the appropriations, in a narrative device familiar from popular romantic comedy genres, making of the wedding a set-piece.[4] For instance, *Much Ado*'s network of interlocking hotel rooms that permit and frustrate romantic ingress and egress is very much the territory of *Four Weddings and a Funeral* (dir. Mike Newell, 1994), among other films of a similar ilk, and indicates an equation of Shakespeare and Englishness that might strike a chord with some elements of the American imaginary. Hence, each adaptation possesses the necessary qualities to be labelled, as Lez Cooke states in a discussion of television costume drama, 'heritage export': 'Englishness' becomes the meal ticket with which appeals are made to a global, postmodern audience.[5]

   In keeping with the Englishness of setting are intertextual allusions to, and a reliance upon, a range of British televisual products (many of which have been successfully transferred to America), making an encounter with *Much Ado* and *Taming* at some level an oddly 'British' experience. The adaptations draw upon comfortable cultures and bourgeois relations to transform Renaissance narratives into 'thirty-something' dramas, episodes of *This Life* and Shakespearean versions of *Cold Feet* (some parts of which were also written by David Nicholls, the screenwriter for *Much Ado*). This twenty-first-century Shakespeare, then, is recognisable through the conventions and pleasures associated with an already established genre, one that Jill Marshall and Angela Werndly typify as a modern 'comedy of sexual manners' centred upon the 'lifestyles, interpersonal relationships, careers and rites of passage anxieties of middle-class young professionals'.[6]

As is characteristic of such thirty-something drama, in *Much Ado* and *Taming*, the stress falls not so much upon narrative as upon personality, with identification encouraged through fast-paced yet intimate camera work. The centrality of the two main couples – Beatrice (Sarah Parish) and Benedict (Damian Lewis) in *Much Ado*, and Katherine (Shirley Henderson) and Petruchio (Rufus Sewell) in *Taming* – to both appropriations is at once established via casting arrangements: 'stars' beyond the confines of the stories proper, all four are familiar to British television audiences through their previous parts in dramas such as *Cutting It* and *Hearts and Bones* and their roles in 'British' films such as *Bridget Jones' Diary* (dir. Sharon Maguire, 2001) and *24 Hour Party People* (dir. Michael Winterbottom, 2002). Both sets of characters are represented as belonging to a recognisable, independently oriented and cynically driven generation. Typical here are journalists and presenters Beatrice and Benedict, 'media types' beloved of thirty-something drama and newly appointed co-anchors on *Wessex Tonight*, a regional news programme. Beatrice is clever, attractive but waspish; Benedict is the suave 'ladies' man' and 'housewives' choice': both are constructed as ferociously ambitious and competitive, placing career over anything resembling a private life. In *Taming*, links to the media world (and both appropriations' easy, in-built dialogue with television culture) are discovered in the opening scene, which sees an incandescent and inadequately briefed Katherine Minola returning to Whitehall to her mild-mannered civil servant after having been 'shown up' on *Newsnight*. The opening, with its 'from-the-knees-down' shots of Kate's tiny sensible shoes pacing political corridors, immediately focuses attention upon a juxtaposition of gender and power, while the music – a version of John Williams' infamous score from *Jaws* (dir. Steven Spielberg, 1975) – puts us in no doubt as to her ferociousness of character. An early close-up reveals Kate shaking with rage, with her first words, 'Fuck it', followed by a resounding smack about the face for the civil servant, highlighting a propensity for violence and an alacrity of angry response. For this *Taming*, then, it is Kate, more so than Petruchio, who is figured as displaying physically aggressive tendencies. A Tory politician in the mode of Margaret Thatcher ('This lady's not for marrying', a pastiche version of the famous 'The lady's not for turning' speech, was the formulation with which *Taming* was announced), Kate is a candidate for the party leadership and is defined entirely by the long hours she spends at the office: the blue files she cradles are symbolically suggestive of a life that is non-existent outside of the work environment.

However high-flying, glamorous and financially rewarding these careers might be, they register as little more than backdrops to the more serious business of romance. The genre of daytime TV and regional programming inside which Beatrice and Benedict function is mercilessly lampooned through parodic camera work in the style of *Brass Eye*, *The Day Today* and *Knowing Me/Knowing You*: hairstyles are exaggerated; colours are outdatedly brash; shoulder pads are over-padded; and the dialogue emerges as overblown, cheesy and insincere. Typically, the features are either frothy or ridiculous: ladybirds deluge the coast, amateur fossil-hunters make a startling discovery, and a local cheese festival has the presenters licking their lips. Notwithstanding Beatrice's occasional protestation about the importance of regional programmes, this is not a career trajectory to take seriously. Likewise, *Taming* makes light work of Whitehall and the social and media frenzy surrounding contemporary politics. Notable here is a similarly parodic quality to *Much Ado*, for Kate's relationships with understated but omnipresent civil servants and MPs are firmly within the mannered range of the *Yes Minister* comedy series. Moreover, as with the TV studio that is the setting for *Much Ado*, everything is 'bigger' in *Taming*. Integral to an excessive modality of characterisation is a parallel magnification of the visuals and materials of the filmic locale. The film is hyperbolic at each level of its vibrant and colourful *mise-en-scène*, from Bianca's (Jaime Murray) fur coats and huge bathtub television to the physicality of Kate's rages and the eighteen-inch height difference between the central couple.

Inside hyperbole, both narratives are organised so as to generate a delicious confrontation between the work and romantic life components. It is suggested that, were she to marry, Kate would be the prime candidate for the leadership: her married status would attract the favourable media and voter response that is simply not accorded the single woman. (As her civil service mentor puts it, there are 'lifestyle issues' standing between Kate's bid for power and its acquisition.) In part because of Kate's standing, the accelerated courtship and disastrous wedding, when they do take place, unfold beneath the full glare of the party and media spotlight. The filmic prominence accorded publicity becomes a part explanation, in contemporary terms, both for the expedition of the wedding and for Kate's begrudging acceptance of Petruchio's behaviour. (The groom's physical force at the altar restrains Kate, but so does his reminder to 'think of all those little voters out there'.) By the same token, Beatrice and Benedict are paired as co-anchors largely because of the chemistry between them. As Leonard (Martin Jarvis), the programme controller, acknowledges, the couple exhibit a much sought-after sexual charge: 'the frisson,' he states, 'is what the public want to see'. Inside this tensely rarefied television world, verbal sparring matches are given full rein. Typical is Beatrice's remark that she watched an episode of Benedict's late-night, bargain-basement show, 'Attic Antiques': 'Is that a pre-record or do you actually have to stay up to 4am?' she asks. His retort – 'It's pre-record: you'd be surprised how popular it is with *middle-aged women living alone*' – is similarly barbed, equating, as it does, an imagined spinsterish audience and Beatrice's own single condition. Here, as elsewhere, her rejoinder – 'You really do put the "w" into "anchor man" ' – points up her superior intellectual prowess even as it hints at a denied mutual attraction.

As the invented prologue to *Much Ado* makes clear, this testy bickering amounts to more than the familiar rivalries (frequently speculated upon in the British tabloid press) of the daytime television sofa. Taking Shakespeare's play as its cue, *Much Ado* establishes a shared past as a context for current conflict. The narrative opens three years previously (an on-screen caption succinctly differentiates between the present and former selves) in order to discover Benedict committing the ultimate *faux pas* in terms of technology etiquette – breaking up with Beatrice via text message. Consequently, in the story proper, reminders of this history lend Benedict and Beatrice's war of words both an ill-tempered subjective edge and a sense of personal journeys as yet unsatisfactorily concluded. This is not least because the parallel montage of the opening sequence, in which each dresses to meet the other, deploys a visual grammar of personal vanity (both narcissistically preen and inhabit excessively tidy, minimalist spaces) in order to suggest a unacknowledged connectivity: as in the play, Beatrice and Benedict are all too alike, confirming their generically and stereotypically thirty-something status. *Taming* elaborates a no less absorbing impression of inevitability by developing a 'will they/won't they' narrative that relies on demonstrating compatibility. Having arrived back from travelling in Australia, homeless and in

debt, Petruchio represents no trophy spousal material; however, his con-
cordant class and ability status are discovered through the gradual revelation of shared backgrounds. The country pile and his titled status (Earl
of Charlbury) compensate for current cashflow problems and confirm
that he is a Tory boy at heart. And, from the first moment (in the lift to
Bianca's shiny modern-art apartment), Petruchio and Kate are established as paradoxically 'right' for each other. As she had earlier assaulted
a civil servant, so does Kate hit Petruchio, with his response – 'You do
that again and I'll hit you back' – suggesting a temperamental equiva-
lence. After the wedding, following his drunken antics at the service, even
Kate's disinterested mother (Twiggy Lawson) is prompted into querying
Petruchio's excesses. Harry (Stephen Tompkinson) admits his friend is
'borderline' but adds, comfortingly, 'Still, they're well-matched'.

Such is the extent of the appropriations' elevation of the main players
and thirty-somethings that the sub-plots and younger characters tend to
be present only as amusing foils. *Much Ado* is a case in point. Within an
approximation of more powerful television entities, Beatrice and
Benedict are joined by the beautiful Hero (Billie Piper) and the handsome
Claude (Tom Ellis), a 'weather girl' and a 'sports presenter' drawn to
each other through a shared youthful naivety and a penchant for wearing
shades of pastel pink. Neither is particularly bright (Hero, for instance,
announces that 'there's only one word for the weather this weekend, and
that's very changeable'), and both are afflicted by traditionalist notions
of passionate earnestness, rushing into marriage at the first opportunity.
Meantime, the depressed, divorcing and demoted Don (Derek Riddell),
a version of Don John, having developed a crush upon Hero after a one-
night stand, pursues her obsessively. Illegitimate behaviour takes over
from illegitimate birth, with a construction of the early twenty-first-
century stalker replacing an early-modern manifestation of the bastard.
Don's prowling practice provides psychological motivation and answers
to contemporary credibility requirements; given the paraphernalia of
cameras and microphones that adorns the studio setting, his villainy
gains an additional plausibility. Likewise, the studio locale offers a neat
conceit for related overhearing scenes: it authenticates the plot to trick
Benedict into falling in love and makes fictionally persuasive that seemingly untranslatable dramatic device.

The idealised yearnings of Hero and Claude are most often deployed in
productive juxtaposition to the cynically aligned Beatrice and Benedict;
indeed, we consistently see the former couple operating as a means of illuminating and offsetting the latter couple's mocking attitudes towards marriage and romance in general. Cast in a similar mould is the relationship

in *Taming* between the sexually assertive Bianca (a globe-trotting bill-board-adorning supermodel) and the younger Italian Lucentio (Santiago Cabrera), which is used to highlight the more genuine romance of Kate and Petruchio. (The lack of language in the Bianca/Lucentio pairing clar-ifies the transparency of communication in the Petruchio/Kate marriage.) In addition, given the peculiar connotations of the appropriations' set-tings, a gallery of minor characters is authorised to play roles as confi-dants, advisors and supporters. As befits the profiling of careerist thirty-somethings, parental figures are largely axed. Gone, therefore, are the roll-call of patriarchs adorning the 'originals' and the patriarchal struc-tures that, as Kathleen McLuskie states, are all too often in Shakespearean drama seen as 'the only form of social organisation'.[7] All that remains in *Much Ado* is Hero's father, Leonard, whose bumbling attempts at pater-nalism are sympathetically spotlighted because of his widower status. *Taming* pursues an even more severe policy of familial amputation. The authoritarian father figure, Baptista, is replaced by a profligate and inef-fectual mother, who is vainly interested in celebrity, the right places to be seen, clothes and her own romantic prospects. Once again, as in *Much Ado*, the gap thereby created is made up by a team of work-mates, all of whom perform personally important functions. Extended familial rela-tionships are replaced by chosen networks in the manner of *Friends*: friends become the new family, operating in such a way as to underscore both a diffusion of traditional authority and the adaptations' shaping sensitivity to the *mores* of British and American comedy drama.

Jill Marshall and Angela Werndly write that the emergence of thirty-something drama over the last ten years taps 'into a particular Zeitgeist' in its concern with 'changing gender relations and both masculine and feminine identities'.[8] Certainly, in *Taming* and *Much Ado*, a preoccupa-tion with the impact of gender destabilisation on heterosexual relation-ships is central. The notion that marriage is no longer necessarily on the cards for women is epitomised by the resolutely single Bianca, who is shown turning down offers because of a devotion to an independent life of luxury, travel and sex on tap. 'I'll get married when Katherine does' is Bianca's way of saying 'I'll never marry', although her consuming, shallow and promiscuous lifestyle emphasises a figuration that trades upon essentially unlikeable traits. But, at much greater length in *Taming*, the 'singleton' stereotype – accomplished but partner-less – is evident in the representation of Kate, whose diary is jam-packed for each day but contains only one evening engagement: 'Take the bins out'. Equally, in *Much Ado*, a satisfying relationship for Benedict and Beatrice appears impossible for either to achieve, despite the satiating signifiers of the opening soundtrack: 'Love is like candy on a shelf, / You want to taste and help yourself' is the resonant refrain of Tom Jones' 'Help Yourself'. The pursuit of career pleasure, it is implied, has blocked off both to amatory fulfilment. Overweening self-regard, sexism and commitment phobia mean that relationships for Benedict are generally short-lived, while the verbal sharpness and defensive feminism necessary for the workplace dictate that Beatrice remains psychologically isolated. The deep complementarity of these single personae is covertly confessed to in an exchange that sees Beatrice and Benedict experiencing with mock-horror the inception of Hero and Claude's romantic intimacy. 'I can't think of anything worse than to have someone say they love me,' states Beatrice, to which Benedict responds, 'Me too . . . that's something we've got in common.' The consensus reveals a shared condition by putting into Shakespearean circulation the confirmed singleton type attested to by the most recent generation of media and popular representations.

Alike in exhibiting a prickly attitude towards their unattached labels, Kate and Beatrice are shown to be subject to almost constant taunts about spinsterhood and questions about their sexuality. Even the beautiful, successful Bianca betrays insecurity when the announcement of Kate's marriage is seen to precipitate her own wedding plans. Most powerfully, the image of a sleepless Beatrice who comforts herself with nighttime drinks and cigarettes coheres with the realisation of a more famous singleton, Bridget Jones, and gains romantic energy from purposefully conjuring both that cinematic counterpart and numerous 'chick lit' equivalents. Like Bridget, Beatrice is glimpsed living the secret life of the singleton – heartbroken and vulnerable, prey to unwelcome attentions and ridicule. A comparable representational method is at work in the imagining of Kate: discovered as an outsider in her own family, her reasons for not attending a party are revealing. Her mother remarks, 'You can't lose your temper and make a fool of yourself in five minutes', to which Kate replies, 'I can.' The rejoinder suggests a fragile and uncomfortable conception of self. Complementing such moments is the covert delight entertained once a soulmate has been secured: for example, references to her wedding provoke half-smiles from Kate, pointing up a conservative cure for the singleton disease. If 'chick lit', as Suzanne Ferriss and Mallory Young argue, 'brings in focus' issues of 'identity . . . femininity . . . feminism . . . consumerism and self-image', then *Much Ado* and *Taming* proceed firmly within the remit of the genre's ideological parameters.[9]

The process is even more marked because in-depth development is rarely allowed the male characters. Hence, Benedict remains largely one-dimensional. When he appears in isolation, for instance, the effect is to stress his vanity only, such as in the scenes where he is seen rehearsing for a range of more prestigious television roles: 'Welcome to *Newsnight*,' he announces (in a strangely sublimated intertextual imitation of Jeremy Paxman interviewing Kate as Tory MP), 'I'm Benedict Taylor.' By contrast, in *Taming*, Petruchio is more elaborately conceived, although this extends only to a situating of his current neuroses (abandoned as a child, he was bullied at the local comprehensive) and is, in fact, more typical of the characterisation of Don, whose marital break-up and rejection by Hero means that he seizes upon a construction of wounded male pride as the private badge of his malaise. At some level, Don and Petruchio, too, are represented as discharging a traumatised masculinity in the interests of re-establishing a specious sense of dominance. In general, men in both adaptations are secondarily positioned, discovered as less intellectually able, and more institutionally passive, than their female peers. Typical is Harry, who either trails in emasculated fashion behind Bianca or complains to his friends about the inversion of contemporary stereotypes. 'I'm on the outside,' he moans to Petruchio, and his comment could stand as an epitaph for any of the surface-defined males in these female-privileged worlds. The dilemma of the modern man, left behind while women flourish, is suggested with particular piquancy in the image of Harry wearing a 'target' T-shirt in the run-up to Bianca's wedding: here, he becomes a literal version of what Sally Robinson has described as the 'marked man', a figure 'pushed away from the symbolic centres of . . . iconography [and] re-centred as [a] malicious and jealous protector of the status quo'.[10] The procedure speaks abundantly to a drive both to flesh out women's roles in Shakespeare and to privilege in television drama in general the centrality of the female protagonist.[11]

II

Working in concert with the appropriations' revisions to male-female hierarchies is a studied concentration upon the plays' conversion-resistant, early modern elements. As characters are subjected to modernising, so, too, are the multiple disguise and dress-related dimensions of the Shakespearean narrative. Thus, the masque becomes, in this reading of *Much Ado*, a fancy-dress party held at the controller's *Footballers' Wives*-style house to mark the launch of the new-format programme. With more than a nod to the similar party episode in Baz Luhrmann's *William Shakespeare's 'Romeo + Juliet'* (1996), *Much Ado* casts Leonard, appropriately enough, as a Shakespearean Caesar, Hero as Marilyn Monroe (the latter's tragic sex-symbol status anticipates the former's apparent death) and Don as a clown – both pathetic fool and sinister pierrot.[12] Interestingly, Beatrice appears as Elizabeth I in a further self-conscious piece of casting which mobilises both the notion of the independent single woman and the recent glut of television commemorations of England's most celebrated female monarch. Expressive, too, are the disguises donned by Claude and Benedict, who, having taken advantage of a two-for-one deal, present themselves as identical knights in armour. This has the effect of demolishing Benedict's 'prince charming' persona (he is too worldly-wise to capture Claude's naivety) and providing an opportunity for Beatrice to launch an attack on the verbal rival she pretends not to recognise.

Taming is marked by no less slick and innovative updatings and substitutions. Dressing in his morning suit prior to the wedding, Petruchio suddenly breaks down in front of the mirror, confessing, 'I can't do it . . . not dressed like this . . . There's something she needs to know about me.' A quick cut reveals the inebriated Petruchio arriving at church on a backfiring motorbike (requisitioned in order to avoid lateness) dressed in a leather skirt, fishnet stockings and high heels. The 'something' that Kate 'needed to know' is unveiled as a modern-day confession of transvestism. Both the need to change, and the corresponding resort to alcohol as a means of allaying nerves, wonderfully situate Shakespeare's Petruchio in a contemporary register while at the same time deflecting the 'original' character's misogyny.[13] Devices that testify to the facility of the update include the rationale for bride and groom being unable to attend their own reception (Petruchio is figured as having mixed up the travel schedule) and Kate's descent, without identifying documentation, into postmarriage helplessness. In the scene following the loss of Kate's luggage and mobile phone, she is envisaged in Renaissance terms: her ripped white wedding dress, and dishevelled progress along a dusty Tuscan road, recalls and parodies the heat-baked landscape of *Much Ado About Nothing* (dir. Kenneth Branagh, 1993) and suggests that a woman denuded of modern accessories comes to resemble an early modern heroine. There is a meaningful gulf between the earlier image of the hair-scraped Kate and this subsequent visualisation of a softer countenanced woman with hair loose: the physical change alerts us to the emotional transfiguration ahead. Because no food has been ordered for the villa, the conversion of Kate, when it does take place, is more of a piece with a species of no-frills holiday that culminates in domestic downscaling and psychological re-evaluation. Although sleep deprivation forms part of this experience, here it takes a romantic form, with Kate being awakened by Petruchio playing opera to a sea of candles: the modern translation insists upon its greater acceptability. All is geared towards the construction of a narrative modality that preserves a taste of the 'source' while simultaneously showcasing an independently contemporary plotline.

As the reincarnation of Petruchio begins to suggest, Shakespearean appropriation enters a crucial phase when its task is to update morality. How best might the early modern ethical paradigm be turned to accommodate an early twenty-first-century mindset? The question is fiercely taken up in both adaptations, but particularly so in *Much Ado*, in which the charge that Hero was unfaithful the night before her wedding is an obvious critical occasion for translation. *Much Ado About Nothing* in its Shakespearean incarnation, of course, discovers Hero's seeming death from shame in the wake of her apparent loss of maidenhood. The unpalatable nature of this interpretation – and its accompanying thematic reification of virginity – are teasingly reflected in *Taming* in the scene where Kate is described by Harry as 'thirty-eight and still a virgin . . . it's not what you want, not these days', the hushed tones of his disclosure underwriting the chasm in standards of desirability and morality that divides the early modern and modern eras. The move is rephrased in *Much Ado*, in which the plot is modified so as to construct promiscuity and infidelity, rather than relinquishment of virginity, the alleged crime. Hence, Hero is arraigned for 'lying, cheating, scheming', with the bald terms of Claude's question – 'Have you slept with Don?' – unfortunately not allowing for the fact that the one-night stand took place some time previously. As the news that Hero slept with the lower-league Don ricochets around the church, only those close to her know that the socially unacceptable sex arose out of a misplaced kindness. 'I just felt sorry for him,' Hero states earlier, an explanation glossed by Margaret (Nina Sosanya) as 'pity sex'. Both the escape from the church and Hero's wedding, then, unfold along an axis of an altogether alternative brand of shame, one engendered from the revelation of an embarrassing sexual encounter. Yet the play is simultaneously returned to in the representation of the effects of the revelation, for, at least momentarily, Hero is akin to her Shakespearean counterpart in being reduced to disempowerment.

Claude is quickly alerted to having been deceived thanks to the 'discoveries' of the security guards, who combine a pompous zeal for 'health and safety' issues with a fascination for television detectives that bespeaks a barely concealed passion for fighting crime. However, whereas in the Shakespearean play Hero is consigned to relative silence, *Much Ado* in its modern guise allows her to recover to deliver a blistering self-defence. Her eloquent wrath degenerates into a physical assault that results in her collapse and subsequent unconsciousness: as the ambulance is called, a black veil descends over the screen, suggesting a theatrical-like closure to this section of the narrative and subliminally indicating the play's abrupt shift into a funereal vein. Equally in keeping with the theatrical metaphor is the way in which the veil, now a type of curtain, is lifted to disclose a hospital's intensive care corridor. Consistent with its strategic policy of reframing Shakespeare inside popular television genres and discourses, *Much Ado* now avails itself of the soap opera cliffhanger: Hero is in a coma, and no medical authority is confident enough to pronounce upon her chances. The Shakespearean resurrection trick finds its analogue in the modern miracle of the idea of coma recovery. Thus, when the life-support machine begins to bleep, Hero comes back to life, to the astonishment of the assembled on-set audience. Earlier Claude is realised weeping over the comatose Hero, eloquent in his regret and sorrow. But such repentance is insufficient for this reading of Shakespeare's romantic comedy. In a new epilogue, Hero and Claude are discovered sitting on a beach and talking over what has happened. Crucially, there is no forgiveness here, only the recognition of a recurring scenario of unwanted paternalism; as Hero explains to Claude, 'I'm bored of being owned – by you, by my dad – I'm going to be on my own for a while.' Despite Hero's adamantine view that she will not marry Claude ('never in a million years'), he continues to plead against her silence ('Say I can hope, please'), suggesting that, in this version, the woman chooses to be wordless only at the point when her erstwhile male interlocutor wishes her to speak.

Because the ethical considerations and moral impasse surrounding Kate in *Taming* extend even further, they are impossible to contain within the epilogue formula. After all, as Penny Gay writes,

> looked at with sober late-twentieth-century eyes, this is a story in which one human being starves and brainwashes another, with the full approval of the community . . . *The Taming of the Shrew* argues that the cruel treatment is for the victim's good, to enable her to become a compliant member of patriarchal society.[14]

Traditionally, directors and filmmakers have diverted attention from such dramatic indigestibility by deploying the frame – the Christopher Sly material from Shakespeare's induction and the anonymous *The Taming of a Shrew* (1594) – either as a diverting bookend or as a series of comic motifs distributed through the course of the narrative.[15] No equivalent tactic is adopted in *Much Ado*, although metatheatrical superimpositions would not necessarily be out of place in a production that is itself inherently self-conscious in filmic terms. (Indeed, it is possible to argue that a vestige of a frame is retained in the cartoon-like flicking between screen images that frequently characterises *Taming*'s camera work.)

Distinctive in *Taming* is an initial rehearsal of romantic discourses, including the enlistment of the 'love at first sight' convention. Constructed as a combination of a bounty-hunter and a gambler ('£50 says you won't get a look in; £50 says you won't want to,' Harry states), Petruchio, on meeting Kate, immediately falls for the woman he has been enjoined to woo. And, even if this is a well-worn interpretive gambit, being mobilised in countless stage productions, its recurrence here is given a contemporary twist. Petruchio's line – 'I like everything about you' – mimics the central refrain of *Bridget Jones' Diary* and endorses the holy grail of self-help sentimentality: 'I like you just as you are.' But more important, however, is the erotic energy that clusters about the Petruchio persona. Even in drag Petruchio/Sewell cuts a masculine figure, and this is emphasised by the sexual undercurrent that runs beneath his edginess and violence. The *Taming* production is always on the sexy side of a fine line between desire and threat, the most obvious instance being the attempted 'rape' scene in which Petruchio chases Kate to the bedroom, throws her onto the bed and exclaims, 'You've teased me long enough.' As Petruchio undoes his belt, the unsettling aggression of the moment, which is seen from his wife's point of view, is compounded by a gasp of desire (the implication is that the husband-assailant is impressively tumescent) and a continued defiance ('Fine, do it!') that is belied by Kate's facial expression of desire. At the last moment, Kate leans her mouth towards Petruchio's face, only for him to break dramatically away: 'I can't do it . . . not until you start being nice to me,' he states, in a farcical dashing of assumed gender roles. The plaintive response – 'Can't you?' – is accompanied by a panning away of the camera that shows the frustrated Kate writhing on the bed in sexual disappointment. Playing upon a sexualised dynamic, the scene rewrites the drama's legacy of violence in terms of a consummation averted, highlighting the ways in which, according to Stephen Greenblatt, Shakespearean comedy 'constantly appeals to the body and in particular to sexuality as the heart of its theatrical magic'.[16]

The actual 'taming' – the moment at which Kate bows to Petruchio's will – is configured as personal reflection, as an understanding that career, upon which an undue emphasis has been placed, cannot be paramount. Joining the couple at their honeymoon villa, Harry engages Kate's lament ('My career's ruined') by elaborating an alternative perspective. Noting Kate's affirmative nod in response to his inquiry as to whether she loves Petruchio, he asks, 'Is your career more important than that?' At the same time as she answers Harry's question negatively, Kate kisses an amazed Petruchio, who follows her to bed. Just before this climactic reconciliation, Kate declines to intervene to prevent Petruchio casting her suitcase, and its prized contents, into the swimming pool. Her comment – 'I don't wear knickers anyway . . . not when I'm on holiday' – shows that she has moved away from a reliance on external possessions, and that a general loosening of attitude is linked to the articulation of a more explicit sexuality. Kate's sexuality emerges to meet Petruchio's, and it is this dynamic upon which the success of the appropriation is wholly dependent.

As the conjuration of 'going commando' unequivocally establishes, *Much Ado* is *par excellence* a modern language appropriation of the Shakespearean 'original', but this is not to detract from the ways in which the play's rhetorical and verbal forms underlie the contemporary surface dialogue. The television script and the Shakespearean drama mime and mine each other in explicit and subtle fashion. Meeting again for the first time, for instance, Beatrice interrupts Benedict's self-serving anecdote to declare, 'I'm amazed you're still talking, Benedict, no one is listening to you.' 'Beatrice – you're still here!' is Benedict's astonished but acid reply. Quick to suggest itself here is the Shakespearean inspiration:

BEATRICE: I wonder that you will still be talking, Signor Benedick. Nobody marks you.
BENEDICK: What, my dear Lady Disdain! Are you yet living?[17]

Via such close wording, the appropriation performs more than the simple retention, in Jean E. Howard's words, of Beatrice's 'witty . . . iconoclastic voice'.[18] The exchange suggests that, in order for contemporary television dialogue to work authentically at moments such as this, only early modern titles and personifications need be disbanded. Likewise, the elaboration of Benedict's rationalisation of his change of heart and his decision to broadcast his feelings immediately brings the anterior text of *Much Ado About Nothing* to mind. The play shows him reflecting:

I may chance have some odd quirks and remnants of wit broken on me because I have railed so long against marriage; but doth not the appetite alter? A man loves the meat in his youth that he cannot endure in his age . . . The world must be peopled. When I said I would die a bachelor, I did not think I should live till I were married. (II.iii.208–11, 213–15)

The appropriation has Benedict predict:

> There'll be some fun at my expense, of course . . . [But] love is just one of those things a man grows into . . . like jazz or olives. After all, the world must be peopled. When I said I'd die a bachelor, I just didn't realise I'd live this long.

Christy Desmet writes that 'appropriation' of the 'Bard satisfies motives ranging from play, to political commitment, to agonistic gamesmanship'.[19] Certainly, at least two of these impulses are operative here, with the adaptation both comically flirting with the prior formulation and gesturing to its precursor in order to improve upon it. In this way, the citation of Shakespeare in *Much Ado* serves both canonical and non-canonical purposes. At once, the narrative is organised so as to encourage identification of the 'original' and, in this sense, *Much Ado* ensures that it makes its appeal to more than one viewer constituency, that it issues reminders of Shakespeare in the interests of advertising and excusing its own translating procedures.

The most famous speeches are particularly interesting in this regard; that is, it is clear that the production teams cater to a presumed audience desire to experience particular lines and exchanges. When Kate and Petruchio wake after consummation, for example, a version of the 'sun and moon' arrival scene (IV.vi.1–23) ensues. A close-up shot of the happy post-coital couple is accompanied by Petruchio's observation, 'How brightly shines the moon,' and Kate's response, 'That's the sun, you pillock.' The dialogue's success springs from the fact that, at one and the same time, Shakespearean language is closely pursued and mockingly abandoned, to the extent that Petruchio appears as the stuffy representative of poetic tradition and Kate as the modernising voice of vernacular realism. No less important is the fact that, in a related departure from the play, in which the 'shrew' is forced twice to submit to her husband's wild claims, Kate is constructed as consistently having the last word. Thus, Petruchio's remark 'You shouldn't contradict me' is immediately matched by Kate's reply, 'You shouldn't talk bollocks.' Indeed, the male genital slang deployed here – 'pillock' and 'bollocks' – might be seen as Kate's metaphorical answer back to a masculinist economy in which she is now, even if contentedly, implicated.[20] More generally, the mood of sexual satisfaction and the suggestion of shared lovers' jokes serve to exorcise any remaining traces of misogyny, as when Petruchio's statement, 'And we'll have no more talk of divorce either, let's make that clear', is immediately followed by a glimpse of him rising from the bed to make breakfast. Role reversal is deflected back upon Petruchio rather than Kate, while the simultaneous invocation and debunking of the dramatic language make it clear that this *Taming* functions according to a multiplicity of verbal perspectives.

Behind the intimacy shared between the plays and the appropriations lie economic and cultural assumptions about how Shakespeare might and must be marketed in postmodernity: the retelling of the Bard is authenticated via a perceived proximity to 'source'. Or, to put it another way, even if Shakespeare is only dimly present, he nevertheless functions as the imprimatur for the revisionary play that unfolds across his *oeuvre*. Moreover, expectations about the universality of the language, and thus constructions of Bardic timelessness, can be perpetuated if departures and additions are seen to be subordinated to familiar and already entrenched narrative structures and contours. Of course, this is not necessarily to suggest that the Shakespearean language is still valid: as reviews of the 'Shakespea(Re)-Told' season testify, both *Much Ado* and *Taming* desacralise as much as they sacralise.[21] Rather, it is to argue that canonically hardened formulations that enjoy cultural currency are reawakened according to the requirements of particular historical situations and predicaments. Petruchio's exclamation, 'Kiss me Kate', which is called after the departing object of his intentions, is indicative of this self-consciously allusive procedure, recalling, as it does, both the 1953 film musical of the same name and a broader trajectory of Shakespearean borrowings and mediations. 'Shakespeare' in 'Shakespea(Re)-Told', then, is neither a monolith nor an easily identifiable reference point, but at one and the same time a prompt for departure and a corpus of revision the utility of which resides in a dense intertextuality.

In both adaptations, direct Shakespearean quotation intrudes at major moments. In *Taming*, self-conscious quotation is mainly the preserve of Petruchio, as when his announcement, 'So I've come to wive it wealthily in Padua', rebounds upon him to mark him as a smart-arse, middle-class, exhibitionist. *Much Ado* follows in the same vein. At the party, Benedict and Beatrice dance stiffly and apart, both mesmerised by the spectacle of Claude and Hero's developing romance. The older couple's mutually sardonic assessment of the match as 'touching . . . a marriage of true minds', a reference to Sonnet 116, quickly descends into mimicry and finally gobbledygook: 'Blah, blah, blah,' Beatrice and Benedict chorus in parodic unison.[22] Viewed through the eyes of Benedict and Beatrice, the ensuing marriage proposal, as Claude drops to his knees before Hero, is understood as a *cliché* to be approved only by the young and foolish. Yet Benedict later returns to Sonnet 116, suggesting that Shakespeare becomes both the instrument of, and the key to, psychological reformation for the cynical older generation. In a romantic ploy, Benedict asks Beatrice to assist in textual explanation as preparation for his best man's address. 'Let me not to the marriage of true minds / Admit impediments' (p. 1962) Beatrice reads, unveiling the finer mysteries of iambic pentameter and subsequently situating the Shakespearean language in modern parlance. At one level, the scene thematises *Much Ado*'s relation to Shakespeare: as much as the narrative aspires to a re-telling of the Bard, it also represents a paraphrase. At another level, the exchange over the body of Sonnet 116 marks both a figurative coming together of like 'minds' and the emergence into an even greater prominence of Beatrice – the assumption of a female-centred interpretive authority. Hers is the intellectual stimulus that enables Benedict to arrive at serviceable, if comically inelegant, glosses of the lines: 'Love's not time's fool, though rosy lips and cheeks / Within his bending sickle's compass come' (p. 1,962), for instance, is recast as 'Even though they – or we – might get a bit knackered, they'll – or we'll – still fancy each other'. As the camera closes and the music swells in keeping with a renewed emphasis upon intimacy, the delivery and paraphrase of the final rhyming couplet – the 'turn' in the sonnet's meaning – is shared between Benedict and Beatrice, suggesting a new understanding that supersedes their earlier mockery and a levelling of previously fractious relations.

That this new understanding impacts upon both Benedict's masculinity and Beatrice's femininity is quickly made clear. Faced with Beatrice's tears and vulnerability, and forced to acknowledge the impropriety of his earlier rejection, Benedict is realised as beginning a transformative development away from the insensitive persona of before. Once again, in the confessional exchange between Benedict and Beatrice in the church, the play is raided as a resource: lines such as 'You know, there's nothing in this world I love as much as you, and isn't that strange?', 'I'll do anything for you' and 'Kill Claude' are little more than close echoes of the Shakespearean reading of this climactic moment.[23] Typically, the dramatic dialogue supports and vindicates the modern appropriation: the long-awaited unravelling of mutually entertained feelings is as idiomatic and vernacular as it is canonically recognisable. If Beatrice's femininity is revealed in this sequence via distress and acknowledgement of the restrictions facing her as a woman, a more traditional masculinity in Benedict is similarly spotlighted and directed.[24] Although Benedict promises 'to make everything all right' rather than to 'challenge' Claude, there is nevertheless a marked movement in the representation of his ethical sense of himself. 'I'm sure he has his reasons', the initial postmodern resistance to judgement, soon transmutes into 'You've done something terrible', the charge with which Claude is confronted.

Interestingly, the assumption of such a form of new heroism accords with popular constructions of Shakespearean morality: notions of honour and integrity are mobilised so as to steer Benedict into a traditional niche – he now appears well suited to knightly attire. And, crucially, the first kiss between Benedict and Beatrice can only take place once masculinity has been properly embraced and executed. Effortlessly placing Shakespearean comedy at the centre of a new sexual economy, *Much Ado* and *Taming* illustrate the ways in which the gender debates of popular culture now privilege questions about changing constructions of masculinity and femininity, and about the relation between the work-life balance and the pursuit of personal happiness in a firmly post-feminist landscape.

III

The narrative preparations for Kate's much anticipated final speech find her back in the House of Commons as leader of her party. A television screen inset shows her as angry and aggressive as ever, while Petruchio appears as the perfect ministerial consort, complete with smart suit and civil servant banter. A discussion over the rights and wrongs of Bianca's pre-nuptial agreement constitutes the believable context for the delivery of Kate's sentiments, since the Italian lover is exposed as an unrepentant gold-digger who does not object when the wedding is called off. In keeping with the conversation between the appropriation and the play, the homily on wifely virtues deploys several lines verbatim even as it supplements the 'original' with qualifying parentheses: hence, Kate will obey Petruchio in everything 'except when I'm running the country'. On the one hand, such writing over the famous paean to domestic subordination demolishes many of its fundamental assumptions, transforming what might appear as a genuine 'taming' into impersonation and performance. On the other hand, the fact that the camera privileges Petruchio joining Kate on the sofa during the delivery of her speech suggests an alternative reading – a set of values that, although shared, are in constant negotiation and a reliance upon, if not promotion of, a necessary personal reciprocity.

The endings of both appropriations self-consciously play upon audience awareness. Although the epilogue to *Much Ado* emphasises resolution in the face of romantic persuasion, the temporal connection between this scene and the ensuing on-screen caption, 'Sometime in the Future', introduces the teasing notion that Hero has indeed changed her mind. The idea is reinforced when the camera cuts to Claude, in wedding attire, rehearsing that by now overly familiar Shakespearean utterance, Sonnet 116. Fetched in by Benedict, who is once again dressed for marriage, Claude is summoned to the altar. Positioned respectively as best man and groom, Benedict endeavours to calm Claude as the music of the bridal march commences. However, when Benedict and Claude change places, we realise that, in an equivalent narrative move to the tricks practised upon the majority of the characters, we, too, have been duped. The appropriation replaces the play's suggestion of a double wedding with a single union, that of Benedict and Beatrice, with Hero and Claude appearing not as bride and groom but as bridesmaid and best man. The cultural capital of Shakespeare notwithstanding, there can be no reconciliation for Hero and Claude at this historical juncture: the famous sonnet, it is implied, works its magic in one context but not another. Instead, as the shared laughter of Benedict and Beatrice indicates, a mature marriage of equals sounds the high romantic note, although in an ironically knowing and muted mode. Unsurprisingly, then, the couple enjoy a final joke: Benedict asks, 'Remind me what we're doing here,' and Beatrice replies: 'I have absolutely no idea.' The perfectly timed smirking expressions, combined with the diegetic return of the 'Just Help Yourself' number, confirm the impression of romantic suitability and comic closure.

In a move that is typical of the hyperbolic timbre of the production, the last scene of *Taming* takes place in the lift with Kate's announcement to Petruchio that she is pregnant with triplets: an excited embrace signifies the holy grail of contemporary heterosexuality – passionate commitment and a still vital sexual attraction. The conclusion comprises an interleaved series of shots of Petruchio at home in a house-husband role, looking after the children, with stills of Kate winning the election and becoming Britain's second female prime minister. Given the fact that the montage of the ending recalls the similar use of still images in both *Four Weddings and a Funeral* and *Love's Labour's Lost* (dir. Kenneth Branagh, 2000), films that subscribe to a 'feel-good' agenda, a further suggestion is that Kate's assumption of power with her family before the door of 'No. 10' is a cause for national as well as ideological celebration. It is the single political moment in two strikingly un-political appropriations and it suggests that a new domesticity is the context for professional success, that gendered adaptations and modifications make for mutually dependent lifestyles. For Shakespeare's singletons, back in fashion and breaking through, the moment has come in triumphant finales that see both Kate and Beatrice culturally centred and politically powerful.[25]

Notes

1. See the BBC website at http://www.bbc.co.uk/drama/shakespeare/listings/shtml.
2. Daniel Fischlin and Mark Fortier (2000), 'Introduction', in Daniel Fischlin and Mark Fortier (eds), *Adaptations of Shakespeare: A Critical Anthology of Plays from the Seventeenth Century to the Present*, London and New York: Routledge, p. 1.
3. *Shakespeare's Happy Endings* was screened on BBC4 on 29 November 2005.
4. For a discussion of the contemporary tendency for film and television to include weddings 'regardless of their relevance', see Chrys Ingraham (1999), *White Weddings: Romancing Heterosexuality in Popular Culture*, New York and London: Routledge, p. 131.
5. Lez Cooke (2003), *British Television Drama: A History*, London: BFI, p. 168.
6. Jill Marshall and Angela Werndly (2002), *The Language of Television*, London and New York: Routledge, p. 49.
7. Kathleen McLuskie (1985), 'The patriarchal bard: Feminist criticism and Shakespeare', in Jonathan Dollimore and Alan Sinfield (eds), *Political Shakespeare: New Essays in Cultural Materialism*, Manchester: Manchester University Press, p. 99.
8. Marshall and Werndly, *Language*, p. 49.
9. Suzanne Ferriss and Mallory Young (2006), 'Introduction', in Suzanne Ferriss and Mallory Young (eds), *Chick Lit: The New Women's Fiction*, New York and London: Routledge, pp. 2–3.
10. Sally Robinson (2000), *Marked Men: White Masculinity in Crisis*, New York: Columbia University Press, pp. 5–6.
11. On the rise of female-centred drama in the 1990s, see Cooke, *British Television Drama*, pp. 185–7.
12. The reference here, I think, is to *It*, the 1990 film version of the Stephen King novel of the same name in which a clown, Pennywise (Tim Curry), terrorises the residents of an American town.
13. Interestingly, whereas the Shakespearean play stresses Petruchio's motley plebeian dress and, through the description of his improperly decked horse, a blurring of human and animal categories, the appropriation elects to favour a more embarrassing entanglement of class and gender transgressions. See *The Taming of the Shrew*, in *The Norton Shakespeare*, Stephen Greenblatt, Walter Cohen, Jean E. Howard and Katharine Eisaman Maus (eds) (1997), New York: W. W. Norton, III.ii.41–64. All further references appear in the text.
14. Penny Gay (1994), *As She Likes It: Shakespeare's Unruly Women*, London and New York: Routledge, p. 86.
15. See Gay, *As She Likes It*, pp. 87–119; Kenneth S. Rothwell (2004), *A History of Shakespeare on Screen: A Century of Film and Television*, 2nd edn, Cambridge: Cambridge University Press, p. 124.
16. Stephen Greenblatt (1988), *Shakespearean Negotiations: The Circulation of Social Energy in Renaissance England*, Oxford: Clarendon, p. 86.
17. *Much Ado About Nothing*, in *The Norton Shakespeare*, I.i.95–7. All further references appear in the text.
18. Jean E. Howard (1987), 'Renaissance Antitheatricality and the Politics of Gender and Rank in *Much Ado About Nothing*', in Jean E. Howard and Marion F. O'Connor (eds), *Shakespeare Reproduced: The Text in History and Ideology*, New York and London: Methuen, p. 180.
19. Christy Desmet (1999), 'Introduction', in Christy Desmet and Robert Sawyer (eds), *Shakespeare and Appropriation*, London and New York: Routledge, p. 3.
20. 'Pillock' originated in the early modern period as a derogatory term for the penis: see Gordon Williams (1994), *A Dictionary of Sexual Language and*

Imagery in Shakespearean and Stuart Literature, 3 vols, London: Athlone, II, p. 1,030.

21. Commentators noted the 'daring' involved in addressing material perceived as 'hallowed' (Paul Hoggart (2005), 'Moving away from the Bard old days', *The Times: The Knowledge*, 5–11 November, pp. 37–8) at the same time as they observed that 'this [the season] . . . is not really Shakespeare at all' (Sally Kinnes (2005), 'Pick of the Week', *The Sunday Times: Culture*, 6 November, p. 59).

22. Sonnet 116, in *The Norton Shakespeare*, p. 1,962. All further references appear in the text.

23. See, for instance, IV.i.266–7, 286, 287.

24. 'If I were a man I would eat his heart' is the modern approximation of the Shakespearean 'O God that I were a man! I would eat his heart in the market place' (IV.i.303–4).

25. My thanks to the Postgraduate Renaissance Discussion Group at Queen's University, Belfast, for organising a stimulating seminar on the 'Shakespea(Re)-Told' season. Ashley Dunne, Adam Hansen, Edel Lamb, Naomi McAreavey and Adrian Streete offered particularly helpful observations.

Notes on Contributors

RICHARD BURT is Professor of English and Film at the University of Florida. He is the author of *Licensed by Authority: Ben Jonson and the Discourses of Censorship* (Ithaca: Cornell University Press, 1993) and *Unspeakable ShaXXXspeares: Queer Theory and American Kiddie Culture* (New York: St Martin's Press, 1998); the editor of *The Administration of Aesthetics: Censorship, Political Criticism, and the Public Sphere* (Minneapolis: University of Minnesota Press, 1994) and *Shakespeare After Mass Media* (New York: Palgrave, 2002); and the co-editor of *Enclosure Acts: Sexuality, Property, and Culture in Early Modern England* (Ithaca: Cornell University Press, 1994), *Shakespeare, the Movie: Popularizing the Plays on Film, TV, and Video* (London: Routledge, 1997) and *Shakespeare, the Movie II: Popularizing the Plays on Film, TV, Video, and DVD* (London: Routledge, 2003). He is editor of the forthcoming *Shakespeares After Shakespeare: An Encyclopedia of the Bard in Mass Media and Popular Culture*, to be published by Greenwood in print and on CD in 2006, and he is currently finishing a book entitled *The Remains of the Play: Alluding to Shakespeare in Transnational Cinema and Television*.

MARK THORNTON BURNETT is Professor of Renaissance Studies at Queen's University, Belfast. He is the author of *Masters and Servants in English Renaissance Drama and Culture: Authority and Obedience* (Basingstoke: Macmillan, 1997), *Constructing 'Monsters' in Shakespearean Drama and Early Modern Culture* (Basingstoke: Palgrave, 2002) and *Filming Shakespeare in the Global Marketplace* (Basingstoke: Palgrave, 2007).

SAMUEL CROWL is Trustee Professor of English Literature at Ohio University, where he has taught since 1970. He is the author of *The Films *of Kenneth Branagh* (Westport: Praeger, 2006), *Shakespeare at the Cineplex: The Kenneth Branagh Era* (Athens: Ohio University Press, 2003) and *Shakespeare Observed: Studies in Performance on Stage and Screen* (Athens: Ohio University Press, 1992). He has also published essays, articles, reviews and interviews on all aspects of Shakespeare in performance and has many times been honoured for outstanding teaching.

RICHARD DUTTON is Humanities Distinguished Professor of English at Ohio State University. He is the author of *Ben Jonson: to the First Folio* (Cambridge: Cambridge University Press, 1983), *An Introduction to Literary Criticism* (London and New York: Longman, 1984), *Modern Tragicomedy and the British Tradition* (Hemel Hempstead: Harvester Wheatsheaf, 1986), *William Shakespeare: A Literary Life* (Basingstoke: Macmillan 1989), *Mastering the Revels: The Regulation and Censorship of English Renaissance Drama* (Basingstoke: Macmillan, 1991), *Ben Jonson: Authority: Criticism* (Basingstoke: Macmillan, 1996) and *Licensing, Censorship and Authorship in Early Modern England* (Basingstoke: Palgrave, 2000); and the editor of *Jacobean Civic Pageants* (Keele: Keele University Press, 1995), *'Women Beware Women' and Other Plays by Thomas Middleton* (Oxford: Oxford University Press, 1999) and *Epicene, or The Silent Woman* (Manchester: Manchester University Press, 2003). He has edited several collections of critical essays, including four volumes, with Jean Howard, of *Companions to the Works of Shakespeare* (Oxford: Blackwell, 2003).

SUSANNE GREENHALGH is Principal Lecturer in Drama, Theatre and Performance Studies at Roehampton University, London. She has published articles on adaptation and the interrelationships of film, television and theatre – most recent is an examination of television *Macbeth*s in a Palgrave collection. Forthcoming publications include a chapter on audio Shakespeare in *The Cambridge Companion to Shakespeare and Popular Culture* and an essay on child performance of Shakespeare on stage and screen in *Children's Literature in Performance* (Lang). She has compiled and introduced the entries on British television for *Shakespeares After Shakespeare: An Encyclopedia of the Bard in Mass Media and Popular Culture*, to be published by Greenwood in print and on CD in 2006. Currently, she is co-editing *Shakespeare and the Performance of Childhood* and writing *At Home with Shakespeare*, which explores the history of the reception and experience of Shakespeare in the domestic and private realm.

SARAH HATCHUEL lectures in English at the University of Paris I Panthéon-Sorbonne and teaches 'Shakespeare on Screen' at the University of Paris VII. She received her doctorate in English Studies from the University of Paris IV Sorbonne in 2000 and also has a postgraduate diploma in Film Studies from the University of Paris III Sorbonne-Nouvelle. She is the co-organiser of a series of conferences on the screen adaptations of Shakespeare's plays at the University of Rouen; has published several articles on the aesthetics of Shakespeare on screen; and is the author of *A Companion to the Shakespearean Films of Kenneth Branagh* (Winnipeg: Blizzard Publishing, 2000) and *Shakespeare, from Stage to Screen* (Cambridge: Cambridge University Press, 2004).

CAROLYN JESS-COOKE lectures in Film Studies at the University of Sunderland. She has published articles and chapters internationally on sequelisation, psychoanalysis, Turkish cinema, and Shakespeare on film – most recent is a Lacanian analysis of Steven Spielberg's *A.I.* for *Screen*. Forthcoming publications include an introductory text on Shakespearean cinema for Wallflower Press' Short Cuts series. She is also co-editing three volumes, *Apocalyptic Shakespeares*, *Film Sequels: New Theories of Sequelisation and Remaking*, and *A Companion to Culture, Memory, and Cinema*.

COURTNEY LEHMANN is Associate Professor of English and Film Studies at the University of the Pacific in Stockton, California. She is the author of *Shakespeare Remains: Theatre to Film, Early Modern to Postmodern* (Ithaca and London: Cornell University Press, 2002), and the co-editor of two volumes of Shakespeare and screen criticism: *Spectacular Shakespeare: Critical Theory and Popular Cinema* (Madison: Fairleigh Dickinson University Press, 2002) and *The Reel Shakespeare: Alternative Cinema and Theory* (Madison: Fairleigh Dickinson University Press, 2002). She is an award-winning teacher and the Director of the Pacific Humanities Centre.

CATHERINE SILVERSTONE is Senior Lecturer in English and Drama at Anglia Ruskin University in Cambridge. She has published on Shakespeare and performance, and recent work includes an article on Shakespeare's Globe Theatre in *Textual Practice*. She is currently writing a book on recent performances of Shakespeare on stage and screen.

ROBERT SHAUGHNESSY is Professor of Theatre at the University of Kent. His publications include *Representing Shakespeare: England,*

History and the RSC (Hemel Hempstead: Harvester Wheatsheaf, 1994) and *The Shakespeare Effect: A History of Twentieth-Century Performance* (Basingstoke: Palgrave, 2002), and, as editor, *Shakespeare on Film* (Basingstoke: Macmillan, 1998) and *Shakespeare in Performance* (Basingstoke: Palgrave, 2000). He is currently writing the volume on Shakespeare for the Routledge Critical Guides Series and editing *The Cambridge Companion to Shakespeare and Popular Culture.*

RAMONA WRAY is Lecturer in English at Queen's University, Belfast. She is the author of *Women Writers of the Seventeenth Century* (Tavistock: Northcote House, 2004) and articles and chapters on autobiography, pedagogy, Shakespeare films and women's writing. She is also the co-editor of *Shakespeare and Ireland: History, Politics, Culture* (Basingstoke: Macmillan, 1997), *Shakespeare, Film, Fin de Siècle* (Basingstoke: Macmillan, 2000) and *Reconceiving the Renaissance: A Critical Reader* (Oxford: Oxford University Press, 2005).

Index